GREECE

ON MY WHEELS

EDWARD ENFIELD

summersdale

Reprinted 2003

Summersdale Publishers Ltd
46 West Street
Chichester
West Sussex
PO19 1RP
UK

www.summersdale.com

Printed and bound in Great Britain

ISBN 1 84024 280 9

Illustrations and front cover by Peter Bailey.

About the Author

After completing a degree in Classics at Oxford and National Service in Germany, Edward Enfield spent five years in the Far East. On his return to England he worked for West Sussex County Council. His first act on retirement was to cycle from the Channel to the Mediterranean and write his book *Downhill All the Way*. He writes a regular column in *The Oldie* magazine and has forged what he calls 'a little mini-career' in journalism, radio and television.

His son Harry likes to call himself a Man of Letters, but this may be one of his jokes, as he is also a comedian.

To my four children

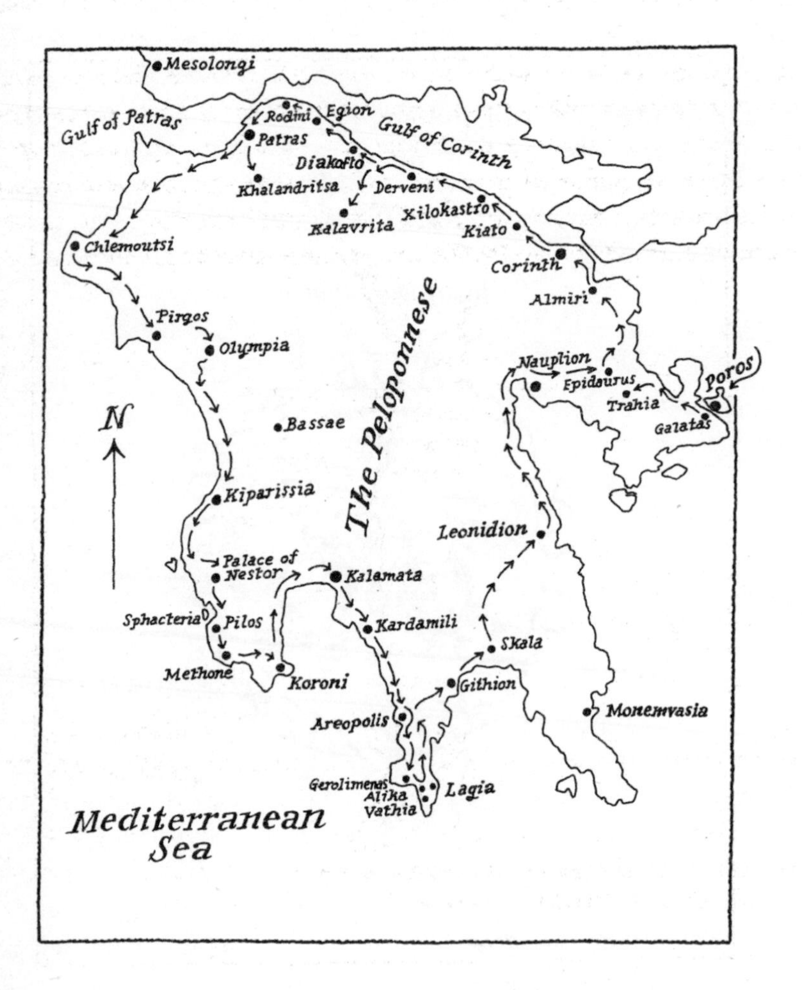
Mesolongi
Gulf of Patras
Rodini
Egion
Patras
Gulf of Corinth
Diakofto
Khalandritsa
Derveni
Kalavrita
Xilokastro
Kiato
Chlemoutsi
Corinth
The Peloponnese
Almiri
Pirgos
Olympia
Nauplion
Epidaurus
Poros
Trahia
Galatas
N
Bassae
Kiparissia
Leonidion
Palace of Nestor
Kalamata
Sphacteria
Pilos
Kardamili
Skala
Methone
Koroni
Githion
Monemvasia
Areopolis
Gerolimenas
Alika
Vathia
Lagia
Mediterranean Sea

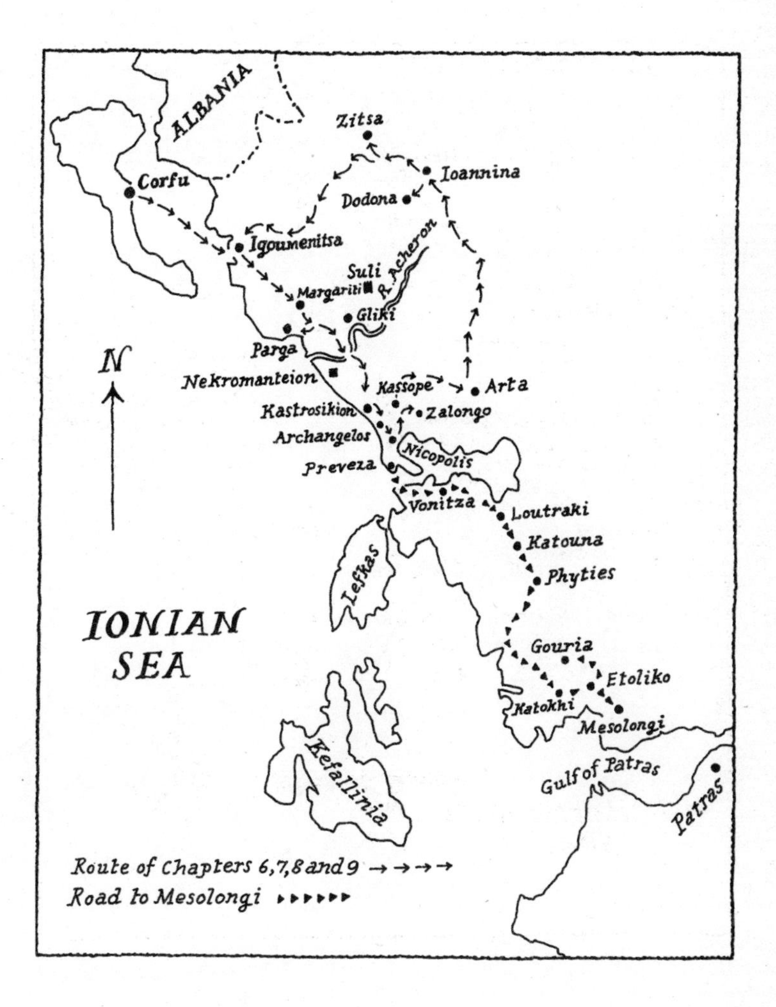
ALBANIA
Zitsa
Ioannina
Corfu
Dodona
Igoumenitsa
R. Acheron
Suli
Margariti
Gliki
Parga
N
Nekromanteion
Kassope
Arta
Kastrosikion
Zalongo
Archangelos
Nicopolis
Preveza
Vonitza
Loutraki
Katouna
Lefkas
Phyties
IONIAN
SEA
Gouria
Etoliko
Katokhi
Mesolongi
Kefallinia
Gulf of Patras
Patras
Route of Chapters 6,7,8 and 9
Road to Mesolongi

Contents

Foreword by Harry Enfield

I was quite surprised at how agreeable I found this book upon first reading it. Surprised only because I don't really think of my father as a very agreeable man. Not that I think of my father very often. One doesn't really, does one? I mean, a father flits through the brain five or six times a month, buried safely in the middle of a thought: 'What should I get Mum and Dad for Christmas?' or 'I must ring Mum and Dad.' Sometimes he is allowed his own thought-sentences: 'I wonder how Dad is? Obviously not dead or Mum would have rung.'

But when was the last time you, I, or anyone other than Woody Allen sat down and had a good long think about their father? For the purposes of this foreword I have had to do just this, and I have discovered that he is actually an agreeable man. The only reason I've been thinking otherwise is because I have a distant memory of his being disagreeable fifteen or twenty years ago. Since then I have vaguely noticed him becoming agreeable, but I'd forgotten to think about this phenomenon and update my mind. I have now done so. It is therefore of little surprise how agreeable I found this book upon reading it.

My father has taught himself that the secret of agreeability in old age is to keep himself away from other humans as much as possible. It is they who make him disagreeable, with their vile looks, hideous gaits and propensity to misuse the English language. In his disagreeable days society made him seethe. Now it makes him sleep. These days he is mostly in fine form, and when we start to annoy him he simply nods off. Recently he came to visit us in London to spend, so he thought, an agreeable hour or so with his latest granddaughter. But

after half an hour, two older grandchildren and at least eight other three- to five-year-olds descended on our house and, with high voices and plastic swords, declared war upon his sanity. My father sat very still for the half hour they were there, removing himself from notice as a stoat will when an owl circles overhead. Upon their exit, he sprang backwards onto the sofa like a startled elf and sank into a deep sleep. Ten minutes later he awoke, once again in agreeable mode. Where once he would have felt trapped and become grumpy, now he is agreeable, unconscious, and agreeable again.

This book has a beautiful pace. It has the pace of a bicycle powered by an elderly man with a bicycle-powered elderly mind. A mind that is peaceful, in part because the humans he meets can be bicycled swiftly away from at the moment of his choosing, and in part because he is in Greece, the country that has been at the forefront of his affections since childhood. He reaches such a pitch of tranquillity that his thoughts occasionally resemble those of a hairy oriental guru, as when a Hellenic lady tries to kill him with her car thrice in an hour: 'I acquit her of any malicious intent though, I just think she lived in a world of her own in which there were no elderly Englishmen on bicycles and she had no idea I was there.'

One of my father's greatest wishes is to die before he becomes a burden to my mother or his children. It is with this at least somewhere in his mind, I believe, that he seeks ever greater mental tranquillity on ever longer cycle rides, so that one day in the not-too-distant future, while cycling along peacefully on some foreign road, he can nod off and literally be bumped off by the nearest passing vehicle. The driver would perhaps be traumatised by dispatching an old

man in such a fashion, and I am sorry about this, but I think that Dad would like it.

One of the things that still makes him cross is the use by the English of American euphemisms. It would thus amuse him to know that he lay under a gravestone containing a euphemism made literal:

Here Lies Edward Enfield
Who Fell Asleep
And Was Promptly Squashed By A Lorry

Preface

This is not a guidebook to the Peloponnese and Epirus, but it is, I suppose, a travel book – an account of a number of expeditions made on a bicycle by a man of advancing years with a smattering of Greek learnt from a tape. Conversations in this book were conducted in that language unless I make it plain that they were in English.

Many interesting and important travellers appear in these pages, such as Lord Byron, Benjamin Disraeli and Edward Lear. They travelled on horseback, but I by bicycle. Baedeker's *Greece* of 1894 says that:

> the horses are generally docile, sure-footed, and possessed of great powers of endurance. Distances are stated in this Handbook in terms of the time taken to traverse them on horseback. As the pace is invariably a walk, an hour rarely means more than three English miles, and frequently means less. A day's journey, as a rule, should not exceed 7–8 hours.

For me, in a hot and hilly country like Greece, eight miles an hour is a fair average, and three or four hours' cycling a comfortable stint. Short of actually hiring a horse, I like to think I could not have followed these travellers more closely by any other means.

When I have quoted from earlier travellers and historians, I have often shortened what they wrote by leaving bits out. The convention is that you should put dots where the bits have been omitted; this can be distracting, so I haven't done it, but I thought I should tell you. I should also say that I have sometimes taken liberties with their punctuation by leaving out superfluous commas.

You may notice some inconsistent spelling of place names. This is partly because the Greeks themselves are not always consistent, but mainly because different interpretations are possible when moving into English from Greek, and from their alphabet to ours. I have tried to give the most common English versions unless I am quoting someone else, when I follow the original.

My thanks are due to Mary Price, then of the BBC, who produced the radio programme *Enfield Pedals After Byron*. This took me into a part of Greece that I had previously neglected. My thanks also to Dr Peter Jones, who read the proof on a train. His great classical learning saved me from a number of errors.

If any of the mixture of which this book consists gives it anything of an original flavour then it would, in the words of Edward Lear, 'be something in these days to be able to add the smallest mite of novelty to the traveller's world of information and interest'.

Part I

The Peloponnese

I am at last determined to go to Greece: it is the only place I was ever contented in.

– Lord Byron to E. J. Trelawny, 15 June 1823

From Sussex to Chlemoutsi

It might be thought that for a man approaching 70 years of age to go bicycling in Greece by himself is a rash act. I would say it is rather like marriage, which the prayer book says is not to be taken in hand unadvisedly, lightly or wantonly; but discreetly, advisedly and soberly. It further says that matrimony should be entered upon in the fear of God, which is also something you may experience in Greece when squeezing the brakes of your bicycle beside a precipice and hoping not to go over the edge.

Well, I wanted to do it so I prepared myself with care. I had ridden across France on a Dawes Tourer with six gears, and in my book about that I poured scorn on the idea that there was any need to have any more gears than six. Then my daughter arrived on a new Peugeot bicycle with eighteen gears, and I found I could not keep up with her. Being unwilling to think that this had anything to do with the difference in our ages, I assumed that bicycle technology must have moved on, so I bought a bicycle that was neither a tourer nor a mountain bike, but was called a hybrid. It was a Raleigh Pioneer Elite, with twenty-one gears, and as far as I am concerned, beyond the Pioneer Elite the law of diminishing returns must set in. It is such a good machine that although you can pay vast amounts more for other bicycles there is very little extra that they can possibly do.

When I cycled round the Peloponnese I took with me a sleeping bag and a body-bag. Actually it was called a bivvy bag, but would have done as a body-bag if I had expired on top of a Greek mountain, which seemed to be a possibility. Its purpose, though, was more to keep me alive than to cope with me dead. It was made of Gore-Tex, and was therefore waterproof. If I wanted to sleep in it I would put my sleeping bag inside, climb in and zip it up, then however much it rained I should be all right. There are two reasons why I might want to do this. The first was that I should be in Greece throughout October when the people who ran hotels or let rooms in their houses might have closed for the winter. The second, and more compelling, reason was that I planned to cycle right round the Peloponnese, which would take me into parts which, from the map at least, looked fairly wild.

The Mani, which is the central of three southern prongs, has a particular reputation for being rugged and formidable. It is a place of treeless and barren mountains where people live in small villages and traditionally have a great liking for blood feuds. Pirates from this area nearly captured Lord Byron, and in the Greek War of Independence the Mani produced one of its greatest generals and two of its better-known assassins. If I was going into places like that it would give me confidence to think that if need be I could compose myself to sleep in my bivvy bag under an olive tree without troubling the natives in any way. When it came to the point I used it twice, more from choice than necessity, but it enhanced the trip as I was much bolder because I had it than I would have been without it.

And so on 2 October I set off. In England a hot summer had come to an end in a downpour that caused a huge crop of mushrooms to spring up, so at 7 a.m. my wife gave me a breakfast of bacon, eggs, sausage and mushrooms as if I was a schoolboy going off to boarding school. She also promised to keep a diary of important events while I was away so that if something exciting happened, such as England winning a test match, she would remember to tell me when I rang up. One of her many merits is that she is always entirely cheerful at the prospect of parting with me for long periods, and I could see she was already relishing the prospect of not having to cook supper and having the whole bed to herself.

From Athens airport I came out into agreeable sunshine to tackle the business of getting to the port of Piraeus. I could perhaps have ridden there, but it did not seem to be a good idea to start my holiday by risking my life in the Athens rush hour, so I asked a taxi driver if he would take me, and he wouldn't. At least, he would have taken me but he wouldn't take the bicycle, which he said was too big. However, further back in the line of taxis was a younger and more dashing driver who, seeing my difficulty, began shouting and blowing his horn to signify that he was ready to make the attempt. When he got to the front of the line we managed to get the bicycle half in and half out of the boot, where it hung precariously secured by rubber spiders while he careered like a fiend through the Athens traffic.

The reason for going to Piraeus was to get a boat to Poros, which, although an island, is only separated from the Peloponnese by a strait of about 500 yards. On the deck of the ferry I had a failure at conversation with a man who thought he could speak English. This idea did not seem to fit the facts. He spoke at length, he waved his hands, he wagged his head, but I had no notion of what he wanted me to understand. He had picked up from somewhere the phrase 'you know what I mean?', which he used as a sort of spoken punctuation mark at pauses in the flow of words. These five words were almost the only ones that I did understand, but luckily he did not want any answer to the question, if indeed he realised it was a question anyway. As he did not seem to want any contribution from me beyond the appearance of listening, I listened for a time and then made some excuse and went inside. I forget what that excuse was, but I think he understood me as little as I him, so I could well have said, 'As the ship is sinking I think I will put on my life jacket' without causing him any alarm.

The boat arrived at Poros in the dark. The waterfront was lit up, and a very handsome waterfront it is, with houses of some age and considerable grandeur rising in a sort of triangle above the harbour. I rode slowly through the warm night, vaguely looking for somewhere to stay and thinking: 'This is *superb*.'

The accommodation problem was solved by a man who came alongside me riding a scooter.

'You want room?'

'Yes, I do.'

'You follow me.'

He rode off. I rode behind. In a few minutes he turned down a sidestreet, stopped opposite a door, ushered me through it and down a sort of open-air corridor smelling strongly of orange blossom. At the end of it he showed me into a clean, sparse room with a shower and a loo, which, when flushed, at first groaned, gurgled and grumbled like any other noisy lavatory, and then emitted a clarion call like a trumpeter summoning a regiment to arms. The room had character, so I took it.

The landlord, whose name was Nicos, proved to be a most helpful man. By some mysterious means he managed always to be around at moments when he could be useful, and in this respect he resembled that Lord Godolphin of whom Charles II said that he was 'never in the way and never out of the way'. After I had unpacked I came out and Nicos appeared, to point out a place where he thought I should eat. I had swordfish steak and a flask of draught retsina under the stars and overlooking the harbour. The other company was a quartet consisting of two women, a man and a baby. The man had a beard and a foolish smile which he directed at one and all, but most particularly at the baby. One of the women opened her shirt and fed the baby; the second was remarkable for her miniskirt, which was transparent and too tight, and I thought it an unsafe garment for a nubile young woman in Greece. They ordered their meal in broken English, and I think they may have been Italian but I cannot be sure.

When I asked for my bill the elderly waiter smiled sadly, went away and returned instead with an apple, peeled and cut into slices. With great reluctance he finally brought me, on a very small piece of paper, the very small bill.

After that I took a stroll along the waterfront where I

could see large, opulent yachts with opulent yachtsmen dining on deck and making the pastime of yachting look almost agreeable. This impression was corrected next morning when I saw them again. They were then preparing for the business of taking the boat to sea, with all the stress and anxiety that always afflicts yachtsmen at such times. One of them was limping along the front with his knee in a bandage and blood seeping through, which is also something that happens to yachtsmen. When my wife and I stayed on the island of Patmos, one of our simple pleasures was to go down to the quayside in the early morning and sit sipping coffee and watch the yachtsmen chain-smoking and shouting at their wives as they prepared for a jolly day's sailing. I am, as you will have gathered, a land-lubber.

The excellent Nicos had tried to persuade me to stay for two nights because Poros, he said, was such a lovely island. At first I brushed the idea aside, thinking I ought to get going, but I later changed my mind. This was not for the reason he said, but because the bicycle was not right as to its back wheel, which was rubbing against the brake, and also the gears began to misbehave, making a noise like a rattlesnake if I tried to engage the lowest sprocket at the back. Nicos told me to take it to a man called Kostas, but Kostas was away; two other bicycle-hire places had no mechanic, and the fourth was shut. Nicos then reappeared to see how I was getting on, and told me to cross on the ferry to Galatas where there was, he said, a good mechanic.

Naturally the good mechanic was missing by the time I found his shop, but his wife was there and we engaged in serious Greek conversation on the subject of gears, spokes and wheels. 'Spokes' are easy as the word is almost the same as the Homeric word for rays of the sun; 'gears' are more difficult but I got there eventually, and just as I succeeded in explaining the problem to the mechanic's wife the man himself walked through the door, fixed it, and would not take any money.

By the time I got back I had concluded that everyone in Poros and Galatas was extremely nice – all the shopkeepers, the people from whom you ask the way, and the very large men on very small Vespas who chat to you while you wait for the ferry. The only people with whom I had difficulty were two middle-aged Americans with bicycles. There seemed to be far more people waiting for the ferry than it could possibly hold, so in an unhappy attempt at jocularity I said that with any luck a fight would break out and give us something to watch. This they regarded as the remark of a criminal lunatic, and they sheered off hastily, nor did we speak further, though up to that point they had been quite sociable.

As I came off the ferry the ubiquitous Nicos drew up on his scooter, wishing to make sure that everything was now as it should be. He then kindly directed me to an excellent sandy beach where I swam in the company of a great many Teutonic tourists, who seemed to be cultivating skin cancer at some expense to themselves in the hire of sun beds, sun mats, sun chairs, and other life-threatening devices. Rather like hippopotami at the zoo, on the whole they dozed in the sun, but every now and then one of them would get up and lumber into the sea, stay there for a few minutes, then lumber out again.

The next morning I crossed on the ferry to begin the tour of the Peloponnese. The boring Americans of the previous day, before they decided that I was a criminal lunatic, had told me they were making a day trip to Epidaurus and back on their bicycles. They pointed at a huge white peak in the distance and said, 'You go over that.'

'I don't suppose you cross the absolute peak,' I said comfortingly, but I was wrong. If you are in Poros and mean, as I did, to cycle to Epidaurus you had better face the fact that you are going to pass over a col only some twenty feet or so below the tip of the huge mountain that you see towering in the distance.

The first ten miles are flat, with lemon, olive and orange groves, plantations of carnations and vegetables, and occasionally something odd like a big warehouse set down in a field with fifty or sixty motorcycles outside. After that I began the serious uphill work with the road winding in a way that, if it were in France, would call forth signs saying 'Virages' ('bends') all the way along. I pedalled away, not hurrying but saying to myself '*siga siga*', this being the Greek for 'softly softly'. Pretty soon I began to feel immensely pleased when I looked back and saw how far below me the sea now was. Then I rounded a corner, and there was the sea in front; I thought I had cracked the climb but I hadn't – there was a long way to go yet.

After about an hour of climbing I stopped to eat the cheese pie that I had brought with me, and by way of entertainment I carried out an experiment on a double line of ants who were marching along in a purposeful manner, some up and some down the hill. I made them a present of a lump of cheese pie that I put exactly across their path to see if this caused them to call a council of war, detail some of their number to carry this valuable offering home, or even just to stop for lunch, like me. They inspected it closely and decided it was nothing more than an obstacle, so they all walked carefully round it and carried on as before. You would think ants would rather like cheese pie, but perhaps it required some superior ant to come and reprogramme them before they could deviate from their preordained purpose in going up and down the hill.

On I went again, now getting off and pushing whenever it got really tough, which it did increasingly often, especially as it was pretty hot. The pushing increased and the cycling diminished until at last I arrived at Ano Fanari, otherwise Upper Fanari (though there seemed to be no Lower Fanari). It is a handsome village of fine stone houses, looking exceedingly prosperous, though how the inhabitants support themselves is a mystery as there seems to be nothing to be done at such a height.

'This,' I thought, 'must be the top,' but it wasn't quite. A little more pushing though and I was over the crest and viraging down the valley on the other side with the wind threatening to blow my sunhat off. Anyone who does this climb cannot fail to marvel at their own strength and pertinacity in getting so high, as the road seems to go on and on down even more than it had gone on and on up. You simply sit there clutching the brakes and looking about you at the hills and the sea. The boring Americans were younger than I, had no luggage, their bikes were lightweight racing models and they had fancy cycling shoes, but even so, I shouldn't have liked to do anything so strenuous as making the round trip all in one day as they proposed to do.

The road is very quiet, so in the long intervals between traffic you hear either country noises or nothing at all. You do not plunge straight down to sea level again, but for a time the road passes through occasional upland villages which, if you were using any other form of transport, you would rattle through without noticing. As is the case in all such remote places, the language becomes increasingly difficult. I stopped to try to buy an ice cream from a man who had no ice cream, and I think he asked me where I came from, but I only guessed that this was what he wanted to know because it is what everybody wants to know. As to what words he used, I have no idea at all and he might have been speaking Hebrew. (The other questions they ask are 'How old are you?', 'Are you married?' and 'How many children have you got?' To the latter question they seem to find my answer of 'four' to be rather impressive.)

Eventually you come down to join a main road and unfortunately there is more climbing to be done before you reach Epidaurus. I bowled into the area of the famous theatre, which is the reason why one goes to Epidaurus, just at the beginning of dusk. I was looking for the hotel where I had stayed many years before, but the only one I could now see was the expensive government-run Xenia Hotel at which I had no intention whatever of staying. In the Xenia garden I got into conversation with a large Dutchman and his wife, who said the service at the hotel bar was awful. I said it was bound to be awful as governments are no good at running hotels, and thus the whole Xenia chain was probably awful. They spoke excellent English but no Greek, so it was rather gratifying to find that there was one language at which I was better than a Hollander, the usual thing being that they put one to shame by their fluency in several languages other than their own.

The mynheer was friendly and forthcoming. He and his wife were staying at Nauplion, also with bicycles, but they had come to Epidaurus by bus because at his age, which was seventy, he was beginning 'to be frightened of hills'. I later found that there are no hills to speak of between Nauplion and Epidaurus, so I don't know why he was frightened.

It was getting dark and I began to think that I should have to sleep in the body-bag, which was not by any means a bad idea in the beautiful surroundings of Epidaurus. I parted on the most cordial of terms with my Dutch acquaintances and set off for a taverna further down the road. My plan was to eat there and ask if I could sleep in their garden, but it was shut. A young man appeared out of the dark and said I would have to go three kilometres on to Ligourio to eat, so I began to pedal in that direction and in no time at all came upon, as I thought, the very hotel that I had been looking for. It seemed to have gone up in the world since my last visit and lost the ramshackle air which it had before, but I didn't mind that. A friendly lady with the looks and manners of a nice vicar's wife gave me an excellent room for 4,000 drachmas, which was at once better and cheaper than Poros, and extremely kind of her as the official price was 7,700 drachmas plus 10 per cent, according to the notice in the room. I had a shower, washed some clothes and went to ask if I could have anything to eat.

'No, not here. I am sorry, you will have to go to Ligourio – only five minutes on the bicycle.'

'What are all those for?' I asked, pointing to the tables and chairs.

'For breakfast. I only do breakfast.'

So I got my bike but as I was about to start I saw another hotel across the road, which was indeed the one where I had stayed before; the one I was now at was a later construction.

'What about there? Can I eat there?'

'You can try.'

So over I went.

'Can I get something to eat here?'

'Certainly. Anything you like. Put the bicycle there, near the flowers, so that we can look at it.'

I chose salad, an omelette and a bottle of beer. Such beer! I had done 38 miles that day, and while the nectar of the gods is of course the most superior drink of all, in mortal terms a bottle of cold Greek beer at the end of the day for a man who had cycled 38 miles over a mountain in the heat must come pretty close. I sat outside beneath a canopy of vines and under a light so I could read. There were a few other people, who I think were members of the family, sitting and chatting or playing draughts in the gloaming. It was 16 years ago that I came before and as it was exactly the same slow-going, genial, vaguely run-down place that I remembered, it felt like coming home.

The next morning I set off without stopping to visit the theatre. This was because I had seen it before under such magnificent circumstances that I did not want to risk spoiling it by going again. It is huge, but the guidebooks vary as to how huge. Some say it seats 12,000 people, some say 14,000, whereas a large British theatre such as the Chichester Festival Theatre seats about 1,200. The most astonishing aspect is a small round stone in the centre of the orchestra. If you stand on this and speak in an ordinary conversational tone then, however many people are milling about, what you say is miraculously broadcast to every one of the seats, even in the top row, which is row 55 (or 54 depending on which guidebook you look at). The theatre is built on the side of a hill, and you might think that the acoustics would be made more difficult by its being in the open air, but it is not so. I believe it is something of a mystery. I read somewhere that an American professor measured every aspect and angle and carved a replica by blasting and burrowing in the side of a hill, and when it was finished it didn't work.

On my visit years before I arrived in the early afternoon and there were people everywhere, so I went away and came back an hour before closing time when the crowd was down to three Italians and me. One of the Italians, a woman, fancied herself as a bit of an opera singer so she stood on the stone and warbled while the two men sat in row 55 (or 54) and shouted 'Bravo!' I climbed up to the top and shouted 'Bravo!' too. Then they all went away, and I had the whole magnificent theatre entirely to myself.

I told the story of the Italian warbler to the Americans on the Poros ferry and they said, 'Who was the opera singer?', thus making it plain that they could see no point to the anecdote whatever. Like a fool I answered, 'Just a tourist,' whereas I should have said 'Callas!' and sent them away satisfied.

Anyway the moral is: when travelling in Greece, stay at the place you want to see. This makes it possible for you either to get up early and be there before the tourist buses arrive, or to go in the evening when they have gone. In the case of Epidaurus the two hotels are by the T-junction where the road from Poros joins the road to Nauplion. If you stand with your back to the theatre and your face towards Nauplion, my advice is to stay in the one on the left and eat in the one on the right. If you are travelling by bus rather than by bicycle, it is perfectly easy to get to this point from Poros and Galatas or from Nauplion, depending on which way you are going.

So, leaving the theatre unvisited this time, I set off in the general direction of Corinth. The road starts with a short climb and then indulges you in a long, luxurious run down, so you sit touching the brakes now and again to keep your speed below 20 mph because of the virages. There are plenty of hills to climb thereafter, but all the same you cannot fail to realise that there is no way to see a country that compares with viewing it from a bicycle. From a car or bus you do not smell the figs and oranges and pines, and cannot stop at a moment's notice to look down on the bays and villages and churches, and above all you cannot savour the silence. The secret of getting a bicycle up a hill is plenty of walking and pushing. If you have, say, 24 pounds of luggage, comfort yourself by thinking that to push it uphill on a bike is certainly easier than lugging it up on your back, which is what backpackers do.

On the first of two particularly long climbs I passed a line of beehives with a man in full protective clothing doing something to the last hive. The bees were buzzing all about him so I shot past at full speed, which was about 5 mph because of the steepness of the incline. After the second climb it was lunchtime and a taverna turned up, so I stopped.

A little while earlier I had been overtaken by a rusty pick-up truck full of rusty crates full of unhappy chickens. This was now parked in the sun opposite the balcony of the taverna, and a small gypsified boy in trousers too big for him appeared from somewhere and began to do something to the truck's wheels with a spanner and a rock. I rather hoped he was loosening all the nuts so that the wheels would fly off and the truck plunge into the sea, as this would probably cheer the chickens up. They looked to have little life expectancy anyway, and to take the driver with them to the next world would give them some consolation. Whatever he was doing, and I am afraid that I have no idea what it was, the boy worked away with great industry, banging at the spanner with the rock at each wheel in turn. After a bit he decided to prise open the bonnet, meaning perhaps to sabotage the engine as well as the wheels, if indeed sabotage was what he intended. There was no sign of a senior gypsy until the boy, in furtherance of his ambition to get the bonnet up, opened the driver's door and I saw a grown-up gypsy asleep on the front seat. When I rode away the gypsy boy was still wrestling with the bonnet and the senior gypsy was still oblivious to what was going on and the whole thing remained a mystery.

It would be quite useless for me to try to describe the beauty of my surroundings. I was trying to decide whether Ireland or Greece was the more beautiful and gave it up because I think it is whichever one I happen to be in at the time. I did, however, wonder about the road signs. If in England we felt obliged, for some unimaginable reason, to put up signs in Greek, should we get them right or would we put the Greek equivalent of 'Reduced Speed. Dangerous Bents. Distance 10 km'? This is what I kept meeting, and you would think that they might have got someone at the British Embassy to look over the artwork before they made the signs. Perhaps they did. Perhaps some Third Secretary at our embassy in Athens thought he would add a pinch of local colour and a dash of originality by doing it like that, and chuckles every time he drives past.

That day's ride was 30 miles, and it brought me to the sea at Almiri, where I slept in the body-bag. The grandly named Biarritz Campsite seemed to be deserted, but I eventually roused from her siesta an old lady who said I should sleep at a particular spot that she pointed out under some particular pine trees. This spot seemed to be no different from any other spot under any other of the pine trees, and as there was no one else there the whole site was available for me to choose from, but I obediently laid out my bag exactly where she said. It was my first experience of a Greek campsite. The cost was a little over £4; the water was hot, the showers and loos were clean, and the showers had a notice: 'No smoking. Only face at the wash basin. Only one person in showers', so the moral tone was satisfactory.

Having settled the camping arrangements, I went and had a swim, or, to be accurate, I immersed myself in the sea for a close encounter with a large, ferocious-looking jellyfish. The Saronic Gulf seemed to be too small for both of us, so I got out and left it to him. That night I was not merely the only camper on the campsite, but also the only diner at the seaside taverna where I ate small pink fishes and a spinach-type vegetable. The fishes were very lifelike, having kept their heads and tails but lost their entrails, and they looked at me reproachfully, clearly indicating that I must bear some responsibility for their predicament. I washed them down with half a litre of draught pink retsina and then went and lay in my bag listening to a chorus of 1,000 frogs with an occasional tenor solo from one particularly gifted frog, unless it was a bird. My father once had a bottle of De Kuyper's gin on which was written:

He who Kuyper's nightly takes,
Soundly sleeps and fresh awakes.

Pink fish and retsina had that effect on me.

The next morning I had to make a decision. I could stay on the main road which followed the sea and should be flat, but involved going through the middle of Corinth, or I could risk taking a minor road going inland via a village called Xilokeriza, which would dodge around Corinth but might go uphill. The Roman poet Horace remarked that 'Not everyone is lucky enough to go to Corinth', but he was speaking of the days when it was a centre of luxury, extravagance and vice. Modern Corinth is a big, dusty, noisy mess, which the lucky people avoid, so I took the small road. It didn't go uphill and did go through pleasant country, and I met a shepherd who was controlling his sheep in the usual Greek way by shouting and whistling and waving his stick.

All Greek sheep behave as if they have been to obedience-training classes. I once saw a man with a big flock of sheep approaching a busy road, and as they drew near he gave the pastoral equivalent of the military order 'Platoon, halt!' whereupon they all obediently stopped. They waited patiently until there was a break in the traffic, and then he shouted 'Quick march!' or words to that effect, and they ambled across the road in a body and started grazing on the other side. They stayed in the same place until he told them to move on, then they dutifully moved. I told him that in England a man would have a dog to help him, at which he was extremely scornful, saying that a dog was only needed in the mountains and was quite unnecessary on the plains. In the tenth chapter of his gospel, St John, in speaking of a shepherd separating his own sheep from some others, says:

> The sheep hear his voice and he calleth his own sheep by name, and leadeth them out. And when he putteth forth his own sheep, he goeth before them, and the sheep follow him for they know his voice. And a stranger they will not follow, but will flee from him for they know not the voice of strangers.

If you watch a Greek shepherd in action you will see all that happening before your eyes.

There was one huge hill visible, but obviously the road was going to go round it and it was not something I should have to climb over. Then I realised, belatedly and stupidly, that this was the great rock of Acro-Corinth that towers above old Corinth and the remains of the Greek and Roman cities of which it was the citadel. Corinth was at one time immensely rich, due to its situation. The isthmus of Corinth, the narrow neck of land that joins the Peloponnese to the mainland, is now cut by the Corinth Canal, but this is a modern affair, completed in 1893. In classical times goods going from east to west or west to east were either landed on one side of the isthmus and shipped again on the other, or else the ships were hauled across bodily. The only road connecting mainland Greece with the Peloponnese passed through Corinth, so the city prospered in consequence and became a sort of Grecian Venice with a touch of Las Vegas.

The Greek geographer Strabo said that:

> the temple of Aphrodite was so rich that it had more than a thousand temple slaves as prostitutes, and it was just as much on their account that the city attracted great crowds and great riches, with the sea captains spending their money very freely.

Ah yes, they would – one can imagine seafaring men getting through their money at a great rate in such circumstances.

The Corinthians later made the mistake of choosing the wrong side in a war between Rome and Macedon, and furthermore, says Strabo, 'behaved so contemptuously towards the Romans that some of them made so bold as to empty their slops on the heads of their ambassadors when they went by their houses'. The consequence was that the city was sacked by the consul Mummius in 146 BC and lay abandoned until refounded a century later by Julius Caesar, as a Roman colony rather than a Greek city. The morals were as bad as ever, at least among the Jews. 'It is reported commonly,' says St Paul, 'that there is fornication among you, and such fornication as is not so much as named among the Gentiles.'

Corinth was sacked by the Goths of Alaric at the close of the fourth century AD, suffered dreadful earthquakes in the sixth and was pillaged by Normans from Sicily in the twelfth. After all this, you are not to expect a great deal to remain for you to see. There are a few Doric columns surviving from the Temple of Apollo in the old Greek city, and otherwise what appeared to me to be fairly ordinary Roman remains, with the remnants of a few shops and a Roman road.

Acro-Corinth I did not visit, and this, I now realise, was a mistake that should be avoided by anyone following in my footsteps. To reach the summit of the great rock above the city meant a choice between an expensive taxi ride or a one-and-a-half hour climb, and all I expected from the top was a view. As there are views everywhere in Greece I thought I could safely give this one a miss, but since then I have discovered from my ancient Baedeker that 'the view was famous even in antiquity'. Apparently on a clear day you can see the Acropolis at Athens to the east, westwards almost to the mouth of the Gulf of Corinth, and to Helicon and Parnassus to the north. Not just that, but the Rough Guide really gets excited about ruined chapels and almost unending battlements, and is properly enthusiastic about the historical importance of its position, not least in the War of Independence. Well, one makes these mistakes, and I left the hill unclimbed and cycled on towards Patras.

There is a super-highway running from Corinth to Patras, and between it and the sea are the old road and the railway. I assumed that the super-highway would take most of the traffic, but there turned out to be a good many cars and lorries left over which took the old road. However, I came to a bridge at Peripiali with a right fork that led to a quiet coast road. 'Quiet' is not actually an adequate word for it, at least in October when everything is shut for the winter. It lets you see what the world would be like after heavy nuclear fallout or a dose of bubonic plague. There is one continuous ribbon of development of smart new hotels, crumbling old hotels, half-built houses, whole-built mansions, apartment blocks and shops – all completely empty. There are discos, bars, restaurants, pizzerias and nightclubs, but life has stopped and the whole lot are deserted. It seemed as if the disaster must have been quite recent, as the cats were still scavenging in the rubbish, so perhaps all the people had run away because they knew of an impending calamity but they couldn't catch the cats to take with them. Occasionally I would see someone going about his business as if everything was normal – one man was even painting his house, and I felt that I should shout to him, 'Flee! Flee for your life! They are coming! It is happening!' But I thought that he might grasp me by the arm and say, 'Where should I flee to? How can I be safe?' and as I did not know the answer I pedalled on, with the Gulf of Corinth on my right and the peaks of Mount Helicon rising majestically on the far side.

On this road they do not tell you where you are. Up on the main road, where life was still being lived, I had no doubt that people were passing out of one village and into the next, but down by the sea it was a continuous anonymous ghost town, and I wondered how the postman managed to deliver letters even before the evacuation. Eventually the road comes to a factory, turns left and brings you to the main road again at Kiato, where, as I expected, people were behaving as if everything was normal. I rode on, and after Xilokastro the supply of hotels and rooms dried up. Mostly there weren't any, and such as there were, were shut. Those people who I asked in bars or tavernas said they hadn't any rooms, didn't know where there were any, and went on with what they were doing.

On I went beside the sea, one village succeeding the next without intermission but with no hotels, and the light fading fast. I was beginning to wonder about the body-bag when I saw an old gentleman sitting outside a taverna with a very battered sign above his head saying that rooms were to let. He heaved himself on to his eighty-year-old legs and painfully climbed the stairs to show me a sparse room with a single bed. The room was perfectly clean except for the sand that had blown in from the beach across the road, and it cost 3,000 drachmas or about £8.50.

I dined in the taverna below, where there was much shouting going on. The old man shouted from habit, generally at the woman who seemed to be running the place and might have been his daughter or daughter-in-law. Outside on the pavement were five men at one table and one man at another table carrying on a single conversation between them at full shout. Occasionally the daughter or daughter-in-law would walk to the door and shout into the darkness. Once I detected the Greek for 'hurry up' in her shout, and this caused a fat boy in a wet bathing costume to come in from the night and waddle, dripping, through the dining room. The television was also on, which I watched with fascination.

In the short breaks between advertisements there was

what seemed to be a combined police-and-hospital soap opera. First a uniformed man in a police station hurled abuse at another man who looked like General Colin Powell and who, not unnaturally, went away. A dark girl appeared, to whom the policeman talked, kissing her at intervals. Then it switched to a woman with fair hair and a man in a suit and what looked like a wig. He was trying to take the clothes off the fair woman, and as they were in her bedroom and she was in a dressing gown it seemed a reasonable idea, but she raised some objection that they were still discussing when it switched to three laughing nurses who were changing sheets in a hospital. Then it went back to the police station where they were still talking and kissing. Then the clothes came off the fair woman. The man was no longer in his suit but was still in his wig, and he and the woman began writhing on the bed. Then there was more of the three jolly nurses, and that was the end of the episode.

When I went to bed, the six men were shouting below my window and the sea was noisily pounding the shore, which I suppose is a soporific sound as I went to sleep at once. I woke later because the men were shouting goodnight to each other at extra volume, but I went back to sleep immediately, waking at 6 a.m. to hear the sea pounding even more vigorously.

When I set off next morning I found that the road towards Patras was still pretty sparsely provided with hotels until Derveni or thereabouts, where things seemed to get back to normal. Any cyclist relying on rooms between Xilokastro and Derveni, or even Diakofto, is living dangerously. Be warned.

I reached Diakofto in good style by about noon, with

the sun blazing away as it had ever since I left Poros. The point about Diakofto, and the reason that people visit it, is the rack-and-pinion railway, which climbs up a mountain gorge to Kalavrita. People arrive by train on the one-track railway from Athens, presumably because they like trains like that, although the buses are more efficient. Then they get off in order to go up and down to and from Kalavrita as they like rack-and-pinion trains even more. Then they get back on the ordinary train and disappear, either in the direction of Patras and Olympia or else to Corinth and Athens. The station is always crowded with elderly foreigners and juvenile backpackers, and the shops and *cafeneia* (cafés) must all be owned by millionaires as they are constantly selling biscuits and fruit or serving food and drink to the people in transit.

I had been worrying as to whether I should attempt a high-level, long and taxing ride through the mountains from Kalavrita to Patras, always assuming that the mountain railway would take my bicycle up from Diakofto to Kalavrita. It was obviously a very hilly route and the body-bag was likely to be brought into play as there would probably be nowhere to stay along the road. 'Exploring' says Samuel Butler in *Erewhon*, 'is delightful to look forward to and back upon, but it is not comfortable at the time, unless it be of such an easy nature as not to deserve the name.' Undeniably the route I was contemplating was a challenge, and my usual response to a challenge is to walk the other way. I learned this from a man I met in Scotland who said, 'I like mountain walking, but I object to getting lost, breaking my leg or falling in a bog – so if it's a challenge, I give it a miss.' I was enormously impressed by this philosophy, which I have adopted on my own account. It was George Mallory, I believe, who said he wanted to climb Everest 'because it is there', whereas I, if a mountain is there, prefer to go carefully round the bottom. On this occasion, though, the Greek Tourist Board leaflet on the Peloponnese gives such a glowing account of the scenic beauties of this route that my inclination was, if I could, to make the attempt.

The matter was settled by the man in the ticket office at Diakofto. I asked him if the mountain railway would take my bicycle up to Kalavrita, and he said most emphatically and definitely that it would not. I think he must have been having an unhappy time that morning, because I subsequently found that the train has a big luggage area where you can easily put a bicycle, and furthermore I met a German couple who had done it. Perhaps I should not have asked.

Anyone who succeeds in getting their bicycle up to Kalavrita by train has three choices. One is to go west towards Patras as I had aspired to do. Another is to go south towards Tripolis, a trip I have done by bus, and the scenery is truly superb but I don't know where you can stay along the way. The third is to give yourself a treat and coast downhill by road back to Diakofto. If any reader of this book does the first of these and could be so kind as to send me a postcard telling me if I have missed anything really important, I should be most grateful.

On this occasion I was not-too-secretly relieved to have the matter taken out of my hands. I went and found somewhere to stay in a house by the sea in a room that was clean and cheap and had a good view. The room belonged to one of the family, a student whose boots were still there, but I was assured that I should not see anything of him other than his boots, and did not. I left my bicycle and walked back to catch the 2 p.m. train up the gorge.

Everybody, not just railway buffs but everybody who possibly can, should go on the Kalavrita railway. I had been before, but I liked it even more this time because I understood how it worked. I had looked up 'rack' and 'pinion' in the dictionary but could not understand the explanation; however, a man I met in Austria demonstrated how it worked with the aid of a table knife and a mustard pot. The knife, he said, represented a rail with teeth, and the mustard pot was a wheel with teeth. If you engaged the teeth of the mustard pot with those of the knife and then turned the mustard pot, it went along. He also said that as a method of getting trains up hills this was very expensive because of the wear on the teeth, so you only used it when essential and otherwise laid ordinary track as if for an ordinary train. Once you know this you can see what is happening on the Kalavrita railway. It explains why a lot of the track is normal and the train rattles along at a great rate; then from time to time a third rail, which is the rack, makes its appearance, and the train stops to engage the pinion. Then the train grinds slowly forward up a steep bit, stops, then speeds off again on ordinary rails.

The real point of this engineering triumph is that it takes you up the rockiest of gorges in the most spectacular of scenery. You look up, and huge crags tower above you, threatening to precipitate an avalanche of rock upon you at any moment. You look down, and there is a sheer drop to a river below into which the train itself might easily be dashed. The train staggers and groans, and you feel that the engine has given out, the brakes will fail and the whole thing run backwards so that you are all killed that way. You pass under unsafe ledges, and the driver hoots at lunatic young people who are walking on the track and would certainly be crushed to death if the train met them in one of the tunnels. It is altogether a most exhilarating experience. The train tends to be full of laughing children and teenagers, but if you bought a first-class ticket you ought to be able to sit by the driver in the first-class compartment at the front and get the best view.

The town of Kalavrita is at the top of the railway and the journey takes a little over an hour. I had stayed there some years before and met a most enterprising Englishman in the hotel. He was a lecturer in health and safety at a London polytechnic, which you would think would be an enervating way to earn a living, but being a man of dash and go he had managed to turn things to his advantage. Noticing that the Greeks were applying for membership of the European Union, he saw at once that they would be overwhelmed with a flood of health and safety regulations originating from Brussels ordering them to stop doing things that they had done since time immemorial and to behave themselves in a way which would never have entered their heads. Instantly he seized the opportunity to corner the market in initiating the Greeks into these mysteries and so made frequent trips to Greece, either to lecture on the spot or to check on the progress of students who had been to England to see the safe and healthy way in which we were managing our affairs. When I met him, a weekend had intervened in the middle of his lectures (I suspect that he generally arranged things so that weekends intervened). Accordingly, he had relaxed in his efforts to stamp out such atrocious Greek practices as climbing into olive trees without a safety net, put a little knapsack on his back and set off for Kalavrita. He had ridden up the gorge on the train that day and was going to walk down it the next, and I was greatly impressed on all counts.

Three-quarters of the way up the railway is the monastery of Megaspeleion, which was visited in 1850 by George Ferguson Bowen Esq. M.A., Fellow of Brasenose College (as it says on the title page of his book). He rode up on horseback through vineyards of currant grapes, many of which belonged to the monks, who could hardly be got to talk on any other subject:

> 'How many inmates are there in the monastery?' we asked.
> 'Three hundred,' they replied, 'and how much do you think grapes will fetch this year in England?'
> 'Is your library in good order?'
> 'No, but our grapes are of excellent quality.'
> 'May we see your church?'
> 'Certainly; we hope you will recommend us to the English merchants of Patras.'

I will mention *en passant* that George Ferguson Bowen also says:

> We may mention *en passant* that the dwarf grape, the fruit of which is so plentifully consumed in England, derives its usual appellation of *currant* from a corruption of *Corinth*, its French name being *raisin de Corinthe*.

To get to the monastery nowadays you get off the mountain railway at Zakhlorou. From there the walk to the monastery is said to take 45 minutes, and it is as well not to try to beat that time as the way is steep and slippery. The scenery is magnificent with the stillness broken, in my case, only by the ringing of bells by goats on the way up and by monks on the way down. During the War of Independence, when the Greeks were in revolt against their Turkish conquerors, the monks defended their monastery with great heroism.

In 1826 they were besieged by Ibrahim Pasha, whereupon, says Bowen:

> The fathers, calling in a brave band of mountaineers to their aid, set the infidels at defiance. They fortified with barricades, planted with cannon, and flanked with excellent marksmen the front of the building, on which side alone it is accessible. Several onsets of the Turks were driven back with great skill and courage.

Ibrahim tried rolling down rocks and burning trees from above but they all fell outside the walls, and he eventually retired, having lost some hundreds of his best troops.

'We conversed' says Bowen, 'with several of the monks who had borne a prominent part in the siege. They piously ascribe to the aid of their wonder-working image the triumph won by their own strong arms and gallant hearts.' This is a reference to their famous portrait of the Virgin Mary painted by St Luke, which I most stupidly forgot to ask to see. I hope no interfering busybody will submit it to any foolish carbon-dating techniques such as those used on the Turin Shroud. There is apparently another such picture in Istanbul, of which they have a 700-year-old copy in one of the monasteries of the Meteora in Thessaly. This I have seen, so I know what it is to gaze upon the Palestinian features of the Mother of Christ as depicted by the hand of the evangelist, and I would not wish to be disturbed in my belief in the authenticity of any of these paintings.

Most unfortunately the building that George Ferguson Bowen visited was burned down in 1934 by a fire resulting from the explosion of a powder magazine left over from those earlier times, and the new one looks like a Hilton hotel that some giant has picked up and glued to the face of a cliff. The name of the monastery, Megaspeleion, means 'the great cave', and it is so called because it is built round the mouth of a huge natural cavern which goes some 90 feet into the cliff face. There were originally cells for the monks within the cave but they now have more salubrious quarters in the Hilton-type building. The monk in charge at the library presides over a display of manuscripts, which are largely of a theological nature. There are also grisly relics of a sort I do not like, such as a mummified hand seemingly belonging to St Theodore. The superintendent monk drew my attention to a cross of gold wire made by a man in Smyrna who devoted 16 years to the project and went blind as a result – which, I am sorry to say, did not seem to me to have been worth it.

The walk down from the monastery is definitely not something to be hurried as it is of the ankle-twisting variety owing to loose gravel, and a stick would be handy. At Zakhlorou there is a hotel and restaurant called Romantso, decidedly ramshackle in appearance but where I would certainly risk staying if alone, as the situation is superb. Whether I would risk it with my wife is another matter altogether.

Those who go to the top of the railway at Kalavrita will find a memorial with the clock stopped at 2.43, the time when a particularly savage atrocity was perpetrated by the Germans in 1943. The Greek resistance had been very active in the area, and in reprisal the Germans took 700 men to the cemetery and mowed them down with machine guns. They locked the women and children in the schoolhouse and set fire to it. At the last minute an Austrian soldier unlocked the door and five women were saved, but all the rest perished.

From Zakhlorou I caught the last train back to Diakofto and dined in the open air with a fine view of the railway station, this being the hub of the whole town. So far on this trip I had eaten only fish but now I ordered souvlaki, lumps of meat on a skewer which can be very good but this time were not. Maybe I had nearly drifted into being a vegetarian, but the meat seemed stringy and stuck in my throat. I was struggling with it when a woman arrived.

The woman was Greek and thin, aged perhaps 40, with orange hair and a smoker's cough, but in other ways not unattractive. She came and spoke to me in Greek, asking if the chair on which she proposed to sit was free. I said it was, so she sat on it and from then on we spoke English. I think I should explain that I am really pretty unsociable, but all my life I have seen my relations with people whom I disliked ripening into friendship against my will. Schoolboys who I did not care for would ask me to tea, and then I was made to ask them back. That sort of thing all too easily leads to an invitation to go and stay in the holidays, which meant days of dreadful boredom in someone else's house followed by the dreadful bore coming to our house. There was a young man at Oxford who thought he had a licence to turn up in my rooms whenever he felt like it and really believed that I was always delighted to drop whatever I was doing and give him coffee. His conversation was almost exclusively about Harrow, where he had been at school. To my enormous delight he failed his exams at the end of the first year and disappeared, without which merciful dispensation I believe he would still be one of my closest friends.

I know all the symptoms when someone is about to fasten themselves upon me in this way, but I have never found a way to head them off. It was rather like that now.

Here was this woman who I did not want to talk to. The meat that I did not much want to eat was not made any better by her blowing cigarette smoke at it. I had no interest in satisfying her curiosity about where I came from, how I got here, and what I did for a living, nor did I much care that she was divorced, lived in Corinth and was on holiday. In a moment of madness I bought her a cup of coffee. I don't know why I did this, but she was sitting there and we were talking and I was drinking, and I asked if she would like a drink and she said she would like coffee, so I ordered it. Then we were stuck. I got to the end of the meat and I could, I thought desperately, get up and say I was going to bed, but would she insist on accompanying me? Fear began to take over, and my conversation became increasingly wild and disrupted.

Then she said she had a headache. Had I got an aspirin? Of course I hadn't got an aspirin. I do not sit at tables outside railway stations with my pockets bulging with medicaments for the use of passers-by, casual acquaintances, or women trying to pick me up, whichever was the right description. Nevertheless the shops on the other side of the station were open, and with that habitual politeness to women with which I am afflicted, I said I would go and get her some aspirin if she wished. She did wish it, and as she did not proffer any money I crossed the tracks and bought some aspirin with my money. When I got back she had gone.

This was unexpected, but I feared it might be temporary and that she would be back at any moment. I put the packet of aspirin at her place, finished my wine and was drinking a cup of coffee when she reappeared in most surprising circumstances. She was parading up and down the station platform on the arm of a young man in the uniform of a corporal in the Greek Army. Evidently her headache was better, and in a matter of minutes she had found a more promising acquaintance than me. I waved the aspirin in the air in a tentative sort of way in case she needed it for a future occasion, but she would not so much as glance in my direction, being wholly concentrated on the captured corporal. He was wearing an anxious, hunted look, which I dare say was my own expression a quarter of an hour before. I felt a good deal of sympathy towards him, but had a much stronger feeling of relief that the problem was now his and not mine, so I paid my bill and withdrew thankfully to find my room.

This was in a house by the sea, on a quiet road with trees but no shops, discos or tavernas. A nearly full moon was shining on the waves, and I was so entranced with the scene and elated with my escape that I walked straight past the house, overshooting it by a couple of hundred yards, and had to turn back to find it.

On the morning after my trip on the Kalavrita railway I had breakfast at the thriving hub of Diakofto, i.e. the station, and discovered that an important invention had been made since my last visit in the shape of a two-compartment yogurt pot, the larger part being full of yogurt and the smaller of honey. One of these and a double coffee set me on the road to Patras, and I soon became entirely reconciled to cutting out the cross-country trip from Kalavrita; in fact, I was positively grateful to the ticket clerk who vetoed it. No doubt the scenery is very fine up there, but so it was down where I was. On the left are mountains, on the right is the sea, and then the foothills of Parnassus on the other side. The old road is not busy, or at least not on Sunday. For company you have the railway and the new highway, and you pass over the one and under the other from time to time. It is the sort of road on which the bicycle seems to hit a stride and bowl along with no effort, checking a little on a slight rise but giving you a rest as it canters down the other side. That great Cambridge rowing coach Roy Meldrum many years ago told me that for anyone who had really mastered the technique that he advocated, it felt as if the water reached up and took the end of the oar and pulled. This made it very much easier for the oarsman who didn't have to struggle and gasp in the usual way. It is a sensation which I felt perhaps half a dozen times under his coaching, and the way the bicycle was going along by itself was rather on the same lines.

There was one tricky moment when I thought I was getting onto the main highway by mistake, but it proved to be the outskirts of Egion, a sprawling, ugly place that I had to go through the middle of. It was replete with ominous signs. The route I followed was marked 'Hospital'; off to the left it said 'Civic Cemetery' in English as if for my special benefit; and most alarming of all, there was a big sign in Greek saying 'Brain Diagnostic Centre'. I had just been thinking that for the cyclist the worst drivers in the world are the English as they go too fast and they come too close, whereas the Greeks, like the French and the Irish, treat you respectfully and give you a wide berth. These signs suggested that I might have been too hasty and was about to come to a sticky end in Egion, so I rode with some anxiety lest I should go through a red light and be taken unconscious to the Brain Diagnostic Centre. Suddenly it was all behind me, and the sea and the open road were back again. The bicycle evidently had not liked Egion any better than I did because it now showed definite signs of bolting, so I slipped it into top gear and gave it its head. Together we sprinted for the best part of a mile until I had to rein it in for a level crossing.

As we flung Egion behind us I saw two cruise ships tied up to a wharf. 'Now there's a rotten way to see Greece,' said I to myself. 'Penned in a ship and crammed with food and facts, then herded ashore at somewhere like Delphi just when it is most crowded with tourists delivered by the busload. Then back to the ship for more food and more facts till you are marched ashore again and made to jostle with the crowds at Olympia. Then they send you home having seen so much and been told such a lot that your brains are scrambled and you are not at all sure where you have been or what it was like.' Such at least is what people say when they have given up the attempt to delude themselves into thinking that it was money well spent. If they can escape from the lectures and the forced marches they can possibly relieve the tedium with what Lord Macaulay said are the two principal diversions of a sea voyage – quarrelling and flirting. Possibly not; they may be too old for flirting and too carefully regimented for quarrelling.

Swan Hellenic recently sent me a brochure for a cruise to Italy that confirmed my worst fears. Venice, it says, is 'one of the most remarkable cities in the world', which is not exactly news. It then says things like: 'Friday. Day at sea. Time to catch up with the lectures', as if, having missed the lectures by going ashore you are somehow going to catch up with them again after they are over. Most intimidating to me was: 'Wednesday. A morning at sea. Relax on deck with a good book from the extensive library aboard.' I can see myself in my cabin reading a Dick Francis novel when the steward enters: 'What's this, Mr Enfield, skulking below with a work of fiction? This will not do at all. Take this volume of Grote's *History of Greece* from our extensive library and get up on deck at once.' As I slink up the companion way I hear him shouting after me, 'And don't let me catch you in the swimming pool – that isn't scheduled until Saturday.'

As a further example of the way you see things from a bicycle that you do not see otherwise, I will now report that on the Greek road sign indicating that children may be crossing, the girl has a pigtail. I bet very few people who have been to Greece have noticed that. The little sister with a pigtail goes in front and her big brother goes behind; they are both carrying their school books and are rather sweet. On the comparable sign in England they appear to be dashing across the road in a foolhardy and irresponsible manner.

At a seaside place called Rodini where I turned off for coffee, my bicycle was much admired by a young man called Georgios who could have served as a model for the boy on the crossing sign. I sat writing in my notebook by the beach, occasionally raising my eyes to admire the hills on the other side of the Gulf of Corinth. Meanwhile, behind me, Georgios was giving a lecture to his friends on the beauties of the gear change, the subtlety of the lighting system, and the ingenuity of the computerised milometer on my bicycle.

From Rodini I arrived in Patras, a terrible place, worse than Egion because it is bigger. What you want to do is find your way through it, which is easy, and get out of it, which is difficult as it seems to go on for ever.

The road, which was busy even on Sunday, went past rubbish of all sorts discarded along the coast, plus an encampment of the dirtiest and most depressed of Gypsies established on a tip. I had ridden 40 miles that day, and the heat and the distance were beginning to tell, so, although still not free of Patras, I began to look for somewhere to stay. There didn't seem to be anywhere, so I went on and on, getting hotter and hotter in the unattractive outskirts of this unappealing city. At last a sign appeared indicating that if I turned left there was a hotel. I wondered very much what I should get in these surroundings – 'insalubrious' was the word that sprang to mind – but what I did get was a clean, quiet and luxurious room with air conditioning (not needed), a bath (very hot water) and a television set. From this I discovered that there is a BBC world television service, something I had not known about before. It showed news, an item about the plight of people making sulphur in India, a film about an English governess in Argentina, and Michael Fish telling me tomorrow was going to be a fine day in Greece.

There seemed to be a mini-drama as I was booking in at the hotel. A thin man with grey hair, wearing black trousers and a white silk shirt, swaggered in, followed forlornly by a pretty but deadpan girl in black. He flung something, I could not see what, at the clerk, who gave him a key, plus a TV control, which the man angrily rejected. He and the girl started towards the staircase in silence, then the man turned back, snatched up the TV control as angrily as he had rejected it before, and they slowly mounted the stairs together. There was no sign of luggage. The next morning while I was loading my bicycle the sultry but sulky girl stalked down the stairs alone, through the hall, out of the door and was gone, leaving me feeling sorry for her without exactly knowing why.

The topic occupying my mind in the night had been whether or not I should deviate to visit Khalandritsa. This would have been the last village before Patras on the cross-country route from Kalavrita if I had come that way. The idea had been put into my head by the Greek Tourist Board leaflet:

> These places and their myriad tiny villages are difficult to describe. To get to know them, you need to get out of your car, walk through the streets, visit their castles and churches, mingle with the people, take a drink with them and clink your glasses in a toast.

About Khalandritsa it said: 'Stone houses, courtyards, narrow lanes, a ruined Frankish castle, countless churches, bell towers with a Western touch. The heart of Achaea begins to pound.'

It seemed a pity to miss it altogether but the clerk in my hotel regarded the idea of going there by bicycle as preposterous. I don't know the Greek for preposterous, and it wasn't what he said exactly, but from the way he reacted there was no other word for it. If I insisted upon doing it I must go back to the middle of Patras and start from there. However much I tried to prove from the map that there must be a shorter way he could not be shifted from this position. If there was a shorter way he did not know it. He did not know how far it was, only that it was too far for a sane man to attempt by bicycle.

The man in the pizza place where I had eaten the night before was more helpful. He too wanted me to go back to Patras but once I positively and energetically vetoed this idea, he acknowledged that I could not have chosen a better place from which to start than where I was now. If I went straight along the side of the hotel as far as a T-junction and turned left, I would come to the Patras to Tripolis road where I should turn right, and after a bit I would see the sign to Khalandritsa and

Kalavrita. He drew me a map on a table napkin that was sufficiently clear for me to go wrong only twice before I emerged on the right road.

The distance to Khalandritsa proved to be ten miles. It was a stiff climb, and at one point the wind blew so strongly in my face that I had to pedal even on one of the rare downhill bits. All the same, it only took me an hour and forty minutes, so as far as getting there goes, there was nothing much to it. Unfortunately there was nothing much to being there either, as the Tourist Board leaflet proved to be a triumph of the copy-writer's art. I did as I was told, got off my bicycle and walked through the streets, but it looked very much like anywhere else. Not all the houses were stone by any means; in fact very few of them were. I did not see a courtyard of any special merit, I couldn't find the Frankish castle, and the countless churches seemed easy enough to count, being three in number. The bell towers looked like any others. I didn't manage to clink glasses, but I bought an ice cream from a man who appeared to be condemned to spend his days sitting in a kiosk with nothing to do. The people were all very friendly, particularly a young man who admired my bicycle outside a *cafeneion*, but I can't say that I quite felt the heart of Achaea pounding. Even so, I was very glad to have made the effort, as it was a great consolation to think that I should not now spend the rest of my life wondering if I had made a great mistake by not going there.

Fortunately Khalandritsa is in a beautiful situation, and the ride back was exceptional because the wind was now behind me so I hardly had to pedal at all, and certainly never with any vigour, until I got to the beginning of the outskirts of Patras. This dreaded town

I then circumnavigated successfully by going on any little road that seemed to be heading south unless it showed signs of going upwards, in which case I branched off it towards the sea.

Then I rode in the direction of Pirgos, and the road became very busy, so the cycling for once was more a means to an end than a pleasure in itself. Still, the road was flat and the wind was behind me so I made good progress at an effortless 17 miles per hour. It would nevertheless be a great boon to cyclists if the Greek government could get a grant from Brussels to make a cycle track beside the railway that runs down the west coast of the Peloponnese, and so get us off this bit of road.

The other thing they need a grant for is rubbish. The Greeks have a serious rubbish problem, particularly a problem with polythene which is to be found everywhere in the form of agricultural detritus. With the rubbish go rats. I only saw one live rat, but I saw plenty of dead ones squashed on the road. If the Greek government could get a grant to get rid of all the litter and set up rubbish-processing plants for the future, and then bring in flogging as the penalty for dropping litter as in Singapore, things would be much better. I expect there are enough horrible policemen left over from the days of the Colonels to administer whatever penalty was thought appropriate, however ferocious.

I was aiming for Chlemoutsi, which the Blue Guide calls 'the best preserved Frankish monument in the Morea'. I like the way they called it the Morea, this being an antiquarian term for the Peloponnese that went out of use years ago. After a time – after a pretty long time, to be truthful – the road arrangements improved because

I got off the new road and onto the old road to Pirgos and arrived at a place called Lehena. The castle of Chlemoutsi is in a village called Kastro, and from Lehena to Kastro the way is clearly signposted and the road peaceful.

As I came into Kastro I saw a sign advertising rooms to let three hundred metres ahead, so I went that way but there was no house with any such notice to be seen. Two Greek girls assured me that it was the house opposite the oil barrel in the road, so I went there and found a courtyard with an old gentleman sunning himself in a plastic chair. I asked him in my best taped Greek if I could have a room for the night, which caused him to leap in the air and bolt into the house like a startled rabbit. A few moments later another man came out to ask in English what it was I wanted. The man whom I had frightened was, I learned, an Englishman from Luton. He and his wife were on a visit to his daughter who had married a Greek. Understandably, the father-in-law was not used to dealing with strange men who appeared from nowhere and started speaking in tongues.

The son-in-law looked rather sorrowful as officially they were shut for the winter, but he said that I had better have a cup of coffee while he thought the matter over. Accordingly, I sat and chatted to the man from Luton who told me that the easiest way to get from England to Kastro was to fly to Zante and take the ferry to Killini, a crossing of a mere one and a half hours. This may be useful information for anyone wanting to get directly to the southern Peloponnese. Then the son-in-law reappeared to say that his wife would have to clean the room but if I didn't mind waiting, it would be done.

'Never mind,' said I, 'if you are shut, you are shut. I can get a room in the village.'

'No, it will be no trouble. My wife will do it.'

I did most fervently hope that the wife was as well disposed to the idea as her husband now seemed determined on it. It was settled that, it being now three o'clock, I would visit the castle at Chlemoutsi which the son-in-law said shut at five o'clock, then when I came back the room would be ready.

After the sack of Constantinople by crusaders in 1204, Greece had a sort of Norman Conquest of its own, except that the conquerors, known as Franks, came from Burgundy, Lombardy and Champagne, as well as from Normandy via Sicily. They carved the country up into feudal kingdoms and turned the Peloponnese into the Principate of Achaea. Many of the castles of Greece are relics of this time, including that at Chlemoutsi which, being designed for the subjugation of the surrounding countryside, was built high up with a view to keeping an eye on things in every direction. In consequence you can see it from a long way off as you approach, and then there is a steady climb to the top of the town to reach the castle. In terms of Frankish castles it seemed to be pretty big. I cannot say how big, but I have seen several smaller ones in England, and I dare say that in circumference it could keep company with Cardiff or Caernarvon, though not quite in terms of repair. The outer wall is in good shape though, and they are putting the rest of it back together so you can see what the huge keep used to be like and get a general idea of the other arrangements. It seemed strange to me to imagine Frankish knights with names like Geoffrey de Villehardouin clanking about in armour and saying things of a medieval nature such as 'Beshrew thee, Jacques, thou art as arrant a knave as ever drew clothyard shaft.' I have never been able to discover what happened to these Frenchmen. The descendants of the Normans who arrived in Ireland with names like de Burgo survive there under the name of Burke, but I have never heard of any Hellenised version of the Crusaders called Boniface or de la Roche. Perhaps they just went away.

There was no one but me at the castle. The iron gate with a padlock stood open, and in case my landlord was wrong about closing time I locked my bicycle to it as a strong hint that I was inside and did not wish to be imprisoned for the night. Outside you cannot walk quite round the perimeter unless you are more closely allied to a mountain goat than I, but by going first to the left and then to the right you cover 95 per cent of it, and the views are stunning, both over the plain of Elis, which is studded with olive groves and pine woods, and out to sea towards Zante.

Kastro and Chlemoutsi were places that I found by accident. That is to say, until I noticed them marked on the map with a symbol indicating they had something special to offer, I had never heard of either of them or of anyone who had been there. Kastro proved to be quite a big and bustling place well provided with rooms and hotels. My landlord, who seemed to have some of the ubiquitous qualities of Nicos in Poros, bobbed up in the middle of the town to see how I was getting on and to tell me where to eat that evening. I was rather regretting having taken a room in his house as there were others more central, but I was wrong. I went back and met my landlady from Luton who took me up to my room and threw back the curtains with a flourish.

There, in a great sweeping arc, was a plain of olive trees and then the sea. The room was ultra-clean with various English touches such as the bed actually being made instead of just left with a sheet and blanket dumped on it, as is usual. Furthermore, to my utmost joy, on the landing were an electric kettle and some teabags. I sat on my balcony, drank two cups of tea, which were the first of the trip, and marvelled at the view. It was the best place at which I had stayed so far, combining comfort with a magnificent prospect.

Later that evening I discovered that Kastro, which seemed to have plenty of churches already, had yet another under construction. It was very big and when I saw it, it was at the grey concrete stage but by now it is probably white. Anyone who has been to Greece will know that Greeks love building churches and do it all over the place. Some are in the form of tiny white chapels in inaccessible places in hills, where I suspect they are tended by devout women and only used for worship on the day of the saint to whom they are dedicated. Some are in towns which, like Kastro, have got plenty of churches already but still want more. If you said in England, 'We have got to double the number of churches in the country,' the reply would be, 'Impossible! The cost would ruin us.' In Greece they would say, 'What a great idea! When do we start?'

I had walked up into the town for dinner and again encountered my landlord, though he may not have been truly ubiquitous but just avoiding his in-laws. At Chlemoutsi I had noticed floodlights in position but had forgotten about them until now, when I found that the castle was beautifully illuminated. My landlord directed me to walk down a certain road from which to get the best view, and I was so much struck with it that after dinner I walked right out of Kastro in the other direction to see the castle from beyond the town altogether. There are few enough aspects of modern life that I approve wholeheartedly, but until recently floodlighting was one. Oxford when floodlit reverts to being the beautiful city it was in my youth, instead of the crowded, scruffy place they now make of it by day. Then I read that floodlighting is bad because it makes it difficult to see the stars, so that was another innocent pleasure ruined.

Dinner that night started as a linguistic triumph. I seemed to have hit upon a vein of high-speed Greek that enabled me to carry out a quick-fire conversation with the waiter. Although I did not follow everything he said, I got it established that I wanted a measure of draught retsina while I wrote some postcards, and afterwards I would order my dinner. When it came to the latter exercise I ordered aubergines, potatoes and small fried fishes. What came, pretty soon, was a basket of bread with a knife and fork; a plate of delicious potato chips fried in oil, which I put to the left; a plate of aubergine likewise fried and wholly delectable, which I put to the right; and to occupy the middle position, nothing at all. 'Ah well,' I thought, 'the fish will be coming,' so I started picking at the potatoes and aubergine while they were still piping hot. But the fish did not come. The vegetables cooled, I ate them faster, my appetite diminished, still no fish! I asked the waiter, who was now dashing about at full speed, and he said they were on the way and that I was to keep calm. 'Siga, siga!' So I surrendered to the ineradicable Greek habit of giving you things when they are ready and not when you want them. I was glad that my wife was not with me. Had she been there I might have felt obliged to make a fuss and either demand fish *now*, or make them take away the vegetables and keep them hot. As it was, just as I finished everything else the little fishes arrived with a few more potatoes, and were delicious.

Olympia, Bassae, Pilos, Koroni

The next day, after two cups of morning tea on the balcony at Kastro, I took a long downhill run with a deviation through a eucalyptus grove to see the Loutra Killinis, the thermal baths of Killini. These have a considerable surrounding development and a most disgusting smell. The bathhouse, apart from the stench of sulphur, was like a hospital with old people like myself or even older sitting in their dressing gowns outside cubicles waiting for something – total immersion, miraculous rejuvenation or death, who knows? The television programme that I had watched in Patras had said that the people in India who made sulphur got terribly ill, so it seemed odd that getting into a solution of the stuff would do good. Anyway, I might possibly have taken a hot sulphur bath out of curiosity had it been the end of the day, but I wasn't going to do it at ten in the morning, so I moved on, heading for Pirgos, from where I meant to go on to Olympia.

From Loutra Killinis there was a good spell of quiet road with the castle of Chlemoutsi looming up on the left, then a long spell on the main road. I got off it by a happy bit of map reading. At a clearly marked turning to Amaliada, to which I could see that I did not want to go at all, there was also a carefully hidden side road marked to Douneika. This seemed to be the right direction, and the road took me on a peaceful trip through an anonymous village with a semi-cathedral under construction as part of the neverending ecclesiastical works programme.

At siesta time I noticed a small white church set well back in an olive grove so I turned down the track to reach it and was about to settle down in the shade when a priest and a farmer arrived, looking rather worried at my presence. I asked if I could rest in the shade of a tree (Lesson 16 of my Linguaphone course) which cheered the farmer up and to which he happily assented. I think they had thought I had some sacrilegious intentions towards the church. This they now unlocked and between them carried in a large brass candelabrum that they had brought in the farmer's pick-up truck. Then they went away and I, like Kai Lung, the Chinese storyteller, unrolled my mat and went to sleep.

My little road rejoined the main road shortly before the Pirgos bypass. I had thought that to go to Kastro from Olympia in one day might be a bit far, but I felt fresh, it was not too hot and Olympia was now only 16 miles away so I rode on. I had left the coast road and struck inland to Olympia for a purpose, which was to see why I hadn't liked the place when I went there before. This may seem a strange reason for coming back, but I thought there must have been something wrong with me as everyone else thought it was marvellous. I made out itineraries for friends who were going to Greece, saying, 'You have to go to Olympia because it is Olympia but you will be disappointed,' and they came back saying, 'You were quite right – Olympia is *wonderful*,' which was not what I had said at all. Perhaps my problem was due to the fact that someone had said to me, 'If you like Delphi you will like Olympia even more as it is so much greener,' so I arrived with enormously high hopes, only to have them dashed. Or perhaps it was the dog.

In one of the Sherlock Holmes stories there is 'the curious incident of the dog in the night-time'.

'The dog did nothing in the night-time.'

'That was the curious incident,' remarked Sherlock Holmes. Unfortunately this Olympia dog did not do nothing in the night-time, it ran around barking. Sometimes it barked directly under my window, and sometimes it ran barking down the street and then ran barking back. Occasionally, by way of variation, it howled. I was not the first to have met this problem. The Irish classical scholar J. P. Mahaffy, just down the road at Pirgos in 1873, says:

> Nowhere does the ultra-democratic temper of new Greek social life show itself more manifestly than in these disturbed streets. It seems to be considered an infraction upon liberty to silence yelping dogs, braying donkeys or any other animal which chooses to disturb its neighbours.

Donkeys I do not mind, as theirs is quite a pleasant sound to wake up to, but a dog yelping all night has nothing to be said for it, and that time I got up in a bad temper.

This time I liked Olympia better, but not all that much better. The town, which has one main street, seemed undignified. It has surrendered entirely to tourism, with signs saying things like 'Fast Food' or 'Joe's Diner'. There are the same sort of jewellers as in most places, but one with the surprising sign: 'YANNIS: Gold Jewellery, Gold Schmuk'. I thought at first that Yannis had a very low opinion of the stuff he was selling, but I later found from the dictionary that 'Schmuk' is just the German for jewellery. Still, I think we might adopt it into English to mean the sort of stuff you get in tourist shops, which is what it sounds like.

There is a greater preponderance of this sort of schmuk at Olympia than there ought to be, and particularly of obscene postcards, statuettes, ashtrays and such like. The postcards are supposed to be representations of things going on on Greek vases, but I have seen plenty of Greek vases in my time, and never with such goings on as are going on on the postcards. If such vases really exist, they keep them well hidden from the general public, and so they should.

As for the situation of Olympia, it is indeed green, with greenery on every side, but nevertheless it is disappointing. All the other major archaeological sites that I have been to, such as Delphi, the Acropolis at Athens, Dodona or Bassae are all in truly spectacular situations and Olympia does not compare. Certainly to my mind it has nothing to offer against the wonderful sensation that you get at Delphi from standing with Mount Parnassus behind you and gazing out to sea over the olive groves. In this heretical aspect of things J. P. Mahaffy more or less concurred:

> When we came to Olympia the prospect was truly disenchanting. However interesting excavations may be, they are always exceedingly ugly. Instead of grass and flowers, and

> pure water, we found the classic spot defaced with great mounds of earth, and trodden bare of grass. We found the Kladeus flowing a turbid drain into the larger river. We found hundreds of workmen, and wheelbarrows, and planks, and trenches, instead of solitude and birds. Thus it was that we found the famous Temple of Zeus.

The archaeological site now is much better. It is very large, very well supplied with trees and there is certainly something remarkable about walking through the tunnel by which the Olympic athletes entered the stadium. All the same, if you took one of the classical Greeks to see it he would say: 'There has been an earthquake, so why don't you put it back together?' and to some extent I wonder why they don't. Some of the columns of the Temple of Zeus have fallen over in an orderly manner, as if you had built a pile of dominoes and then knocked it over, and it looked a simple enough job to rebuild them by stacking the drums up again. When Olympia was at its peak there was a conglomeration of temples, treasuries, porticoes, official buildings and some 3,000 statues, and it was doubtless a fine sight. Now it puts me in mind of London in the future, as imagined by Lord Macaulay 'when some traveller from New Zealand shall take his stand on a broken arch of London Bridge to sketch the ruins of Saint Paul's'.

Still, I wandered about happily enough. Olympia in its heyday was not a town in its own right like Athens or Corinth, it was just a place for having a festival every four years, so I suppose that most of the time there were few people about. It was like that now, which was a definite improvement upon the last time that I came.

In the high and palmy days there were three parts to Olympia. There was the great architectural complex in and around the Altis, the word 'Altis' being local dialect for 'grove' and signifying the sacred grove of Zeus. In this were the temples of Zeus and of Hera. Then there was the stadium, where the athletic events took place, and parallel to the stadium was the hippodrome for the equestrian events, but the hippodrome has since been washed away.

The Greek word 'stadium' is a measure of distance like the English word 'furlong', to which it approximates, a stadium being 212 metres. The distance from the start to the finish of the track at Olympia is exactly this, which is why it is called the stadium. It helps the imagination to know what was going on, and there were eight events in the stadium: three ordinary foot races plus one in armour; the pentathlon (foot race, long jump, discus, javelin and wrestling); and then boxing, wrestling, and a grisly affair called the pancration.

The races were run in heats of four, so you can conjure up a vision of the competitors as they are conducted in through the tunnel. Their names and cities are announced, and they then line up on their marks. The single foot race was a one-stadium sprint, and the double involved doubling round a post and back to the start. The long-distance was twelve laps round the stadium and came to about 4,800 metres. I cannot discover the length of the race in armour. After that came the wrestling, for the best of three falls, and then the boxing.

When it comes to boxing, J. P. Mahaffy becomes entirely scornful. Having first said that the boxers wore a weighted glove with spikes on the wrist (in which he may have confused the Roman gladiatorial glove with the Greek athletic one), he then, being a sporting Irishman at heart, gives us a two-page lecture to prove

> that the Greeks did not box on sound principles and that any prominent member of the Prize Ring with his naked fists

> would have easily settled any armed champion of Olympian fame. The principles of increasing the weight of the fists is only to be explained by the habit of giving swinging or downward strokes, and is incompatible with the true method of striking straight home quickly. In Vergil's description a boxer is even described as getting up on tip-toe to strike his adversary on the top of the head – a ridiculous manoeuvre which must make his instant ruin certain, if his opponent knew the first elements of the art.

J. P.'s interest in it all helps to bring the thing to life. When it comes to the last event, the pancration, he is dismissive:

> Little need be added about the pancration, which combined boxing and wrestling, and permitted every sort of physical violence except biting. Such contests were not to the credit of either the humanity or the good taste of the Greeks, and would not be tolerated even in the lowest of our prize rings.

However lukewarm I might be about the sacred grove, there is nothing wrong with the museum. There are some particularly fine bronzes, and it always surprises me that in the sixth and fifth centuries BC they could work in bronze with such astonishing elegance and accuracy while making comparatively crude figures in pottery. The statues though, as always, and particularly in the case of the Elgin Marbles, made me think that if you took one of the great Greek sculptors such as Phidias or Praxiteles to see them, he would say, 'They are all broken; you must have got them off a tip. Why don't you get some new ones?' Then if you took him to the gardens of Fontainbleau, which are full of statuary, he would say, 'Now this is more like it!' I fear that if you showed him a Henry Moore sculpture he would say, 'Nice piece of marble – lend me a chisel and I can make something out of it.'

In the museum there was a woman in a black trouser suit staggering around with a video camera on her shoulder that weighed, at a guess, about two stone. She kept recording stationary objects, muttering as she did so. I thought at first that she was swearing to herself at the weight of the machine, but later supposed that the thing could hear as well as see and she was recording a commentary such as 'This is a black-figure vase, so called because the figures are black.'

It struck me again how intensely boring is the life of a museum attendant. They can stand, they can sit, and once in a while they can tell someone not to touch, but beyond that, nothing. I first realised this when I did an enormous favour to the attendants at the National Portrait Gallery in London by taking my beautiful actress friend Lorraine Chase there because I thought it would interest her. It did not interest her half as much as she interested the attendants. They left the pictures to look after themselves, and I could have stolen a couple with ease while they trotted round after Miss Chase, drawing her attention to particular points in the portraits and pleading with her to come and see them again. We only went to the Victorian Gallery, and I think it was the high spot of their year. Next time I must take her to liven things up among the Tudors and Stuarts.

But to get back to Olympia. I enjoyed the stay, in spite of the hard things that I have said about the place. Among the tourist schmuk I tracked down some reasonable postcards which I bought from a very old man who had been a general in the war. He had been in the Resistance, blowing up German installations, which called forth my utmost admiration. His daughter, who was fussing about the shop, seemed to think that by now he was incapable of selling postcards without muddling the change, but this was absurd. A man who can dynamite bridges can certainly sell postcards, it was just that his mind was far away as he talked of old times.

'Anthony Andrews!' he said suddenly.

'Film star!' I replied, feeling rather well informed as I am not up in film stars.

The old man nodded enthusiastically. 'Archaeological professor – Athens,' he said, and from his poor English and my inadequate Greek I made out that there is or was another Anthony Andrews who spent the war dynamiting things in Thessaloniki before going in for archaeology. It was strange to find a man with a history of such heroic exploits selling postcards in a schmuk shop, but I viewed him with enormous respect, both for the terrible risks he must have run and because the Greek Resistance pinned down several German divisions that Hitler would have been glad to send elsewhere. As the elsewhere was probably Russia I dare say the Germans in question were glad enough to be pinned down.

After this I had an encounter with a plump American who was waddling down the street in bright Bermuda shorts. He stopped at my table and eyed me with a look mid-way between hope and despair. 'You speak English?' he asked.

'Fluently,' I said.

'You English?'

'Yes.'

He looked suspiciously at the notebook in which I was writing. 'You a reporter?'

'No, I have a bad memory so I make notes, otherwise I forget what has happened.'

'I am a quantity surveyor,' he announced, as if that somehow underwrote the strength of his memory.

'My father-in-law was a quantity surveyor,' I replied. 'He seemed to spend his time taking off quantities. Is that what you do?'

'Not any more,' he said. 'I'm the boss.'

The fact that I had a quantity surveyor in the family and had mastered this technical phrase about taking off quantities seemed to reassure him. He lowered himself into a chair and came to the point which had obviously been troubling him.

'Tell me,' he said. 'What is a guy supposed to do in a place like this?'

Now that was a bit of a surprising question but I took it in my stride. 'Most people go and visit the ruins.'

'Ruins!' he said scornfully. 'If I see any more ruins I hope they're in better shape than these ones.'

'You could try the ones at Athens.'

'Athens is a dump,' he replied morosely.

'Have you been to the museum?'

'Most things are all broken up,' came the answer.

The case was desperate, but in what he said I could detect an echo of some of my own feelings, so I was not without sympathy. 'I expect you could get a copy of the *New York Times*,' I offered.

'I didn't come all this goddam way to read the *New York Times*.'

What was I to do? Did he hope I would invite him to join a poker game, point him at the casino or direct him to the nearest brothel? Anyway, what was he doing wandering about on his own when he ought to be part of a tour party?

'You staying here?' he demanded, a question that struck

me full of fear that he might propose that we dine together, when he would regale me with stories of Quantities that I have Taken Off. Mendaciously I told him that I was only passing through and would soon be moving on.

He rose to his feet. 'Ah well,' he said and paused, searching his mind for some jovial phrase with which to part from an Englishman. Finally it came to him.

'Tally ho!' he said inanely, and then waddled off on his melancholy way.

I stayed two nights at the excellent Pelops Hotel run by an Australian lady called Suzanna. She said I should climb the hill of Kronos because the wild cyclamen were out and I would get a fine view of the Alpheios Valley from the top. I did my best to follow her instructions and climbed two different hills but possibly neither was the right one. The first had wild cyclamen but no views as there were too many trees at the top; the second I reached by a rough road running beside a chain-link fence topped with barbed wire, the strands sloping inwards to prevent the people inside from getting out. Within there was a modern building with glass domes that looked like a sports hall but might have been a prison or a lunatic asylum. There was no fence on the other side of the road, but there were some promising and inviting woods with wooden towers that looked as if they were for fire-spotting. I advanced upon one of these but met two men who were most upset by my being there, said I shouldn't be, and insisted that I go away. I went back to complain to Suzanna that she had nearly got me arrested, and under close cross-examination she admitted that it was some years since she had been that way herself so it was possible that trees had grown up on the hill of Kronos to block the view. The lunatic asylum she said was a camp for Olympic athletes, so I suppose the barbed wire slopes inward to stop them from getting out and breaking training.

By way of recompense for having led me such a dance she told me where the real people eat, as opposed to Joe's Diner or Fast Food. The place is called the Kladeos Taverna, and there are two ways to find it. One is to locate the small gate out of the museum compound that leads to a footbridge, because the taverna is just there by the bridge. The other way is to ask someone where it is, but I suspect that this is a more difficult way as it is pretty well hidden. If you can find it, it is properly Greek, which is not easily come by in Olympia.

The next morning I breakfasted in the hotel on a cold boiled egg and a certain amount of tobacco smoke contributed by Suzanna, who kindly came to join me and stationed herself by an open French window, out of which she blew smoke with limited success. From time to time she would disappear out of the window altogether because some Italian tourists were advancing or some French ones were retreating. Sometimes she did this in mid-sentence: 'Isabel Allende,' she said, and I looked up from my egg to find that she had gone. A few minutes later she came back from another direction.

'What about Isabel Allende?' I asked.

'What about her?'

'You said "Isabel Allende" and went out of the window.'

'Her books are marvellous,' said Suzanna severely, as if I should have been able to work that out for myself. The upshot of this fragmented conversation was that when I got home I sent her Isabel Allende's book *Paula*, which Suzanna wrote to say 'is now stained with my tears'.

And then I parted from Olympia, from Suzanna and, for the purposes of this book, from J. P. Mahaffy because he went inland whereas I went back to the coast road. Before I leave him, though, I will quote one last passage from his writings because it seems to me that some friendly muse must have seized the end of his pen and guided it to produce a piece of beautiful and vivid, but perhaps disturbing, prose. He came across some goats, and describes the scene like this:

> Further on we met other herds of these quaint creatures, generally tended by a pair of solitary children who seemed to belong to no human kin, but, like birds or flowers, to be the natural denizens of these wilds. They seemed not to talk or play; we never heard them sing, but passed them sitting in curious vague listlessness, with no wonder, no curiosity in their deep eyes. There, all the day long, they heard no sound but the falling water, the tinkling of their flocks, and the great whisper of the forest pines when the breeze touched them on its way down the pass. They took little heed of us as we passed, and seemed to have sunk from active beings to mere passive mirrors of the external nature around them.

The day on which I left Olympia was Friday the 13th. Suzanna had seemed to be very worried by this, so when the bicycle began to make a noise as if it were falling to pieces I assumed that her gloomy prognostications were about to come true. It turned out to be just a buckle of one of the carriers rubbing against the wheel, and having put that right, I was able to enjoy the undiluted pleasure of the country road leading to the Alpheios Dam, at which point the Alpheios becomes a river of respectable size. The same lovely road goes on to join the main road, which is not so lovely but is not bad.

I was heading for Kiparissia and rather more than halfway from Olympia one passes the turning to Bassae. Now Bassae is a remarkable place so far as it is a place at all. It exists in the form of a great Doric temple of Apollo, bigger than the Theseion at Athens, and was built by Ictinus, the architect of the Parthenon. It stands in solitary splendour with no other buildings except a hut for the custodian. It was raised in a wilderness as an offering to Apollo in gratitude for deliverance from a plague; it is no small affair, and when I went there on an earlier trip I got lost.

The whole undertaking was hazardous. I arrived by bus at Andritsena, which is the nearest place to stay, and put up at a rickety hotel with a precarious wooden balcony overhanging a gorge. The only place I could find for a meal served nothing but fat mutton that had been seethed for several weeks in tepid oil. Next morning I took a taxi to the temple (which they just call 'the pillars') and dismissed the driver because the Blue Guide said 'the 2½ hours' walk through the valleys is rewarding'. The custodian of the pillars said that the way to walk back was to follow the something-or-other, a Greek word I did not recognise at first, but eventually realised was the Homeric word for a water-course. I followed the water-course until it divided in two, and there being no way of knowing whether to go right or left, went right and found myself plunging downhill through waist-high grass and bracken, unable to see where I was putting my feet and with little idea of where I was going. I thought: 'If I break my leg I shall die, because nobody knows where I am.' My wife was in England and had no idea of my whereabouts. The custodian of the pillars had forgotten about me, and the taxi driver had lost interest. Possibly sometime next day the hotel owner might begin to wonder what had become of me, but I don't suppose a search party would have been organised until long after my demise. However, my luck, which had kept the hotel balcony from collapsing into the gorge and had warded off food poisoning from the seethed meat, held once more. Eventually I arrived at a cottage where a man was skinning a sheep hung up by the back legs, and he put me on to the right track so that I got back unscathed.

I did not go back now on my bicycle, but it is a deviation I would recommend to anyone with a car or an adventurous spirit. To see some parts of this temple, which is officially called the Temple of Apollo Epikourios or Apollo the Deliverer, you have to go to the British Museum. They have got some of the frieze from the cella, or inner chapel, of the temple which they acquired in a manner that seems to me to be fairly discreditable. One of the discoverers was Charles Robert Cockerell, later a most distinguished architect but then a young man of 22. The archaeological party was a mixed bag of Europeans, who the Greeks of that time used to lump together under the collective title of 'Franks'. Cockerell describes the dig of 1811 (as quoted in the British Museum catalogue of 1846) like this:

> On the top of Mount Cotylium, whence there is a grand prospect over nearly all Arcadia, they established themselves for three months; building round the temple huts covered with boughs of trees, until they almost formed a village, which they called Francopolis. They had frequently fifty or eighty men at work in the temple, and a band of Arcadian music was constantly playing to entertain this numerous assemblage; when evening put an end to work, dances and songs commenced, lambs were roasted whole on a long wooden spit, and the whole scene, in such a situation, at such an interesting time, when every day some new and beautiful work of the best age of sculpture was brought to light, is hardly to be imagined. Apollo must have wondered at the carousals

> which disturbed his long repose, and have thought that his glorious days of old were returned.
>
> The success of our enterprise astonished everyone, and in all the circumstances connected with it, good fortune attended us. Just at this time Vely Pasha was removed from his government; we should have been much embarrassed by our agreement with him, which made him proprietor of half the Marbles, but he was now very glad to sell us his share; and scarcely were the treasures put on board a vessel ere the officer of the new Pasha came down to the port with the intent of seizing the whole; but they were then safe.

Discussion rages to and fro over the Elgin Marbles, and whether Lord Elgin robbed the Greeks of them or saved them from the Turks, but about the Bassae Marbles the British Museum has little more than a laconic notice that 'in 1811 a group of architects and artists discovered the sculptures. Their finds were eventually auctioned and acquired on behalf of the British Government'. This seems to me to gloss over a very shady deal with a discredited Turkish Pasha, and the action of the museum could almost amount to receiving stolen goods.

But, to get back on track, I passed the turning to Bassae and somewhere along the line fell in with the first touring cyclist I had met. He was an Australian and his name was Pate, or possibly Payt, which was short, he told me for Pater or possibly Payter. He was a cyclist of the heroic variety, having ridden here from Scotland by way of Ireland, France and Italy, including crossing the Alps. Apparently, if you work for the same firm in Australia for ten years they give you three months' leave, to which he had added his four weeks' annual leave and was devoting it to cycling.

We were both going to Kiparissia but I let him get ahead. Then as I was riding along the seafront looking for a room at Kiparissia and finding only an expensive hotel, I came to a campsite, to be greeted by Pate. He had taken off his cycling helmet from which he emerged looking like Socrates, a thick-set man with a bald head and a beard. I joined him on the campsite, which was overrun with large domestic rabbits – black, white, grey and brown – that were apparently immune to cats, of which there were several. The rabbits were very tame, in fact rather too tame, as I had to shoo them out of the way to spread out my body-bag, and they woke me up in the night by coming to see what I was, rustling in the undergrowth and stamping their feet the way rabbits do.

That evening Pate and I ate by the sea in a taverna which the old man watering plants outside said was open, much to Pate's surprise as it looked as if it had gone bankrupt. It was Pate's second day in Greece as he had crossed to Patras from Brindisi and ridden to Olympia the day before. There he had a disappointing meal in Fast Food or Joe's Diner, but tonight it was different. We sat in the open air a few yards from the beach and feasted upon spinach, potatoes and a sort of fish which they say are in season from October to March, after which they get too big. Pate, with a properly adventurous spirit, started with some ouzo, went on to draught retsina and finished with Metaxa brandy, remaining entirely sober all the same.

I have on my shelves at home a book published in 1835 called *The Adventures of a Gentleman in Search of a Horse*. In this the anonymous author makes the remark that 'The next greatest pleasure to benefiting one's self is to do good to others.' My own pleasure in this meal was greatly increased by the good I had done to Pate. He had been in favour of passing the taverna by, on the grounds of bankruptcy, but I had prised it open with my taped Greek and in the same language conjured up this excellent meal, which Pate devoured with evident relish, every element in it being new to him bar the potatoes, but including the Greek coffee.

Next morning Pate brewed me tea on his camping stove, and we parted. I set off early because I wanted to get going before the sun was too hot, and Pate stayed behind as his washing was still wet and because, he said, he preferred cycling in the 'hate'. From Kiparissia it was a fine ride on a very quiet and countrified road to a place called Filiatra, after which it became even quieter because I took the coast road rather than the main road. I was cycling through olive groves and passing unlikely signs in the middle of nowhere saying things like 'Disco' and 'Camping'. All these places were shut, and it is difficult to believe that anyone finds them even in season. Then I was seduced and entrapped by a fishing village called Marathopoli, where I had no intention of staying, especially as it was only 11.30 when I got there. There were little fishing boats buzzing about, two tavernas on the waterfront looking out towards an island called Proti, and a place with rooms overlooking the sea with rocks immediately below from which to swim. One of the tavernas was painted blue and its wicker-bottomed chairs were also blue, so it looked like a postcard. The island of Proti, which was uninhabited but had a fort on it, looked like a Divine Folly placed there by the Almighty to enhance the seascape.

The room I was offered was not so much comfortable as palatial. The whole place was irresistible, and there being no point in resisting the irresistible, I took it. Then I swam off the rocks, had lunch and slept from one o'clock until after three o'clock.

That evening I walked about, and Marathopoli gave the impression that it was ready to receive visitors – indeed, that it intended to welcome them (the people in the shops being extra friendly) and that it had convinced itself that visitors will come, but they won't unless something is done. Potential visitors will all take the main road to Pilos because the turning at Filiatra is unmarked and can only be found by close enquiry on the spot.

The important thing is, when in Filiatra, to demand to be shown the minor coast road to Marathopoli. This will enable you to enjoy, as I did, the spectacular display put on by the sun as it sinks behind Proti, which it did that evening for my entertainment alone. I viewed it from a blue chair at the blue taverna after dining on a pork chop and a delicious sort of pickled aubergine that the taverna owner was rather worried about. He said Greeks liked it a lot but he was not sure about barbarians – not that he said 'barbarians' but it was what he meant, 'barbarian' being the classical word for anyone whose native language is not Greek. (Instead of speaking properly in Greek, barbarians made a funny noise when they spoke, sounding to Greeks like 'bar-bar-bar'.)

Next morning I set off for Pilos, meaning to call in at the Palace of Nestor on the way. I stopped for coffee at a place called Floka, where six men and one old woman were sitting outside chattering. My arrival struck them dumb at first, then they began to chat among themselves till I pulled out my map, whereupon I became the centre of attention. Where was I going? Where had I come from? Was I Italian? They huddled round to look at the map, to encourage me on my way, and to compliment me on my amazing Greek. The old lady said that she herself found Greek a hard enough language because it had so many words and was astonished that an English barbarian should even attempt it. I felt that my efforts at conversation were, in Dr

Johnson's phrase, 'like a dog walking on his hind legs. It is not done well, but you are surprised to find it done at all.'

I went on my way to the Palace of Nestor with their good wishes, but whether it is worth going at all is an important question. To me the visit is essential, the palace being the scene of a most vivid passage in the *Odyssey*. The young Telemachus, searching for his father Odysseus, arrives by sea to consult Nestor. He finds Nestor with his sons in the middle of a feast on the seashore and is given the traditional Homeric welcome, which amounts to saying: 'Do come in; do sit down; you must have something to eat and drink; later on you must tell us who you are.' In this case, when Nestor finally gets round to the 'Who are you?' question, he puts it like this: 'My friends, who are you? Where have you come from? Are you at sea for any particular purpose, or just cruising about as pirates?'

Piracy was, at this time, perfectly respectable. The historian Thucydides, writing in the fifth century BC, tells us so:

> There was no disgrace attached to this profession. On the contrary, it was considered rather distinguished. In the ancient poets the question they always asked of those who arrived by sea was 'Are you a pirate?' There is never any suggestion that those who were so asked would deny the fact, or that those who wanted to know would reproach them with it.

That is all very well, but I have never been able to discover how the conversation went on from there. Did the pirates say, 'Yes, we have come to burn your town, rape your wives and daughters, and carry off your gold and silver,' to which their hosts replied, 'Let us give you a little more to drink before you start'? It seems to be carrying hospitality a little far.

Anyway, when Nestor discovers that the young man is the son of Odysseus, he is so delighted that he insists on his coming back to the palace for the night. This is the palace you now enter, at the gate by which you presume they entered. You find yourself in the Great Hall where more drinking happened; you see where Nestor sat presiding; you see the hearth round which they gathered, and the very bath which you imagine Telemachus used, it being part of the hospitable routine to offer visiting strangers a bath.

This bath is marvellously well preserved, but the use to which it was put caused Mr Gladstone (the Prime Minister) and other nineteenth-century scholars a good deal of embarrassment. In a bald and simple translation, what Homer says about the proceedings might be rendered like this: 'Meanwhile fair Polycaste, Nestor's youngest daughter, bathed Telemachus, then when she had bathed him and anointed him with olive oil, she put on him a fine cloak and a tunic, and he came out of the bath looking like a god.'

To Victorian scholars the idea of a princess of the house of Nestor actually washing a young man in the bath, rubbing him over with olive oil and then putting his clothes on for him was deeply distressing. There are sixteen words in the Greek of Homer, which my edition of 1886 discusses in a footnote of about seven hundred words. All the similar passages in Homer are carefully examined in an effort to see what the general practice may have been. Among them are some awkward lines describing how Odysseus is given a bath by Circe, where the language is almost identical with the Telemachus passage but has the unambiguous statement that Circe herself 'poured water over the head and shoulders' of Odysseus. Mr Gladstone's comments on this passage were these: 'The statement that the water was poured over his head and shoulders, as he sat in the bath, evidently implies that what may be called essential decency was preserved,' and again, 'She gave him water to wash with, pouring it over his head and shoulders, and then leaving to him the substance of the operation which was not completed by this mere act of affusion.'

As an added crumb of comfort, the editor says that 'the scantiness of light in Homeric rooms was itself a veil – a consideration applicable to all cases of indoor bathing, whatever we take the women's part to have been.' Even without this helpful comment, Mr Gladstone expressed himself satisfied 'that the statements of Homer give no ground for sinister or disparaging imputation.'

I was delighted to have seen the bath that gave rise to so much scholarly discussion. I have to say, though, that in other respects the Palace of Nestor needs a good deal of imagination. Apart from the hearth, the bath and an impressive burial chamber in the car park, what you actually see is a big corrugated iron roof, lots of low walls and some bits of string. There are also notices saying 'Guard Room', 'Oil Store', or 'Stairs to Upper Storey'. Otherwise the wild cyclamen were in great profusion; the oleanders were in flower; and there were lots of hibiscus, bougainvillea and roses. Still, if you have no great interest in Homer I should give it a miss and take the coast road to Pilos, which is a lovely little town with an interesting history, particularly in connection with two important battles.

In 425 BC, the Athenians bottled up a Spartan garrison on the off-shore island of Sphacteria, and after a stout resistance of 72 days the Spartans surrendered. This may not sound much of a story, but the effect throughout Greece was profound. It was always supposed that Spartans died, but never surrendered, whereas now 292 soldiers laid down their arms and capitulated. The effect was as if nowadays such a number of Israelis were to come out with their hands up and surrender to the Palestine Liberation Organisation. The military reputation of Sparta was greatly tarnished as a result.

In later years Pilos was called Navarino by the Venetians, and eventually passed into Turkish hands. Then, during the War of Independence when the Greeks were engaged in shaking off the yoke of the Ottoman Empire, the Turkish garrison was besieged by a strong force of Greeks and starved into surrender. The agreed terms were that all valuables were to be given up and the Turks transported to the coast of Africa. Then, says the historian W. Alison Phillips, 'a dispute arose as to the way in which the women were being searched', to which he adds the sinister footnote 'Lemaitre, page 76 is more explicit'. The dispute developed into a general massacre of the Turks, who had been disarmed and were defenceless.

> Women, wounded with musket balls, rushed into the sea, seeking to escape, and were deliberately shot. Mothers, robbed of their clothes, with infants in their arms, plunged into the water to conceal themselves from shame and were made a mark for the inhuman riflemen. Greeks seized infants from their mothers' breasts and dashed them against the rocks. Children, three or four years old, were hurled living into the sea and left to drown.

The War of Independence was all too frequently carried on like that, by either side.

The counter-attack came in 1825 when Ibrahim Pasha arrived from Egypt, landed at nearby Methone, recaptured Navarino and proceeded to lay waste the Peloponnese with fire and sword. According to a philhellenic yachtsman called Gambier Parry, 'a slave market was opened at Modon [Methone] for the sale of captives of both sexes, who were crowded in dungeons, loaded with irons, unmercifully beaten by their guards, and often murdered in pure wanton cruelty.'

At this point the attempt of the Greeks to secure their independence was virtually lost, but as in Bosnia in the 1990s, so in Greece in 1827, foreign powers intervened. England, France and Russia came forward with a proposal for a Greek principality under the general sovereignty of the Sultan of Turkey and a demand for an immediate armistice. This the Turks, being on the point of victory, not unnaturally rejected. The three Great Powers had anticipated such a rejection so far as to say that their proposal should, if necessary, be imposed, but 'without the use of force'. How the rampant Ibrahim was to be stopped without the use of force was by no means clear.

On 20 October 1827 a combined English, French and Russian fleet, under the command of Admiral Sir Edward Codrington, sailed into the Bay of Navarino. Their hope was, officially, says Gambier Parry, 'that the presence of the fleet might stay the effusion of blood without provoking hostilities'. However, possibly by accident, a shot was fired from one of Ibrahim's ships, and there followed the last naval battle ever to take place between sailing ships, in which the Turkish fleet was effectively destroyed.

Admiral Codrington was to some extent in trouble in England for exceeding his orders. The French and Russian governments were delighted, however. In 1828 the French landed an expeditionary force to oversee the evacuation of Ibrahim's troops, and the soldiers, having nothing much to do, built the greater part of the modern town of Pilos.

The Turkish reverse at Navarino at a time when they had virtually crushed the Greek revolution so completely turned the tables that the establishment of an independent Greece at last became a possibility.

In Pilos today you will find the Square of the Three Admirals, with statues of Admiral Codrington; of Admiral de Rigny who commanded the French squadron; and of the Russian Admiral, von Heyden. It made me feel good to look at them. Although well aware that the British government was most anxious to avoid a breach with Turkey, Admiral Codrington concluded his general orders for the Bay of Navarino with Lord Nelson's famous words: 'No captain can do wrong who lays his ship alongside that of an enemy,' and so altered the course of history.

As well as being a really nice town where the waiters do not shout at you in the streets, as they do in the more obvious tourist places, Pilos has a treasure that they do not bother to tell you about, in the form of its castle. It is Venetian-Turkish, having been built by the former and adapted by the latter. To reach it you walk out on the road to Methone and turn right at the first bend, then there it is – enormous. They are doing marvellous restoration work, and the keep has a fine courtyard from which you can walk right round the huge vertiginous battlements. It is from there that you can get a proper view of the mouth of the bay and see that the entrance, which is narrow enough anyway, is further divided by rocks and an islet. The only possible formation for the allied fleet to enter the bay was line ahead, which it did with Admiral Codrington's flagship leading. Had the Turkish batteries that commanded the entrance opened fire as the ships sailed past, they could perhaps have altered the outcome.

Within the castle gate you can wander all over the vast

grounds, where you will find a lovely church in mellow golden stone. Lovely it is outside at least, though falling to bits inside. This was October, but I can tell you as a bit of extra information that if you can contrive to go in May the wild flowers in the castle grounds are perfectly superb. Finally, unannounced in any guide or leaflet that I have seen, just inside the gate on the left there is a building which houses a fine display of watercolours and prints, mostly from the nineteenth century and chiefly of soldiers, heroes and scenes from the War of Independence. It is called the René Puaux collection, and it is a treat to see for anyone with the least interest in Greek history.

I love Pilos, as I hope I have made clear. I stayed at an excellent hotel, the Nilefs, which is set back from the front so it is quiet, but only about fifty yards from a sandy beach. When I arrived the lady who owns the hotel was cracking walnuts by pounding them on a brick with a long brass pestle. She threw the debris, both shells and nuts, into a bowl for sorting out later, but before showing me to a room she picked out a good handful of nuts and gave it to me.

At Pilos a multilingual waiter posed me a problem to which I did not then give a satisfactory reply, and cannot think of one now.

'If a Frenchman says "*Merci*",' he said, 'I reply "*De rien*". If a German says "*Danke schön*", I say "*Bitte schön*", but what if an Englishman says "Thank you"? What is the answer to that?'

'If he is an American,' I said, 'you can say "Don't mention it".'

He was not to be fobbed off. 'But what if he is an Englishman?' he persisted.

There he had me. The current fashion is to say 'No

problem' or even 'No problem at all' but I don't care for either of them. Possibly 'Not at all' would do, but as I don't say that myself, I don't see why anyone else should.

'I think,' I said, 'you should just smile.'

'I can manage that,' he said, and retired to the kitchen.

Next morning my first pause was at Methone. From Pilos to Methone you go steeply up, sharply down, and then there is a long, flat run and you are there. The Venetian fort is the great point of interest, and very fine it is. This is no half-and-half affair, no little hilltop fort, but a vast seaside construction of which it is difficult to guess the area. Perhaps it is about forty acres, but possibly more. There is sea on three sides, which beats impressively against the rocks and hurls up spray in any kind of wind. Here too the spring flowers are stunning, with a strong line in yellow poppies.

I came upon two men who were excavating. They had a big rectangular sieve with two handles at each end, rather like a stretcher. The method was that one would shovel earth and rock onto the sieve while the other watched. Then after a little while they would each take an end and pick it up and shake it, so that they were left with a sieve full of rocks that they tipped onto a pile. Then they did it again. It was difficult to see what this was achieving except a big heap of rocks and a tidy pile of earth, but near where they were working was a stone arch that looked like the beginning of a tunnel or storeroom, so I expect the centre of the fort has a lot of buried chambers waiting to be dug out, and perhaps this was what they were doing.

There was to me a sort of mystery about Methone. From an earlier visit I remembered it as a very small place, with just one hotel and a few houses clustered around the beach, but this time it was a great deal bigger. There would be nothing odd in that if they had built a lot of new houses, but the houses in question did not look new, they looked quite old, so I had no way of knowing how the transformation came about. Later, in the seclusion of my study at home, I was able to establish that an old Blue Guide of 1973 gives the population as 1,330, whereas my up-to-date road atlas now gives it as 1,173, so Methone has been shrinking rather than expanding in recent years. I can only give this as a remarkable example of how you can have a recollection fixed in your mind with complete clarity and absolute certainty, only to find out that it is altogether wrong.

On a later visit my wife and I stayed very happily at the Giotta Hotel by the sea, and other things being equal I would warmly recommend Methone as a place for an overnight stay, or longer for beach lovers, as there are good hotels, rooms to let all over the place, and super-excellent fish to eat. In my case, though, other things were not equal. I had ridden a mere seven miles and wanted to get on, so after a thorough visit to the fort I rode off on the road to Koroni. My plan was to break the journey between Poros and Koroni at a place called Finikounda. My Pilos landlady had assured me that I should find somewhere to stay, contrary to the evidence of my old Blue Guide, which suggested that there was not even so much as a paved road across from Methone to Koroni, so I half expected to find tiny villages with large churches and small *cafeneia* but nothing more. Not a bit of it! The road is excellent, and the whole of the coast has been developed for visitors with invitations to hotels and campsites all the way.

The second climb of the day was up and down again to Finikounda, which proved to be a pretty village with two expensive-looking hotels and a few signs offering rooms. The trouble with arriving there in the early afternoon was, I found, that all the landladies were out, or asleep, or had gone to Kalamata, so they were difficult to find. The only one I could raise offered me a room I did not like for more than I wanted to pay, and as the road sign said I was within 18 kilometres of Koroni I decided to go on.

It was two o'clock. It was hot. It was all very well for Pate, whom I had left drying his clothes at Kiparissia, to say he liked cycling in the 'hate', but he was a man who had ridden over the Alps and revelled in it. I thought the heat of the day was something to avoid, but now I plunged into it and likewise into the third climb of the day, which turned out to be the stiffest since the epic ascent between Poros and Epidaurus. Curiously, it was quite enjoyable. The road was empty as all the sensible people were asleep. Once up among the hilltops the surroundings were sensational. There was a coffee-stop just before the summit, and the run down was cooling and refreshing, but the whole day was tiring – extremely so, although I had only ridden 30 miles. I stumbled into the first room I found in Koroni and had a shower. At six o'clock I ate an excellent pizza on the seafront; by seven-thirty I was in bed and slept until seven o'clock next morning.

I made a very wise decision to stay two nights at Koroni. It would have been a great mistake to hurry round the castle and then dash off to Kalamata. Also my legs were protesting rather, and I thought they needed a rest. Shortly before leaving on this trip I read a statement by someone or other that most of his mistakes in life had been made by hurrying. Being entirely determined not to blunder in the same way, I set off on a thorough search of the town until I found Rachel the baker and bought two croissants. Then

I strolled to the grocer and bought a pot of yogurt and honey and a carton of peach juice. Then I found a man with a huge pile of foreign newspapers – from yesterday and the day before and for several days before that, so goodness knows what he meant to do with them all – from whom I got the *Sunday Telegraph*. Then I went to the balcony of my room and had a leisurely and excellent breakfast, reading the paper and thinking how nice it was to be out of England during the Tory Party conference. Then it was time for a large Greek coffee in the square and some more newspaper reading. Then it seemed to be the moment to explore the castle.

This proved to be a surprise because it is inhabited. It is not inhabited in the sense that Belvoir Castle is inhabited by the Duke of Rutland; it is inhabited because people have built houses within the walls. When the Turks, who were the last owners, moved out, the local people moved in with their chickens and their olive trees and their vines, and built houses here and there. If you look carefully you can see signs of underground chambers and such things, but there is no indication of any archaeologists meaning to do anything about them. Possibly by now it is too late because of the people living there with their chickens, and anyway it is very pleasant as it is.

You enter the castle by an imposing gateway. The main path goes up to another gateway, through which you pass into a chapel. Entering by the north door of the chapel, you are immediately confronted by the south door, through which you pass to a large spic-and-span white church built next to a mellow old church which is but a stone's throw from another white church with a graveyard. As all of these are supplementary to the churches in the town, one of which is very big and one of which is still under construction, the people of Koroni are clearly of the opinion that when it comes to church building you cannot have too much of it.

Walking round the graveyard, I felt the need to do a calculation. I had a pen but nothing to write on so I hunted about until I found an old cigarette packet on which I wrote the ages of all the people in one row of graves, taken at random. They were 85, 74, 73, 70, 90, 71, 98, 84, 80 and 91, which, rounded down to the nearest whole number gives an average length of life of 81 years. I do not suppose that the Greek health service had been prolonging their existence by transplanting their organs or anything like that, and as the Greek way of life ought to carry a health warning because all the men smoke and most of them get fat, this length of life is surprising. It is said that Arachova, near Delphi, is such a lovely place that nobody ever wants to leave it, even for the next world, and the people of Koroni may feel the same. Otherwise it must be that the secret of long life is for all manual workers to knock off by two o'clock, and for everyone to have a long siesta, and for most men to spend hours and hours sitting in *cafeneia* chatting and smoking and playing with worry beads under cover of sipping minuscule cups of coffee – such being the norm of behaviour in Greece.

As a town Koroni has a certain charm. It appears to be adjusting to the idea that it is almost on a tourist route but hasn't quite got there yet. There are one or two perfunctory jewellers that obviously do no business. The newspaper man has his foreign papers for which there are no customers, but on the other hand Koroni has two banks and a travel agent. There are lots of tavernas along the front, and it is important to be seated there at sunset. This is because the bay seems to be entirely encircled by mountains so that as the sun goes down behind the hills on the left, the shadows rise on the right until only the peaks are illuminated, then this light is finally extinguished as the sun disappears altogether. This is an effect I have not seen elsewhere and admired very much.

After Koroni, Kalamata was the place I had to go to, much as I disliked it after a previous visit. It is a climb to get out of Koroni, but not a bad one. Thereafter comes a gently rolling road, sometimes by the sea and sometimes not. The road gets a bit busier after the main highway from Pilos comes in from the left, pretty nasty around Messene and perfectly horrible when you join the road from Tripolis on the outskirts of Kalamata. You approach the centre of this great, dirty, bustling Patras-type city with sinking heart, only to find that they have kindly provided a loop road clearly marked to Areopolis, which takes you round the greater part of the nastiness and brings you safely out onto the road to the Mani. So far so good. At about two o'clock, having put Kalamata safely behind me, I turned into a likely-looking hotel, reached for my passport, rapped out a great oath and slammed my fist down on the counter with a bang that greatly startled the lady behind it. I had left my passport in Koroni.

I now deeply hated the woman from whom I had taken a room there. For some reason she had come bustling in while I was finishing my breakfast on the balcony, chattering something about getting my room ready, seizing my bags and carting them downstairs, and generally creating a fuss and flurry. In all this nonsense, having settled my bill and loaded my bicycle, and she having disappeared, I set off, glad to have nothing more to do with her, but forgot about the passport. The only thing to do now was to leave the bicycle where it was, wait for a bus to Kalamata and catch the first onward bus to Koroni. This second bus arrived at Koroni at 4.30 and left at 4.31, refusing to wait while I dashed to get my passport. There was a bus back to Kalamata at 8.30, arriving at 10.00, but how or whether I should get on from Kalamata and back to my hotel that night was what you might call an open question.

I stormed into the house where my passport was, to find the stupid woman absent and a stupid man snoozing in his pyjamas.

'Passport!' I shouted. He looked blank. 'Passport!' I shouted even louder.

His face cleared. 'Bravo!' he cried, taking my passport from the top of the dresser, and chattering some nonsense about how they thought of posting it to the address of my next of kin.

'Have you come from Kalamata?'

'Yes, by bus, and I have to go back by bus.'

'It goes at five.'

Here my Greek failed me, as I did not know the Greek for 'Rubbish!' so I shouted, 'Half past eight!' and left him.

Now it may be thought that it was my duty to remember my own passport, not the landlady's; I don't agree. It was she who asked for it, and she should have seen that I got it back. Left to myself I would never have parted with it. The only revenge I can take is to say that no one should take rooms in the square at Koroni, as these are rather noisy and run by people who don't give your passport back.

However, before the day was wrecked by this exasperating episode, I had stopped for morning coffee at a place where a group of able-bodied Greeks were prolonging life by doing nothing. They were extremely impressed by my cycling, and the landlord quite certain that I could not possibly get from Koroni to Kalamata in one day, the distance being about thirty-five miles. Then the conversation turned to olives, as the best olives and the best olive oil in the world come from Kalamata. They said that much of the oil is bought by the Mafia and adulterated with Spanish, Italian or Turkish oil before being sold as Kalamata oil. The only place to get the real stuff was in Kalamata itself. Nearly all the olives on the trees were still green, but I had tried eating one of the rare black ones, and it tasted rotten, so I tried another and it tasted sour, like a sloe.

They explained that olives have to be soaked in brine for a week, then transferred to fresh brine for another week, whereupon they are edible. The olive harvest would be at the end of October; they had had no rain since April so this year's crop was likely to be a light crop of small olives. All of this I had leisure to reflect upon as I ate a meal on the waterfront at Koroni for the second time, and waited for the bus. There proved to be a reasonable connection from Kalamata to my hotel, which hotel was a good one and restored my equilibrium.

Interlude ~ Greek Ancient and Modern

I suppose it all started when I was ten years old, which is when I began my long and only moderately successful struggle with the classical Greek language. What a language it is! William Makepeace Thackeray, author of *Vanity Fair*, simply hated it: 'I was made so miserable in youth by a classical education that all connected with it is disagreeable in my eyes, and I have the same recollection of Greek that I have of castor oil.'

I think he felt like this because he was bullied and flogged a lot at school, but I was not, so it did not affect me like that. All the same, as a language, classical Greek is a formidable opponent. I will pass over the general difficulties of grammar; never mind the peculiar moods of the verbs (and Greek verbs have many moods and are decidedly moody); let us draw a veil over the accents which are subject to most difficult rules, and in my hands at least serve almost no purpose beyond decoration; let us not embark upon the oddities of the little words called particles; I will just illustrate an aspect of the problem with a point about vocabulary. Humpty Dumpty said boldly, 'When I use a word it means just what I choose it to mean – neither more nor less. The question is, which is to be master – that's all.' And that's all as far as the Greeks went, very often.

For example, if you look up the word *skêptô* in the lexicon (Greek dictionaries are always called lexicons), it says: 'To prop, support, stay: hence, to let fall upon'. Hence? Wherefore 'hence'? Why should a word which when applied perhaps to a roof mean *both* to prop it up *and* to let it fall on top of you? Or again, if you look up *alastor* it says 'an avenger; one who suffers from divine vengeance', and it doesn't seem to bother anybody that the word for one who exacts vengeance also does duty for one who suffers from it. The word *antilêpsis* means, among other things, 'a help and support' as well as 'an attack or objection'. It would puzzle English lawyers if a word such as 'legatee' meant both one who leaves a legacy and one who inherits it, but I don't think it would have worried the Greeks.

Nevertheless, through all this difficulty there shine some of the brightest gems of European literature, and I got to like it sufficiently to study it, along with Latin, at Oxford. Then, one day at breakfast, at the age of 50 I said, apropos of nothing much: 'Everyone seems to go to Greece nowadays except for me, who has been grappling with the language, on and off, for forty years.'

'Go then,' said the rest of the family, so, rather to their surprise, I bought a fortnight's return air ticket and went.

I wish now to pause and explain something about Modern Greek, though I should say that I am neither a scholar, nor a natural linguist. This last I proved in Hong Kong when trying to learn Cantonese. Chinese is made up entirely of monosyllables, and I believe that in Cantonese there are seven different ways of pronouncing each one, though they all sounded much the same to me. The moment when I gave up trying to master the language was when I asked for a teaspoon and got a bottle of ginger ale. Quite possibly I thought I was talking Cantonese and the waiter thought I was talking English because my way of saying 'teaspoon' in Cantonese sounds a good deal like 'ginger ale'. Whatever the explanation I decided thereupon to throw in the towel.

All the same, poor linguist that I may be, I never like to descend upon a country without knowing something of the language. When we went to Italy several years ago I dutifully worked through a tape from the public library, which my wife thought was a complete waste of time as obviously everyone we met would speak English. When we got there and found that far from everyone spoke English, instead of marvelling at the fluency with which I could conjure up a double room with a view and a bath she would address such questions to me as 'What is the Italian for clothes-peg?' and when I didn't know, made it pretty plain that this proved I had been wasting my time, as she had said.

Anyway, before going to Greece for the first time I thought I had better do something to bring my ancient Greek up to date. I assumed that what I could remember of the Greek of Homer would not get me very far, in which

I was right, and that in the period between his time of about the eighth century BC and the twentieth century AD the language must have changed almost out of recognition, in which I was wrong.

I got a little Berlitz tape called *Greek for Travellers*, and fairly soon it dawned on me that the pronunciation taught to schoolboys in England is simply crazy. It was invented, or at least worked out, by Erasmus in the sixteenth century, and it would have been much better if he hadn't bothered, especially as there was a rival pronunciation on offer derived from Modern Greek by a German scholar called Reuchlin. Anyone taught the Ancient Greek in the modern pronunciation would immediately realise that the Ancient and Modern are all one language anyway, and to move to and fro between the two would be very much easier.

Everybody finds this if they delve at all into Modern Greek. Byron wrote in 1810 that 'I speak the Modern Greek tolerably, as it does not differ from the ancient dialect so much as you would conceive, but the pronunciation is diametrically opposite.' As for the language itself, J. P. Mahaffy, our Irish professor, says 'There is really very little difference between the language of Plato and that of the present Greeks. The present Greek will read the old classics with the same trouble with which our peasants could read Chaucer.' I fancy that not many of our peasants read a lot of Chaucer nowadays, but something like this became clear to me on my very first acquaintance with Modern Greek. One of the phrases I had got off pat from my Berlitz tape was the Greek for 'What do you call this?' On this trip my principal, if not only, conversational gambit was to point at things and say, 'What do you call this?' On the slopes of Mount Pelion I came across two old men and a mule. 'What do you call this?' says I, pointing at the mule.

'*Moolari*,' say they.

I looked rather despondent. 'I thought it might have been *êmionos*.'

'Of course you can say *êmionos*,' they replied with great delight and generally indicated that they thought, upon reflection, that it was considerably the better word. The point of which is that *êmionos* is the word that Homer used for the animals which, among other things, drew the wagon which carried home the corpse of Hector, so the word had come down entirely unchanged in about 2,700 years.

There are lots and lots and lots of words of which the same could be said, and as I found that quite exciting I thought I should look further into the matter, so I got some Linguaphone tapes. Now it is my belief that the Linguaphone course never teaches the language it purports to teach, it teaches something else, which should be called a Lingua-language. Lingua-French and Lingua-German are, I am quite sure, different from the languages that they speak in France and Germany. They are a great deal nicer, for a start. If you learn Lingua-English you would say, in carefully modulated tones, such things as 'Please may I have another one', whereas the native population say 'C'd ivor nuther' or possibly 'Gisser nuvver'. I therefore go about Greece asking carefully for another one, at which all the Greeks are greatly surprised, as they are gisser-nuvvering.

Odder yet, my Linguaphone tapes, which I bought second-hand from a friend, are very old, and therefore lead me to make remarks like 'What time does the steamer depart?' or to expect to get on the airport scales myself because in Lingua-Greece at the time of my tapes they always weighed the passengers as well as their luggage.

When I am on form I think the effect is rather as if, in England, some pre-war BBC announcer had returned from the grave with a very limited vocabulary. The effect upon Greeks is delightful. They frequently demand to know where I had learnt such beautiful Greek, the like of which they have never heard, which is not surprising as no other living person ever speaks it.

Before leaving the subject I should like to explain the word 'Romaic'. It occurs in the chapter on the Mani, and was used by a priest talking to Edward Lear, and means simply 'Greek'. The Greek language was spread by Alexander the Great throughout his conquered territories. The Romans later succeeded to the Macedonians, and when, in the fourth century AD, the Roman Empire split into two parts, Greek became the language of the eastern court at Byzantium (later Constantinople, now Istanbul). The Greeks adopted the name of their Roman conquerors and used it until quite recently. I recall that Patrick Leigh Fermor, the scholarly author, once provoked the surprising question 'Are you a Roman?' when he said something in perfect Greek.

Kardamili and the Mani

Next day I prepared to strike into the Mani, the middle promontory of the Peloponnese. It is an area which fascinates everybody. Patrick Leigh Fermor wrote a whole book about it called simply *Mani*, which I found too learned to be readable.

Major Gambier Parry, who never set foot on it but merely coasted along on his yacht in 1887, tells us all about it, calling the place Maina and the inhabitants Mainotes:

> The southern end of the promontory is almost wholly barren, and it was here that those swarms of pirates, who were the dread of all attempting to navigate these seas, chiefly had their homes. Unable to find subsistence in their exposed and rocky

> country, the southern Mainotes depended largely upon the success of their piratical raids, and thus they infested the coasts, and, after the manner of Greek pirates, established regular centres for collecting tribute from the neighbouring towns and villages.
>
> But if the Mainotes were wild, reckless and independent as pirates, they were scarcely less so as klephts [robbers] ashore. The cliffs of their iron girt coasts and the hurricanes which were associated with them, rendered the Mainotes tolerably safe from invasion, while the rocky and precipitous passes of the northern border made an attack by land a matter of no ordinary difficulty. There was no limit either to the privations they were prepared to suffer, or the heroism and daring they were ready to show in the defence of their country and their liberty.

Thinking that in such an area there might be no banks, I started by riding back into Kalamata to replenish my money supply. The last time I had visited the centre of Kalamata it appeared to have been invaded by Gypsies. The whole place was then full of tents, and the benevolent town council had allowed pegs to be hammered through the asphalt and the tent dwellers to set up television sets with big, permanent-looking aerials, and further to make themselves comfortable with the portable solar-heating panels. They looked quite cosy and well established, and only afterwards did I remember that there had been an earthquake some weeks before and that these were the unfortunate people who had lost their houses.

Kalamata now has no tent dwellers, nor any sign of devastation. It has banks, but otherwise I don't honestly think it has anything else in its favour. It is a place where it is easy to get stuck at the bus station for several hours, and to relieve the awfulness of this particularly awful bus station, it is possible to go to the market. To do this, walk towards the sea, turn left over the first bridge that crosses the river, and left again. If, having seen the market you are still desperate, it is also possible to visit the undistinguished castle, which is up on your right from the market. Beyond that, I can think of nothing else worth doing.

So, having got my money, I hurried out of Kalamata and set off for Kardamili, whereupon the day turned into the best of the trip so far. The road divided, and I had a choice between going left and inland to Kardamili, or right along the coast to Stoupa. As my excellent tourist map of Messenia made it absolutely plain that you cannot possibly get to Stoupa without going through Kardamili on the way, this was a mystery. Having a general preference for coast roads over other roads, I havered to and fro as to which to take, but decided in the end that perhaps the people who put up the signs knew best, and the way to Kardamili was the way they said, so I went left. I have no regrets.

First of all, there is the road. As you look ahead you see a dramatic pass towering above you. 'Am I going to go through that?' you wonder. Indeed you are. The road, which is superbly engineered, winds up and up. You can pedal all the way if you want, though I got off and pushed from time to time in order to savour the majestic grandeur of the hills, the peace and the silence. Once you are up, then down you go through a series of virages ending in a triple S-bend and a bridge, where you are at the bottom of a gorge. Now the Grand Canyon in America is, I know, the gorge to end all gorges and by comparison this one may be nothing much. Furthermore I know that in Greece itself there are other gorges supposedly finer than the one I was in, but as far as I am concerned this one was good enough and I seek nothing better, because it is a very fine gorge indeed.

From the bottom of the gorge I climbed up again, still pedalling and occasionally walking. As I went, two cyclists whizzed by in the other direction, waving as they passed. I reached a vantage point, stopped and looked down at their tiny figures far below, shooting over the bridge and then settling to the long climb on the other side. 'Ants,' I thought, 'that's all we are, mere two-legged crawlers on the face of the earth.' Only in this case they were two-wheeled crawlers.

Then, secondly, there is a monastery, or rather convent, the same word doing duty for both in Greek. Not long after the Kardamili turning was a sign indicating that somewhere around was an ancient monastery. It did not say where it was, it just put you on notice that it was thereabouts, and I did not think any more of it. Then as I approached the second summit of the day there was a sign in Greek which the Messenia map translates as 'Moni Androumpeitsas'. The road down to it was a kind of steep, bumpy concrete drive, so rather than ride I parked my bicycle and walked along. When packing my panniers I always used to put my trousers on top so that I could get at them easily if I wanted to go into a church. This time though, not being sure as to what I should find, I strolled along in my shorts.

I came upon a well-kept walled building with a locked iron door. As I walked round to see if anyone was about, a dog started barking, so I picked up a stick in case it attacked me and went back to try the door again. This time I noticed a bell-pull, which I rather timidly tugged, and in a matter of minutes it was opened by a nun, perhaps twenty years younger than me and dressed in black.

'Can I come in?'

'Yes, you can come in.'

'Am I all right in my shorts?'

'No, but I will lend you a skirt. No, not like that – tie it at the front.'

So I put on a skirt, or more accurately an apron, which covered my knobbly knees in front but let my legs be seen at the back. This ridiculous arrangement somehow satisfied the decencies.

It is a funny thing about this nun but I have never before been in the presence of a woman who, within the space of a minute at most, made me feel that she had got me absolutely weighed up, knew exactly what I was like, and so was able to treat me with a kind of amused tolerance in the absolute confidence that I would do whatever she said.

We were in a little compound, beautifully clean, with flowers and shrubs in great profusion. The living quarters were round the side, and in the middle was a small stone church which, if I understood her properly, my newfound friend said was 700 years old. She opened the door, and I went in to find candles everywhere, a handsome screen, and peeling frescoes on the dome and walls. It was unrestored, untouched and totally peaceful. She watched me with a kind of contagious calm, not fidgeting, not interfering, not pointing anything out. I said it was very beautiful because I couldn't think of anything else to say, at which she smiled.

Might I photograph the church?

Yes I might.

Could I photograph her?

No I could not. But I should photograph in that direction as it is really beautiful.

So I did as I was told, and then she asked, would I like some loukoumi?

Oh, yes please.

Very well, but I must promise to send copies of the photographs when they were printed.

Certainly.

So she said I was to sit on a bench while she wrote the address for me, then I should have my loukoumi, which we would know as Turkish delight. When she came back with a slip of paper, she gave me, with mock severity, a little lesson in Greek. When saying I would send the photographs, I should not have said 'Certainly', I should have said 'Gladly', so we went through that part of the conversation again, and this time I got it right.

But it was when she handed me over to another nun that I realised she had read me like a book. It was my first experience of love at first sight, which, at my age you may think was leaving it rather late. This new nun looked to be about twenty years old, although she may have been older, as I expect people age slowly in such surroundings. I cannot say that she was beautiful, because everything above her eyebrows and below her mouth was covered up, but even so I have never seen eyes so expressive of intelligence, humour, contentment and tranquillity all at once. I could have gazed at her for hours, and I think she would have remained entirely calm under such scrutiny. She led me down some stairs, and I asked what I should call her. 'Sister,' she said, and what a lovely person she was to have as a sister! In the room below she held out a big tray of loukoumi, so I took a piece and tried to lure her into conversation. The first nun had told me that this one spoke English, but she said firmly that as we were in Greece we would speak Greek, which limited things – not that she was unwilling to talk, but I found it hard to keep up. Actually I don't think her English was up to much. I said to her in Greek: 'It's very hot indeed today. Now say that in English,' and she replied with the one word 'hot'.

There were some religious objects in the loukoumi room that you could buy if you wanted, and as I looked at them she watched with the same unhurried tranquillity as the first nun had displayed outside the church. I felt it as a positive force, and thought that if I hung around for long enough I might catch it. However, having spun things out for as long as I could, I thought I had better go, so she led me out. She, too, would not let me photograph her but I got her to take a picture of me in my skirt, which she took like anyone else, first holding the camera sideways, then upright, to see which was the better shot. This surprised me, as I was by now so overcome that I expected her to have some specially saintly way of taking a photograph, or else to be wondering what was this strange worldly object I had put in her hands. Then she let me out, and as I turned to thank her she imprinted on my mind, I hope for ever, the impression of her gentle smiling face, expressive of her absolute conviction that within the convent walls at least, everything was exactly as it ought to be.

I sent the photographs, of course – how could I not? – and that was my last contact until the following Christmas but one, when an envelope arrived with our address but no name nor even the country. Inside was a small hand-made card with a cut-out of the nativity on the front, and on the back in spidery Greek was written: 'At the holy festival of the birth of Christ and the New Year we wish you health and happiness of spirit. May your years be peaceful and blessed by the Lord. With best wishes,' and then it was signed 'Mother Superior, nun and servant of the Lord'. Now that was a delightful thing, to think that in that remote corner of Messenia I had been thought about to the extent of making and sending me a card. I like to think that it was the young one who made it, though the elder one wrote it.

From the convent I swooped down upon the village of Kardamili. In Kardamili there are several stone towers scattered about, which make it plain that this is the beginning of what they call the Deep Mani. The purpose of the towers, which you see everywhere from Kardamili onwards, is explained by Gambier Parry thus:

> Social life in Maina was overshadowed by the presence of a fearful evil. In no country, not even among the Pathans on our Indian frontier, could blood feuds have been carried to greater length than they were formerly in Maina. The northern portion of the country was rich, and silk, valonia, and cotton were to be found among its exports; but how, and by whom was a great part of the industry of the country carried on? By women and children. The male portion of the community rarely left the immediate shelter of their own houses. The houses were in reality forts. They were built as towers; one low door, situated many feet above the ground, and approached by a stone stairway standing apart from the building, alone gave ingress; a board, or moveable platform, connected the stairs with the doorway, and thus acted as a drawbridge; the walls were all loop-holed and no lights were burnt at night for very fear; the lower floor was used as a stable, and all day long men watched their enemies from their own vantage grounds.
>
> Feuds descended from father to son, and revenge was handed down by will. Children were not exempt from risk; boys of tender years were murdered to balance the account of their forefathers, and the female portion of the population were alone safe from the hand of the assassin. To the women, therefore, fell the lot of cultivating the country, and

> assassination, as has been aptly said, remained the privilege of Mainote gentility.

It is all very tranquil now; in fact it is lovely. I had thought I would spend one night in Kardamili, but it had such an encouraging atmosphere as I strolled about that evening that I resolved to stay for two. Kardamili is developing quickly, but is far from spoiled. There are plenty of rooms to let, some in superior stone mansions but mine in a quiet modern block set back from the road. My landlady gave me a huge, luxurious room for 5,000 drachmas – about £14 – for the one night, and when I said I wanted to stay for another night she tried to give me the second night for nothing. I managed to get her to accept another 1,000 drachmas, but even so for the two nights it was the cheapest of my stopping places and one of the best.

Another of this lady's merits was that she did not ask for my passport, and so could not forget to return it. Also, she gave me two cakes. While I was eating these cakes I said in an attempt at conversation in my stumbling Greek, 'There is a famous Englishman …'

'Liffermer,' she said.

Of course it was very stupid of me not to have grasped immediately the import of what she was saying, but I was concentrating on my Greek rather than on anything she might have to contribute, so I ploughed relentlessly on, '… who lives in Kardamili …'

'Liffermer,' she said again.

'… and has written a book …'

'Liffermer,' she said, nodding enthusiastically, at which point it dawned on me that she was saying 'Leigh Fermor' who was the very man I was talking about. The last thing I wish to do is make fun of her pronunciation, which was 90 per cent accurate and no doubt far better than my Greek.

Certainly I should have realised that she was alluding to the fact that the great Patrick Leigh Fermor lives in, or rather outside Kardamili. I call him great not because I am enthusiastic about his writings, which I am not, as I have hinted, but because he fought with the Greek resistance during the war, and organised the capture of General Kreipe in Crete. In my eyes all such heroes are to be venerated.

Just as heroic, if not more so, were the people who helped them. When Allied soldiers arrived by air or sea it was often the women of Greece who sheltered them and guided them through the mountains to join the resistance. Their menfolk were tortured and shot, and whole villages burnt in reprisals, but they never wavered. The price they paid was first brought home to me in the 1980s when I arrived at the tiny settlement of Osios Loukas, at the end of a minor road somewhere between Athens and Delphi. The last bus of the day put me down and went away. According to the guidebook, there would be rooms to let at the restaurant, but when I asked they said coldly, 'No.' I explained as best I could in my then even more limited Greek that as the last bus had gone I was in a fix. A small group assembled to discuss the matter, talking excitedly in a way I had no hope of understanding. The decision arrived at was that a priest should be sent for, so one was fetched from the nearby monastery. He duly arrived, in black canonicals, tall hat and flowing beard, and proceeded to interrogate me. Once he had been assured that I was English and had verified the fact from my passport, all difficulties melted away. Of course I could have a room, and dinner as well, and I spent a lovely evening in that most peaceful place which, alas, no longer provides for travellers. The explanation was that at the nearby village of Dhistomo, on 10 June 1944, 218 villagers were killed in a reprisal massacre by the Germans, leaving only widows and children. It had been assumed, as it was quite often assumed, that I was of the nationality responsible.

My Kardamili landlady and I agreed that Liffermer was a very fine fellow indeed, and very wise to choose such a lovely place to live in. Then she gave me a small sugary-looking lozenge wrapped in foil 'for tonight'. I could not make out what I was supposed to do with it – whether swallow it, wash with it or what. It had the word 'Bayer' on the outside, which is a pharmaceutical name, and although too small to have a bank, Kardamili has a pharmacy. This worried me rather as I had seen other tiny places with pharmacies and began to fear that the Greeks were turning into a nation of hypochondriacs like the French, who are said to spend more on pills than they do on books and newspapers. Still, there it was, this pharmacy to be made use of, so I went and asked the pharmacist what the lozenge thing was, and she said it was for mosquitoes. It was to put in the electric mosquito-zapper in my room, which makes it lucky that I did not suck it, as I had been half inclined to do.

There are two supermarkets in Kardamili, one of which is run by a Greek family from Melbourne, who, as well as working from dawn till midnight, act as bankers, counsellors and Citizens Advice Bureau to visiting tourists, arranging their taxis, making their telephone calls, and advising them on excursions. Opposite the supermarket is a sign to Old Kardamili, by following which you get among ruined towers, some of which have been turned into houses, and come upon the fine old church that they put on the postcards. It is also one of the ways you can get into the mountains behind the village where there are marvellous walks. The flowers can be beautiful, particularly the massive bougainvilleas and a shrub with a whitish bell-shaped flower which I later found out is called datura.

Datura, like oleander, is said to be poisonous, and there are those who exclaim in horror if they see them in England, saying that they come in the category of things fascinating and fatal to children, who are bound to eat them and die. As oleanders grow everywhere, and datura widely, in Greece you would think most children would be dead, and so would the goats, but they are not. I did, however, have a narrow escape from death in Kardamili, not from datura but because I had to run for my life from a man who was roaring up and down on a tractor waving a hand-held lance and spraying olive trees with an organophosphorous insecticide and a fine disregard for the safety of passers-by.

For those who have not come across it, that figure of speech ('spraying with insecticide and a disregard for safety') is called a zeugma. 'She went home in a flood of tears and a sedan chair' is a well-known example from Dickens, and I introduce the explanation to save a footnote about my dinner that night. I dined in Lela's Taverna by the sea and ordered red mullet, which turned out to be like pink sprats with a doubtful taste, so I wondered what they had been feeding on. Behind me, out of the darkness, I began to hear the voices of two Englishmen who might have been Oxford dons or men from the Treasury, or men wishing to pass themselves off as something similar. The name of Maurice Bowra, the Oxford classical scholar, came floating through the night, and then there were snatches like this:

'Anthony Hope – a marvellous writer.'

'Yes, but one feels so *frightfully* sorry for Rupert of Hentzau.'

'Oh, one does, one does.'

And then, about someone or other: 'He went off to Spain with another man's wife and a small fortune.'

'A zeugma! A zeugma! "Went off with another man's wife and a fortune!" How marvellous! A zeugma!'

I paid my bill and went off myself without casting a glance in their direction, having an unfounded fear that they might somehow try to make me join them. The next night I catered for myself in my self-catering apartment, giving myself paté and cheese from the supermarket and making myself mildly intoxicated with ouzo from the same source.

That second evening, as I sat on my balcony I heard the pitapat of feet and a handsome black mule appeared, trailing a rope around her neck and followed sedately by two donkeys. They turned into the empty space opposite and began to graze on the vegetation. Then they found a big pile of white builders' sand, or possibly cement, on which they played king-of-the-castle for a time, until the mule rolled on it, shook herself, and sent white clouds into the air. I waited to see if this was part of a planned excursion, hoping that some human being would appear, perhaps leading a goat to make up the party, but nobody came. There was no barrier between them and the main road, and at home I would have caught the mule by the rope and tied her up, but here I did not like to interfere.

A woman in black came out of her house, walked circumspectly all round them and went back indoors. I could bear it no longer so I went and stood between the animals and the road, waiting for something to happen. A man arrived, and I asked him if it was all right for the animals to be loose, and he said he didn't know and went away. Then they started moving back the way they had come and began grazing on some ferns outside a house, which caused a furious woman to come out with a stick and chase them up the hill into an olive grove. She had an American-speaking daughter with whom I was able to discuss the problem in depth, and she agreed that it might be wise to tie the mule up, but the furious woman had so intimidated the mule that I could not get near. I left the animals to graze among the olives, hoping that they would not come pitapat back in the dark and get run over, and I neither heard nor saw them again.

Leaving Kardamili for Areopolis, which I did next morning, you climb immediately up a steep hill. Very soon I came upon yet another animal trailing a long rope, this time a donkey. There was no havering about on my part. I parked my bicycle and seized the end of the rope, which sent the donkey off full tilt into an orchard, dragging me behind it. Donkeys are stronger than I am, but I snagged the rope round a tree and brought it up short, and thus we advanced in sharp bursts from tree to tree until we were well clear of the road. There I tied it up and left it.

Ahead of me was an enormous climb but I was quite undaunted, feeling I had altogether got the hang of it. I just cycled and pushed alternately and thought my thoughts meanwhile, and then gave myself the usual agreeable surprise when I looked back to see how far below me the sea was now.

A year later my wife and I came the same way by bus, and to anyone so travelling this or any mountainous road in Greece, I would recommend that you sit exactly behind the driver. You will then be able to see why I think that Greek bus drivers are all descended from the old Greek heroes, who were themselves descended from gods, and so it is that they have inherited the gift of being able to see through granite rock. Only thus can one explain the way they swing the bus boldly onto the wrong side of the road to take a blind corner without checking the bus's speed or bothering to sound the horn. According to my observation, the driver usually sits under the 'No Smoking' sign, smoking cigarettes at the rate of three per hour, frequently negotiating the corners with one hand as there is a cigarette in the other. By the law of averages they ought, from time to time, to have a head-on smash, but they never do, which is how I know they have x-ray eyes.

There were two enormous advantages to the climb on which I was now engaged. The first was that I had the towering majesty of Mount Taygetus above me, the sight of which was uplifting to the spirit. The second was that by leaving the coast behind, I also left all campsites, hotels and rooms to let and passed through a series of beautiful villages which have not caught on to this sort of thing and are quite untouched. I came upon one which appeared to be anonymous as there was no sign with its name either on entering or on leaving, but from the map I think it was Langada. It had a fine-looking restaurant under a huge, spreading plane tree, noble stone houses and a lovely church of ornate stonework. It was just the sort of place I had expected Khalandritsa to be when I went there to sample the throbbing heart of Achaea.

The church door was open so I put on my ecclesiastical trousers and went in to find a priest sitting there writing out lists. He got up and showed me round, pointing out that the walls had at some time been plastered over, and that here and there the plaster had been hacked off to show murals beneath. I left a small amount of money as my contribution to the hacking process, and the priest gave me his blessing – or at least, I think that was what he was doing.

The road then ran downhill, and I turned off it because I liked the look of a village called Itylo. As I was walking around I met a man who spoke good English.

'There are many churches in Itylo,' he said.

'Greeks love building churches,' I replied. 'They do it all the time.'

'Here it is because of the feuds. Each family had to build its own church and would not go to the church of another family. Even now, when somebody dies the service can only be held in the church of that family.'

(This was most useful information as it explained to me next day when I arrived in Areopolis why the old part of the town seemed to be made up of a mixture of Maniot towers and Maniot churches in equal proportions, one tower and one church per family. I got a room in an Areopolis tower, and I thought 'I shall be able to find it in the dark because it is the one behind the church,' until I realised that every tower was behind some church or other.)

In Itylo there are two interesting inscriptions on a terrace that seems to belong to the main and superior church, and is therefore perhaps available to all regardless of family feuds. The first is given in French and Greek and can be translated something like this:

> From here in 1675 eight hundred Ityliotes, victims of history, had to leave their country. In Corsica they founded the villages of Paomia and Cargese, living and working in dignity and with respect for their traditions. In October 1991 a delegation of Cargesians, led by the Mayor Jean Zanetacci and the Archimandrite Marchiano, came to erect this plaque in the presence of the Mayor of Itylo, Nicolaos Panayotinis; of Madame Angela Zervolea, honorary Mayoress; of the Priest Nicolaos Katra and of the people of Itylo.
>
> This plaque is dedicated to the two towns and will be witness to their brotherhood across the centuries.

That to me is a cheering sort of inscription, though what it meant by 'victims of history', and how 800 people who couldn't even bring themselves to share churches could get together to emigrate, and why they hit upon Corsica as the place to go to – these all were mysteries. I just hoped that by 'respect for their traditions' they did not mean that they carried on shooting each other.

I later found out more from Edward Lear's book on Corsica, where the town of Cargese is known as the *village Grec*. Lear travelled with a Greek servant from the area of Suli, and before reaching Cargese he says:

> I had told my Suliot servant not to speak Greek at first, by way of having some merriment when our knowledge of their language came to be known; but this plan fell through by my own inattention; for from a window of one of the first houses I pass there looks out a Greek priest with a venerable beard who makes me a bow and waves his hand, to which salute I unthinkingly reply '*Kalee sas eemera!*' Good morning! and naturally elicit 'What! Do you speak Romaic?' for when these Greeks came to Corsica the *hellenic* tongue was unknown as such.
>
> The colony, according to him, came to Corsica under Genoese protection, about 1626. I had heard of the migration of these Greek settlers from the Morea, and of the persecution which had at one time made their adopted land little less undesirable than their own. Long since they have disused all national costume, and very generally the use of the Greek language. Thus, in two or three more generations their family names will be the only remaining proof of their nationality.

The Itylo inscription indicates that the connection has been kept up more carefully than Lear expected. The full story I have since discovered in Patrick Leigh Fermor's *Mani*. The Itylotes emigrated to escape from the infidel Turks into a

Christian country, and were granted land in Corsica by the Genoese, who ruled Corsica at the time. The persecution Lear speaks of arose partly from the antagonism of the native Corsicans, and partly from the hostility of the Roman Catholic establishment to their Orthodox religion.

The other inscription, in Greek, is more sombre. It reads: 'The finest duty of any man is to die for his country. Murdered by the Communists 15 February 1944 ...' and then follow twenty-two names, with ages from 17 to 55. Below that it says 'Fallen in the Battle of Arne, 26.10.47 ...' and then six names, with ages from 17 to 44. The Germans began their withdrawal from Greece in 1944, and it is a terrible aspect of the history of Greece that Greeks were fighting each other both before and long after the departure of the common enemy.

So it was in a slightly sad mood that I set off from Itylo to Areopolis, an easy and simple ride. Areopolis is a funny sort of place. It has an old bit and a modern bit. The old bit is cobbled streets, tower houses and stone churches with barrel roofs, quite unlike the usual sort of church you find in Greece. The place to stay is at the NTOG Tower, failing which I believe there is a hotel somewhere on the beach. However, the main thing you do from Areopolis is go to the Diros Caves.

These magnificent caverns you visit by boat, or at least you get to them by road and then you get in a boat. My visit coincided with what seemed like a Women's Institute outing, a gathering of forty or fifty women shepherded along by a tall priest in a tall hat. As the only man apart from him, I was given pride of place in the bows of one of the little boats, each of which holds about eight people. The boatman shoved off, and thereafter generally pushed us along by using his paddle as a sort of punt-pole, pushing with it against the sides of the cave. The circuit takes half an hour, and we went gliding forward, sometimes through vast majestic caves with huge stalactites and stalagmites of different colours, and into vast chambers which they have called the Cathedral, the Pink Apartment, or the Cavern of the Dragon. Sometimes we crept through tiny tunnels, carefully keeping our fingers inboard so as not to get them squashed. The route is well lit by electric lights, but there are chambers of Stygian blackness on either side. The silence was broken by the dripping of stalactites, the occasional splash of the boatman's paddle, and cries of delight from the Women's Institute. It would not have occurred to me to have broken off a piece of stalactite as a souvenir, but had it done so I would have been deterred by the stern notice in the leaflet which they give you with your ticket: 'The cutting of even the smallest piece is sentenced to two years' imprisonment.'

My plan for the next two days was to complete the circuit of the Mani and get back to Areopolis on the second evening, the most promising place for a night's stop being Gerolimenas. On the way next morning I turned down a side road to look at a deserted village of tower houses. There were no people, but some heaps of builders' rubble and a few indications that someone was about to restore one of the towers, or had thought of doing so but had given up. The striking thing was that in whatever direction one looked one could see, on every little hillock, another cluster of deserted tower houses. It was obvious that at one time this part of Mani was thinly spread with people, so arranged that from every point of view one lot of people could see another lot of people who they could hate and shoot at.

They must have found it comforting that whatever happened, they would never run out of enemies.

On the left as I rode on were the peaks of Mount Taygetus, grey in bright light but brown with any passing cloud, and brown altogether by evening. On the right were olive groves and the sea, or, at one point, the sort of landscape they call a gulch in a spaghetti Western. Later it became stone-wall country where, as in Gloucestershire or Ireland, they had taken the rocks out of the middle and piled them into walls round the sides. Mostly they were growing olives in the cleared bits, but I came upon three or four undeniable fields each with a cow in the middle.

About here I was overtaken by a bus which reminded me of Bangkok, a remark that needs some explanation. When my then employers sent my wife and me to Bangkok in 1958, it was a place where nothing worked properly. The water was not fit to drink, the electric light was too weak to read by, the streets were full of rabid dogs, the mosquitoes were like minor dragonflies. We loved it because the people were so nice, but they were not good at managing things, and among the things they could not manage were neon lights, although they were very fond of them. They put neon lights all over the city, some of which did not work at all but most of which worked in part, saying things like 'C ca ola' or 'Pan merican irways'. Contrary to the general rule, there was one blue sign in a central spot which every night with absolute reliability flashed on and off saying 'Magirus Deutz'. All night it said it, over and over: Magirus Deutz, Magirus Deutz, Magirus Deutz. During the fifteen months we were there I never knew it to fail, but equally I never found out what it meant. I never met anyone who had bought a Magirus Deutz, or had dealings with Magirus Deutz, or had any more idea than I what this insistent message was supposed to mean. Now in the Mani a bus went by which, in big steel letters on the back, had the words 'Magirus Deutz'. So then I was able to come back and tell my wife that I had at last solved the mystery, and that a Magirus Deutz is a *bus*.

I was not sure how I stood for hotels in this part of the world, so if there was one in Gerolimenas I was going to take a room there, and there was, so I did. It looked pretty good from the outside and from the inside had a fine view of the harbour. Otherwise it was all right for an old soldier but would not have done for my wife, owing to there being no private bathroom and the shared one lacking certain amenities she is keen on, such as a seat on the lavatory. I call it a shared bathroom but there was no one else to share it so it was effectively mine but not, as they say, en suite. Still, I believe this hotel was the right choice. I later found two others, but they were much more scruffy on the outside and so were probably worse on the inside.

All that night there was a fearful wind, with a lot of flapping of canvas and slamming of doors and blowing about of empty plastic bottles. In the morning the sky looked as if it was bound to rain but everyone I asked said that it wouldn't, and they were more or less right except that there were a few showers later on. It was, however, altogether different from any earlier day. I set off along a flat and level bit of road with the bicycle veering all over the place, and had to get off for fear of being blown over. Even in Ireland I had never met a wind like that. Now the gloomy prospect before me was to shove the bicycle uphill, sometimes into a headwind, sometimes with a sidewind, according to the bends in the road. I struggled on, hoping that once I got right into the hills there would be some shelter from the gale, and to some extent there was. At least, the wind seemed to drop a bit as I got higher up.

Now, I always regard maps as infallible, and if I go wrong it must be my fault, but this time it was the map published by a Mr Toubi which was wrong and not me. My plan was to go round the tip of the Mani Peninsula and up the east side back to Areopolis. Mr Toubi unequivocally showed that the way to do this was to go through Vathia, a place celebrated for the number of its towers, so for Vathia I set off, and after a vast deal of climbing and fighting the wind, I arrived. There were the famous towers perched on a hillock, and just to make sure that the road came out on the other side in the direction that I wanted to go, I asked a lady who was throwing out her rubbish.

'No,' she said, 'if you want to do that you must go back to Alika.'

In fairness to Mr Toubi I wish to say that he is not the only mapmaker to get this wrong. I have another map which is equally misleading, but also a recently acquired road atlas which gets it right, and shows that the road into Vathia is a dead end. To make a circuit of the Mani, at Alika you should aim for Lagia, not Vathia.

Why, you may wonder, am I making such a song and dance about this? Partly, of course, to stop other cyclists from falling into the same trap, but mainly because I have since made an important discovery about Vathia. Some of its famous towers, I now know, have been converted into pensions by the National Tourist Office of Greece. If I had known that at the time I would have passed on through Gerolimenas with the intention of staying at Vathia. Had I done so, it would not have worked because by this time in October the towers were shut for the winter. This I discovered from a German couple who make their appearance later in these pages, because they had arrived in Vathia hoping to stay but had to go back to Gerolimenas.

No reader who now feels thoroughly confused can possibly be blamed, so I will state my message with unadorned clarity. If I wanted to do it again, I would cycle from Areopolis to Vathia and stay the night in one of the towers, having first telephoned to make sure that they were open for business. Then I would go back to Alika, over the top to Lagia, and back to Areopolis to complete the circuit of the Mani.

As it was, I rode from Vathia to Alika, cursing Mr Toubi and his misleading map. In this I was unfair, as a watchful Providence was keeping a protective eye on my progress.

From Alika I turned in the right direction and struggled a little way forward before deciding that the whole thing was hopeless. There was an enormous hill in front of me, its top shrouded in mist; the gale seemed to be about Force 8 and the rain was spitting in my face. 'If I try that it will kill me,' I thought, so feeling rather cowardly, I turned back. After a hundred yards or so there was a place which looked to be a possible source of coffee, and a man outside it who said that whether it was or not depended on how the lady inside felt. He spoke excellent English and the conversation developed to the point that I said I had wanted to go right round the peninsula but could not face the hill, and so was on my way back to Gerolimenas.

'We will take you over the top in our lorry,' he said.

He was there to shoot quail, or would have been if the quail had not been put off by the wind, which was spoiling the shooting as well as the cycling. He had a car and opened the boot to reveal a nest of pointers all curled up together like a nest of vipers. He told them to wait there, which was hardly necessary as he shut the boot on them and they couldn't get out. Then we heaved the bicycle on to his friend's lorry and set off. On the way up he told me about quail shooting. The birds come from Egypt in spring and go back in October. Quails on their way to Egypt are creatures of habit and always settle on particular bushes to rest, and over the years he had got to know which bushes they favoured and so where to find them. There are, he said, lots of other birds including snipe, woodcock and some black bird he did not know the name of. Heather is pretty abundant so perhaps if you let some grouse go they would thrive and improve the shooting still further.

Shooting used to be quite the thing for Englishmen on holiday in this part of the world. In 1874 Mrs Annie Brassey was yachting off Corfu with her husband, three children, four friends and thirty-three assorted servants and crew members of the yacht *Sunbeam*. In her book *Sunshine and Storm in the East*, Mrs Brassey records that the gentlemen landed for a day's sport

> with some sailors to beat for them. They had a pleasant morning on the whole and saw quantities of game – three and four woodcock rising from one bush at a time. They brought home a good many woodcock, and a few snipe and quail but failed to secure any wild duck. Pigs they did not attempt. Last year Sir David Baird and his brother killed five hundred head in four days, pig, wild duck, woodcock, snipe and quail; and five guns of another party killed four hundred and twenty couple of woodcock in two days.

This mass slaughter sounds to me, as a man who does not shoot, to be worthy of Scotland at what I suppose is its best. You see signs forbidding you to shoot in rural Greece, which is presumably to preserve the game for the landowners, but I have never seen birds in any quantities to suggest that the shooting is one-tenth as good as it was in Mrs Brassey's day.

I should have been sad not to have seen both sides of the Mani, and I can say with certainty that I could never have accomplished that climb on my bicycle that day. The hill was enormous. The road was rough and the wind was buffeting the lorry about so that I thought that if there was a disaster waiting for me on this trip it might take the form of the door flying open and me going over the cliff. My friends, though, took me safely to Lagia, which I think was rather further than they meant to go on their own account. There they set me down at a *cafeneion*, instructed the surprisingly beautiful lady in charge to look after me, shook hands and departed.

I refreshed myself at the *cafeneion* and feasted my eyes on the owner for as long as seemed reasonable, and then set off on the downhill ride, which was terrifying. The road is narrow, winding, full of pot-holes and spasmodically reverts to being a mere patch of gravel. The wind still blew and I hung on to the brakes, now thinking that the preordained disaster might be that I should simply ride over the edge rather than fall out of a lorry. I arrived at the bottom in a trembling state, and there the road became an up-and-down sort of thing, passing through occasional nameless clusters of houses with no signs, so I did not know where I was. I hadn't provided myself with lunch and began to think I might faint before I got back to Areopolis as there wasn't anywhere to buy anything, except for one village where a grumpy baker-lady said the cheese pies were all gone and she hadn't anything else. Eventually, at a place not on the map and whose name I have forgotten, there was a *cafeneion* into which I staggered and asked if I could have something to eat. Things were looking up.

'Yes,' said the lady, 'you can have a salad.'

'No, not salad – it is not salad weather.'

'Well, what would you like?'

'A sandwich?'

'No – no sandwiches. But what about rice and spinach?' And here she pointed to a plate piled high in front of a fat man.

'That,' I said, 'would do nicely.' I have forgotten the exact Greek name, but a mixture of rice and spinach cooked in a sort of broth and served piping hot out of a cauldron proved to be just the thing for a man in my condition, especially if helped down with draught retsina from a glass of about one-third-pint capacity. Provided you have been fortified like that, the journey then becomes pretty simple. You have some biggish hills between you and Areopolis as you cross from the sea on the east to the sea on the west. After a bit you see a sort of defile and think 'Perhaps I will go through that,' which proves to be exactly what you do and soon you are running downhill to join the main road to Areopolis. My Australian friend Pate had a guidebook which said that the thing to do was leave your gear at Areopolis and do a quick 60-kilometre circuit of the peninsula, and Pate was the sort of cyclist to do it but I am not, so I was right to break the journey at Gerolimenas.

I had had a rather unsatisfactory room in Areopolis two nights before, but this time I got into the NTOG Tower which was a complete success. I had a fine bedchamber (one could call it nothing less), with walls about three-feet thick and well able to withstand the blast that was raging outside. Everything was on the grand scale – the staircase, the furnishings, the towels, the hot water. The only snag was that on the television below I had seen a weather forecast which seemed to say that the whole of Greece was due for thunderstorms next day. The manager, who was watching, drew the same conclusion, so I asked if there was a bus to Githion, this town being my first objective for the next day. There was, at 8.30 a.m. In consequence I spent some time poring over maps, wondering if winter had arrived to abort the expedition and whether I should now have go to Githion by bus, and then to Sparta by bus, and then to Athens by bus.

Any idea of catching the Githion bus was put paid to by three factors. First, the sky next morning was perfectly clear. Second, the lady who arrived to cook breakfast said it would be fine down here and the thunder was only in the north. Third, the front door was locked and she did not turn up to unlock it until 8.25 so I could not have caught the bus anyway.

The room and breakfast cost the peculiar sum of 6,169 drachmas, which at 365 drachmas to the pound worked out at the equally peculiar sum of £17.33. Considering the luxury of my surroundings and as the breakfast was a tumbler of freshly squeezed orange juice, a cold hard-boiled egg, a large cup of Greek coffee, butter, toast, jam and cheese, I reckoned it a bargain. Government-run Xenia hotels may not be up to much but this government-run NTOG Tower was superb.

As I left Areopolis I survived three attempts by a lady to kill me. First, she swung her car across the road in front of me and jammed on the brakes so that I nearly ran into the back of it. Then, after I had passed her she started up and overtook me, nearly crushing me against the kerb at a corner. Then she stopped again and opened the door as I was overtaking for the second time so that I nearly ran into that. I acquit her of any malicious intent though, I just think she lived in a world of her own in which there were no elderly Englishmen on bicycles and she had no idea that I was there.

Monemvasia, Leonidion, Nauplion, Poros, Athens

Once I got clear of the homicidal lady of Areopolis I was on the road to Githion, which is a delight. From the first it shows a general preference for going round the sides of mountains rather than over the top, which is how I like roads to behave. It does not seem to climb very much, and then it goes down for a long way, and just as you think it must in the course of nature go up again, it levels off and then mysteriously it goes down again. How a road manages to repay so small an ascent with so long a descent is a puzzle, and I can only assume that, starting from Areopolis, you are further above sea level than you realise. Anyway, from Areopolis to Githion it was what, in the army, used to be called a cushy doddle. The roadside greenery was pleasant after the bleakness of the Mani. The wind still blew, but was much abated; the sun provided a comfortable autumn warmth, and I had a cosy inner glow from thinking that I had not taken the coward's way and the bus. (A zeugma! A zeugma!)

I had been to Githion before. The waterfront is picturesque but my wife and I had found it a bit of a dull place, and I had no great desire to stay there again. You can get boats from Githion to the islands of Kythera or to Crete, and I went to the shipping office to see if I could also get one to Monemvasia, which might have been a pleasant thing to do. Yes, they said, you can, and it goes via Kythera, but not today as the wind was so bad yesterday that the boat did not sail and the schedules are in confusion. So it was not just the quails that were grounded and I reduced to hitching a lift on a lorry, but the shipping was messed up as well. This introduced a note of caution. Monemvasia was to be my last stop on the Peloponnese, and I hoped to catch a boat from there to Poros, so completing the circuit, and thence the ferry to Athens. Clearly, I must take care not to be in Monemvasia relying on a boat which would not arrive because of the wind, and so cause me to miss my plane.

So, being still in cycling mode, I set off for Skala, which looked from the map as if it might have a hotel and was certainly within reach of Monemvasia the next day. An easy ride it was, and Skala did have a hotel, called the Alsos, which means 'grove'. It is set back 30 yards from the main road, is quiet, clean, cheap and overlooks a grove of lemon trees, hence its name, so I recommend it as a hotel. Skala, on the other hand, looked at first glance to be one of those long, dusty, uninteresting towns that no one would stay in unless they had to. At second glance it proved to be exactly that. Still, it had a nice enough taverna where I had dinner with a German couple who waved me over to their table as I walked in. They said they had seen me somewhere further back and were also staying at the Alsos. He seemed to understand, but not to speak, English, and she to do both, so she and I conducted the conversation with him as audience. He, it appeared, was a successful lawyer given to working hard in short bursts and then taking frequent cycling holidays with his wife.

'What's it like cycling in Germany?' I asked.

'Very good,' said she.

'Give me some routes,' said I, 'but be careful because whatever you tell me to do I shall probably do it, so take it seriously.'

So with a pen from my pocket and table napkins from the taverna she wrote out two routes. On one napkin she wrote:

Romantic Street: (Neuschwanstein)
Füssen/Allgäu
Schöngau
Landsberg
Augsberg
Nördlingen
Dinkelsbühl
Rothenburg
Würzburg

On the other napkin she wrote:

Passau (Germ)
Wien (Austria)
Only Bike-Streets on the Donau

I think, but I am not certain, that of the two the Romantic Street is the easier, and the ride by the Danube from Passau to Vienna the more taxing. I have since done the first with enormous pleasure, and hope to live long enough to do the second.

Then the discussion turned, as it always does, to the question of where we were going tomorrow. I said I was going to Monemvasia. She said they were going to Leonidion.

'Not in one go!' I said. 'You will have to stay halfway.'

'In one day we can do it,' she replied. 'Also our map shows there is no hotel between here and Leonidion.'

I expostulated, protested, pulled out my map and showed them that the road climbed to something between 1,600 and 1,800 metres, and told her that they would certainly kill themselves in the attempt. But no – they had done such things before and they were determined.

The truth is that I had considered this route when planning my trip at home and rejected it. If you look at the map you will see that to make a complete circuit of the Peloponnese, so far as the roads allow and if starting and finishing at Poros, the proper thing would be to go from Skala, where we were, over the mountains to Leonidion; from there to Nauplion; and from Nauplion to Poros. Going to Monemvasia and then to Athens by boat, was, in effect, cheating. Going by Leonidion, however, looked altogether too tough. I had no idea what I should find in the mountains. There didn't seem to be much in the way of villages, and the Blue Guide said there were wolves. I didn't fancy being in my body-bag with wolves tugging at the corners to get me to come out so they could eat me. Any number of disasters might overtake me; I might disappear and never be heard of again, so, in a word, I had decided to funk it.

Next morning the German bicycles had disappeared by the time I left the Alsos, so away I went for Monemvasia. As I passed the turning to Leonidion I thought 'It doesn't look too bad.' As I went on I thought, 'I managed the climb from Kalamata to Kardamili.' Then I stopped the bicycle and thought, 'I know they are twenty-five years younger than me, but one of them is a woman. If a woman can do it, surely I can.' (The logic of this is admittedly crazy, as a woman has climbed Everest, which I could not.) Then I thought, 'Perhaps I should just have a look,' so I turned round, rode back, and started along the Leonidion road. After a mile I had to admit to myself that I had broken my own rule of Never Succumb to a Challenge and was now committed to the hazardous mountainous road into the unknown.

I will also say that I missed out Monemvasia with less regret because I had visited it before, but if you have never been there I urge you strongly to go. It is one of the gems of the Peloponnese, and everyone that can possibly visit it should certainly do so, so I will tell you about it. Monemvasia is built on a rock just off the coast of Laconia in the south-east. You can get there by bus, boat or Flying Dolphin (easy from Athens) and when you first get there you will wonder why you bothered to come. On one side is a beach and an ordinary-looking town, and on the other a long causeway leading to a rock which looks like pictures of Gibraltar but does not seem to be anything special. You trudge along the causeway lugging your baggage with you in the heat, go around a corner, and there before you is a hole in the rock big enough for a horse or donkey to go through, but too small for a car. You go through that and there bursts upon you a wonderful inhabited Byzantine city of narrow cobbled streets and handsome houses; of churches, walls and battlements; of towers and flowers; of sea views and dark alleys, with a fine open square in the middle.

The Blue Guide says it is 'melancholy and evocative'. It is a place where you want to wander about by night when it becomes quiet. Also you need to climb right up to the citadel and to the church of Agia Sophia, which is a thing to be done in the cool of the day. These are powerful arguments for staying in the old town rather than in a hotel by the beach across the causeway. It is usually easy enough to get a room, which will probably have a magnificent outlook and where you will be woken to Monemvasia's nearest approach to heavy traffic in the form of a horse or donkey clopping along with bags of cement for the builders who are restoring houses further on. Unfortunately, on our last visit I arrived with my wife on a Friday and there was to be a christening, a wedding and a funeral all on the Saturday, so the town was full. We slept, I recall, in a cellar with a small bed and no view but with plenty of mosquitoes and three large cockroaches.

Do not be put off. The big hotel is called the Malvasia and other hotels and pensions are coming into being all the time as the builders repair old houses in increasing numbers. My special tip for readers of this book is that you should go to the restaurant To Kanoni (which means 'the cannon' and is near the big gun in the central square) and consult the lady there. She is called Maria and furthermore is most helpful and has a whole house to let at her disposal. Staying on the rock is more expensive than the mainland and after our experience with the cockroaches we lugged our baggage back to the other side and booked into an excellent hotel by the beach. The swimming was better, and we sat on our balcony looking out at the citadel in a state of high contentment, so there is a lot to be said for staying first on one side and then on the other.

Monemvasia was once a thriving port and fortress, and used to be called Malvasia by the Venetians, and Malmsey by the English. Malmsey wine was produced in the nearby islands and shipped from Monemvasia, and in 1478 George, Duke of Clarence was drowned in a butt of it, or so it is said.

As for the present day, the restaurants, especially To Kanoni, are very good in the old town, and if you sit at a table in the street you may be tapped on the shoulder by a cat which wants to let you know it is there. If you give it a fish-head or a backbone a riot breaks out as all the other cats start fighting and disputing which of them should have it. For swimming off the rock, the best place is a sort of platform beside the causeway, and the first time I went there I met Mr Kapoor.

Mr Kapoor, as his name suggests, was an Indian, but he lived in Canada. He was sitting on the platform in his shorts and a good deal of gold jewellery, and his wife was sitting in her sari and a great deal more jewellery. There was a girl, who I later learned was Dutch, sunbathing a little way away. Mr Kapoor, as I quickly discovered, had one obsession and two jokes. His obsession was money, because when I told him my name in response to his introducing himself, he replied, 'Enfield Electricals – quoted on the Toronto Stock Exchange at 1.75 dollars.' The greater part of his conversation revolved around the ingenious bargains he had struck, and in particular the knock-down price at which he had got a suite at the Malvasia Hotel by haggling relentlessly with the management. The first of his jokes was to say to me when I went swimming: 'Is the water very wet?' The second was to tell me his profession. 'I am a dam engineer,' he said archly, waiting for me to laugh, or possibly hoping that I would ask what was so damnable about engineering. When I came out from swimming he returned to the subject of his suite at the Malvasia which was so magnificent that he proposed to hold a party there, to which he hoped I would come. As I walked away I heard him saying to the Dutch girl, who had now gone swimming: 'Is the water very wet?'

Rather to my surprise, Mr Kapoor's party actually took place. He buttonholed me in the street next day and said I should come at eight o'clock after I had eaten. The company consisted of Mr Kapoor and Mrs Kapoor (who never said anything at all), the Dutch girl, two American schoolteachers called Mort and Brenda, and me. Mr Kapoor entertained us with tea which he had found in the cupboard left by a previous guest, and otherwise plied us with stories of people he had astonished by telling them he was a dam engineer, or called on us to admire the suite he had got at half-price (which was, indeed, splendid). Later he worked round to dropping heavy hints to Mort and Brenda that he would greatly welcome a lift in their hired car to Nauplion, to which place they were going and to which he wished to go but was faced with the prospect of paying the bus fare. I admired the stolidity with which Mort and Brenda let these hints pass over their heads as if they had not noticed them – which they certainly had, as I met them at breakfast the next day, and they were speculating as to whether Mr Kapoor ever bought so much as a Coca-Cola without trying to beat the price down, if indeed he did not try to get it for nothing.

Some years later when my wife and I were going to

Monemvasia a drama took place on the bus, conducted in high-speed Greek that I could not properly understand. A burly policeman armed with a pistol and dressed in black like a Nazi stormtrooper materialised from nowhere, pounced upon two men and handcuffed them together. Then he ordered the man next to me to produce his papers, which he duly did and was left in peace. Then the policeman eyed us all up and down and seized on a man in a seat in front of me, who had no papers and was hauled off and handcuffed to the other two, the three of them all squashed up together in a seat for two. There they sat, with the policeman towering over them fingering his pistol and everyone on the bus turning round to stare at them. Nobody seemed to have any sympathy for them except for me, who thought they might be illegal immigrants flying from persecution. I suggested to my wife that she should create a diversion by pretending to have an epileptic fit. Thereupon I would overpower the policeman, seize his keys, unlock the handcuffs and let the poor refugees make a break for it. It seemed a good plan but she wouldn't do her bit so I couldn't do mine.

At some point along the way the bus stopped and other policemen in black led the captives away looking very thin, very dirty, very poor and very sad. Later on in Athens my wife got into conversation with a lecturer in mathematics who had spent seven years in Bristol and therefore spoke excellent English. He said there were two types of policemen, the ones in black who could arrest people and the ones in blue who couldn't. From what I have seen, both the black ones and the blue ones carry pistols, so the logic seems to be that the blue ones are not allowed to arrest people but must be allowed to shoot them. Anyway, the lecturer said the three arrested men were probably escaped prisoners as there had been a major jail-break three months before, so possibly my wife was right in declining to pretend to throw a fit.

Who knows what further adventures I might have had if I had gone to Monemvasia for the third time? Not wishing, however, to be outdone by a pair of Germans I turned my back on that amazing place and my face towards Leonidion.

The road up, all the way, has a nasty surface of large pebbles stuck together with tar and interspersed with holes. From the map I could not tell whether it just went up to, perhaps, 1,700 metres and then down the other side, or whether it went up to, say, 1,500 metres, down to 1,300 metres, up to 1,600 and so on, such being often the way with mountain roads. It started with a steady rising gradient up which I puffed, sometimes riding and sometimes walking. Then at some 8 miles out of Skala I came to a crossroads where there was good news in the form of a notice declaring that someone whose name I have forgotten had rooms to let in Kosmas, which was 16 kilometres ahead. That was inspiring. Come what might I could, if necessary, push the bicycle uphill for 16 kilometres, otherwise 10 miles, as long as I knew that there was a room at the end.

So I trudged resolutely on, the road now getting steeper and so increasing the proportion of trudging to pedalling. Then a battered pick-up truck came from the other direction with two extremely excited Greeks wishing to tell me that there were two other cyclists only two kilometres ahead.

'So,' thinks I, 'that is all the start you have got, my German friends,' and I had to quell an inclination to hurry and try to overtake them.

And then: Where had I come from?

From Skala.

Bravo! Where was I going?

Leonidion.

Bravo! Bravo! (in chorus). From here to Kosmas it is all upwards and then from Kosmas all downwards.

How far from here to Kosmas?

Ten kilometres.

So there, at a stroke, was another anxiety removed. There was to be no terrible up-and-down switchback among the mountain peaks but a mere six or seven miles to go, then it would all be downhill.

On I went, and the landscape became extremely beautiful and extremely steep, so I was walking almost all the time. I could see the road winding off above me to the right, and as I finally reached the turn, there it would be winding off to the left. And so we went up together, the road, the bicycle and I, winding to the left, winding to the right, up and up and up. There was nothing happening. There were no houses or side roads, no crops or goats; just mountains and me. I got a second wind and was perfectly happy going along like this, not even wondering when it was going to end, when suddenly a thin, white marble column appeared.

'I do believe it is the top,' I thought, and it was. The summit took the form of a war memorial to which two men were putting the finishing touches in the shape of marble paving slabs. The distance from Skala was 20 miles, and it had taken me just over five hours.

At this point there was a burst of autumn colour. There is nothing surprising, you may say, about autumn colour on the 25th of October but I hadn't seen any anywhere else. There was none on the way up, but here at the top was a blaze of chestnut trees in two big clumps and lots more on the slopes of the mountain on the other side. Kosmas was a little further on, and as I rounded a corner just over the crest of the hill the way was barred by a big plastic pipe on barrels with a small arrow indicating, rather diffidently, that I should take a little muddy track to the left. It seemed an odd idea, but I went that way and narrowly dodged a Fiat Panda coming up, with two girls also clearly wondering if this could possibly be the right way. We were, I think, reassured by the sight of each other; perhaps it wasn't a mistake, and if it was, at least neither they nor I were alone in making it.

In time the narrow muddy track joined a narrow cobbled track, which unexpectedly burst into a wide square with plane trees and a huge church. Here again I was accosted by two more excited men in a pick-up truck. There was the usual 'Where have you come from?' and so on, and they too were keen to tell me about the Germans. 'They are here!' they said, but they weren't, as far as I could see. I looked around expecting to see their bicycles propped up somewhere but I didn't. I would like to think that they had found the climb too much for them and had retired exhausted to the Rooms to Let, but I have no evidence for this and fear the more likely thing is that they just sailed on serenely down the other side. I never saw them again to find out.

As for me, I was hungry, it being two o'clock, so relying on my rice-and-spinach experience I went into the decidedly down-at-heel *cafeneion*, to be greeted with huge enthusiasm by two elderly parties who were finishing their lunch. After I had explained where I came from ('Bravo!') and that I wasn't a German and a few things like that, I ordered what seemed to be the safest dish, which was soup. What you get if you order soup in the coffee place in

Kosmas resembles, more than anything else, the worst kind of Irish stew. If you can imagine a soup-plate with the ribs of some departed sheep swimming in a thin but fatty yellow liquid, that is it. It was mitigated by a lemon, which relieved the fat a bit, and it was just possible to drink the juice and pick a little at the bones. I ordered a glass of wine to go with it and got a small carafe of pink unresinated wine with a powerful kick. It had the sort of indescribable flavour that wine writers talk about when they say things like 'ripe bananas with a hint of woodsmoke and wild herbs'. If pressed I would have said that this was a raw spirit with a hint of rosehips and juniper.

When I first went to Greece, terribly bad food seemed to be the usual thing, but now it has got much better. At that time I assumed that they put resin in the wine in order to disinfect the food in the stomach. There are many explanations as to why retsina is resinated, ranging from the idea that the taste was supposed to put the Turks off drinking it, to the notion that the keeping qualities were thus improved, but I was pleased to find that in 1894 Karl Baedeker was of my opinion. In Baedeker's *Greece*, under the heading 'Rules of Health' (in big black print) he says 'The good qualities of the resinous wine are highly extolled by those who are used to its peculiar flavour, especially in stomachic derangements occasioned by the unusual food.' My first bottle of retsina seemed to me to be perfectly disgusting, my second bottle utterly delicious, and I have drunk it both pleasurably and medicinally ever since. Although I have ventured into fairly remote parts I have never, so far, suffered any stomachic derangement.

In this case the raw spirit and rosehips worked just as well as resin in the matter of disinfecting the Graeco-Irish stew, and the whole concoction nerved me for the ride down. It might be best to say that this was indescribable and so not attempt to describe it, but I will risk it. Speaking factually, I sat on the saddle and for thirteen miles did nothing at all except squeeze the brakes to stop myself from going over the edge of the precipice beside the road. There was no traffic at all so I rode in the middle to avoid getting vertigo and plunging into oblivion. The autumn colours continued to be superb all the way down – chestnut, oak and beech, supplemented by heather which seemed to be blooming out of season. I think the road must be quite new because it does not appear at all on the map that I got for my first trip to Greece in 1979. From Kosmas onwards the only sign of human habitation is a monastery stuck on a rock as you get towards Leonidion. In terms of solitary grandeur the Mani is nothing to it, for the Mani is dotted with tower houses wherever you go, whereas from Kosmas you just wind down an empty canyon for mile after mile till at last the road levels out and you get a glimpse of the sea. The distance that day, from Skala to Leonidion, was 38 miles.

Leonidion, when you reach it, proves to be a town of streets that could hardly cope with one-way traffic but are crammed with two-way traffic. My since-acquired road atlas has bits of extra information such as that Leonidion has two hotels, but as I never discovered the name of the one I stayed at I cannot warn you to avoid it. It was very scruffy, and I have no record of having eaten anything, so I think there is no reason for anyone to visit Leonidion except for the bicycling reason that I did. The thing to do is to get away quickly. As you leave, the road goes up and you look down on trim market gardens, rectangular and impeccably tidy vegetable plots, and orchards of military precision and correctness. It was rather a relief after the barren grandeur of the day before.

I was heading for Nauplion and nobody knew how far away it was. Vagueness about distance is evidently a hangover from the days when the roads were very bad. The landscape painter Hugh Williams, writing in 1817, says 'In Greece a journey is generally computed by time; their tracks always have no measured miles. No carriage could travel them and, indeed, I do not believe there is a single vehicle of this description in the whole country.' Although they now have very good roads it is still the custom to measure distance in time, like this:

Question: How far is it to Argos?

Answer: One hour.

When you explain that you are on a bicycle this is considered to be a good joke which it takes them some time to get over. When you finally press them for a statement in kilometres they take a wild guess as they haven't got a clue. At my hotel they said the distance to Nauplion was 100 kilometres. About a mile along the road a man told me it was 70 kilometres. After ten miles I stopped for coffee and they said it was still 70 kilometres. The way I went it turned out to be almost exactly 80 kilometres, or 50 miles, from start to finish which, after the strenuous performance of the previous day might seem a daunting distance but I took it easy and enjoyed it.

Another Greek habit when it comes to roads is to paint slogans on them, and there were plenty on this road. Sometimes they were just the names of political parties, such as Pasok, and sometimes they were the names of people. They had two things in common. They were all expertly done, not as a rough scrawl with an aerosol or paint brush but all looking as if they had been done professionally by the men who paint 'STOP' or 'GIVE WAY' on the roads for a living. Also they were all very faded, so perhaps they only paint slogans when elections are pending and there hadn't been one for some time and there wasn't going to be one soon. A sign which puzzled me for a time was, or would have been were it in English letters: N.D. YIANNOPOULOS.

I didn't know what N.D. meant and wondered whether the message was 'Good old Yiannopoulos' or 'Down with Yiannopoulos' but later realised that N.D. meant New Democracy which was just Mr Yiannopoulos's political party.

The road goes up and down at first, and as I paused on a rise for a moment a car drew up and out leapt a Jehovah's Witness. I feel very sympathetic to Jehovah's Witnesses because of a pair who visit us at home. They are father and son, the boy now being about ten years old, but when they started he was about six. They come at weekends, and it seems to me a shame that the lad, who is silent and looks depressed, should have to spend his Saturdays and Sundays trailing round after his father watching him receive rebuff after rebuff, instead of going in for boyish pastimes like football or fishing. I am not sufficiently sympathetic to enrol as a Witness, but the technique I have for ensuring friendly dealings is to say, 'This is a devout Catholic household, and we all have our own ways of worshipping the Almighty.' My wife is a Catholic but I am not, so it is stretching the truth rather, but I consider it to be in the best of causes. It works well enough in Sussex but I could hardly stand on the Greek highway declaring myself to be a Catholic household, even if I knew how to do it. I am not sure how I got out of accepting a copy of the *Watchtower*, which is their magazine, but I did it somehow and we parted on amicable terms.

Between Leonidion and Nauplion you travel a very long way without seeing any signs to suggest where you are going or how far away anywhere is, but after a place called Astros they begin to tell you that you are heading for Argos and they start giving you the distance. Then 12 kilometres before Argos there is a sign suggesting that you may prefer to go to Nauplion anyway, which you do by turning right. From there it is a 13-kilometre ride with the sea on the right and eucalyptus trees on the left, which later give place to rather grotty salt flats and failed nightclubs, or so they look. I stopped for a moment to put on a pullover and a car drew up. Out jumped another Jehovah's Witness. 'This is for you, my friend,' he said, pressed a *Watchtower* into my hand and drove off.

In Nauplion I made for the King Otto Hotel. I do not say that everyone should stay there, because if you have to have a private bathroom you had better not as you will not get one. Otherwise you should. It is a handsome old house in the middle of things, and as you go through the front door you see a fine spiral staircase winding up to the first floor. All the rooms have ceilings about fifteen feet high, and it is extremely clean and always seems to have been freshly painted. In the right weather you should have breakfast in the garden, where they give you Madeira cake.

The King Otto has more style than any hotel I know, and in common with all Greek hotels, has no fear of fire but thinks something terrible may happen to you in the bathroom. The most succinct fire precaution notice I ever came across was in a hotel in Japan where the placard read: 'In case of fire shout "Kagi" and leave the building.' Greek hotels dispense with even this elementary instruction and say nothing at all about fire, but they equip the bathroom with mysterious strings which I have often pulled in the hope that they might make the light come on or the water get hot, and then realised I have sounded the alarm. Nothing ever happens, though, so it doesn't matter. I think these alarms must be required as a matter of law but are never attended to, as a matter of practice.

After being in such relatively wild and minor places it was pleasant to be in Nauplion wandering among the brightly lit jewellery shops and seeing white-coated waiters in opulent restaurants. As a city, Nauplion is the best I know in Greece barring Corfu. The Plateia Syntagma is paved in marble and half is devoted to smart eating places and half to small boys playing football. Eating an ice cream there is like doing the same in St Mark's Square in Venice, but a great deal cheaper. The comparison is not far-fetched as Nauplion is a Venetian city, overlooked by the Venetian castle of Palamede. (There are a thousand steps to Palamede and when I climbed up I was greeted with a round of applause by a party of French tourists, to whom I politely raised my hat.)

The harbour is magnificent. I have seen a good many harbours in my time, including Hong Kong in its prime, but my favourite of all is certainly Nauplion, not only by day, but also by night, when you sit on the waterfront watching the lights of cars twinkling down the hills on the other side. There is a pleasant museum with thick walls where you can shelter from the heat of the day and marvel at how clever they were at making things in 6,000 BC and even more so in 1,400 BC. Nauplion is also the jumping-off place from which to visit Mycenae and about Mycenae I have nothing whatever to say that you would not find in a guidebook except that it is a good idea to take a torch so that you can get a proper look at the inside of the Tomb of Agamemnon.

In Nauplion you can find the place where John Capodistrias, the first President of Greece, was assassinated in 1831. He had quarrelled with Petrobey, the 'King of the Mani', who had been one of the first to take up arms in the War of Independence. Capodistrias shut Petrobey up in prison, but foolishly left Petrobey's brother Constantine and his nephew George at liberty. A meeting of reconciliation was arranged by a Russian admiral, but at the last minute Capodistrias flew into a passion at something he had read in the *London Courier*, and when Petrobey arrived under guard, refused to see him. At first the old man was speechless with rage that he, head of the clan Mavromichales, 49 of whose kinsmen had died fighting the Turks, should be so treated by a man he regarded as a Corfiot upstart who had never struck a blow for Greece in his life. Then, as he was led back through the streets to prison, he stopped at his brother's house and called out. Constantine and George rushed to the window to ask how he had got on. Petrobey pointed to his guards. 'You can see,' he said, and passed on. That was it. Under the code of the Mani only one course of action was possible, and next day, as he mounted the steps of the church of St Spiridon to hear mass, Capodistrias was shot in the head by Constantine and stabbed in the heart by George.

I would have liked to stay in Nauplion for a second night, but it was now Friday and I had to fly home from Athens on Monday. One possibility was to stay in Nauplion on Friday night and ride to Epidaurus on Saturday. From there I could go on to Galatas and Poros on Sunday, catch an early boat from Poros on Monday morning, and the plane that afternoon. I could, but there was no safety margin, no allowance for thunderstorms, high winds and disrupted shipping schedules, nor any contingency provision for mechanical failure or me falling off my bicycle.

So what about the bus? Could I perhaps cycle to Epidaurus on Saturday morning and then get a bus to Galatas, arriving in Poros that evening with a day in hand? I went to the bus station to enquire. I consulted the lady whose job it was to answer questions, a task which she clearly found tedious, if not absolutely beneath her. She said that the only suitable bus left Nauplion at twenty past two, although the notice said two o'clock, and when I pointed out the discrepancy, she shrugged her shoulders. She further said that it got to Epidaurus at three o'clock and that whether the driver would take my bicycle would be up to him, about which she declined to express an opinion. That did not seem to have advanced matters very far and rather than risk finding myself at the Epidaurus bus stop at three p.m. on Sunday faced with a bus that would not take my bicycle and a plane about to take off within 24 hours, I reluctantly decided to leave Nauplion that morning.

From Nauplion to Epidaurus is 16 miles, which, to a man in my then state of fitness was merely what racehorse trainers call a pipe-opener. I was there comfortably by half past twelve, lunched at the tumbledown hotel, and was told by the waitress that the bus would arrive at half past two. I was at the stop at twenty past two, made two unsuccessful attempts at flagging down buses that were going somewhere else, and when the bus to Galatas arrived at three p.m. brought it to a halt. I asked the driver if he could take my bicycle and he, in a morose and surly manner, said 'No,' and drove off. I thought that was pretty rotten of him. The bus had no passengers at all so the luggage part cannot have been full, and I am sure that with goodwill and ingenuity we could have managed to fit the bicycle into the boot, but I did not get a chance to try.

My first thought was, 'Lucky I didn't stay in Nauplion.' My second was that I should stay at the Epidaurus hotel where I had stayed before, but it was shut, or else everyone was asleep. My third was that I should ride on to a place called Trahia, and get a room there with an old lady running a *cafeneion* who had told me on the outward journey that she let rooms. Failing her, there was the body-bag or the possibility of a lift in a pick-up over the hill, but there was no chance of my riding all the way in daylight and I did not fancy trying to do it in the dark.

So I set off. From every rational point of view it was a mistake. The old lady gave me a room all right, but I had overlooked the fact that she was garrulous, deaf, given to shouting and spoke no word of English. She kept engaging me in high-pitched conversations, and if I did not understand, which I usually did not, she turned the volume up. I meanwhile was shouting back answers to her remarks which sometimes seemed to hit the target and satisfy her, but more often missed it altogether and caused her to scream even louder. I tried retreating to my room and reading by the inadequate light, but she kept barging in to shout some more. The only thing to do was to go out to a bar and drink a bottle of beer and then sneak back to my room. It was an awful room, and I slept in my sleeping bag, not liking to trust the sheets. The so-called bathroom arrangements were unspeakable.

But, as always on this trip, even the things that went wrong turned out to have done so for good reason. The result of being in such a terrible place was that I left as early as possible, when the mist was still in the valley and clouds on the mountain tops. The sun somehow managed to shine in between and it was unbelievably lovely. The result of the churlish behaviour of the grumpy bus driver in making me ride over the mountain again to Galatas was that I perfectly astonished myself by the ease with which I did it. I suppose it is obvious that a man who has ridden some 700 miles up and down hill in something under four weeks will be fitter at the end than he was at the start, but compared with the outward journey when I toiled and struggled to the top, this time I simply strolled up and rolled down. In fact, I hardly settled to the task of getting up when I found I *was* up, then coasted down, bowled along the flat, went straight on to the waiting ferry and arrived to find Poros in an apparent state of turmoil.

It was actually in a state of celebration in honour of Ochi Day, which they had combined with the First Greek Yacht Festival. Ochi Day is kept as a public holiday because on 28 October 1940 Mussolini issued to General Metaxas, then Prime Minister, an ultimatum demanding unrestricted entry into Greece and the right to occupy certain strategic points. His reply, which has become a treasure of Greek history, was 'Ochi!' (No!) Without stopping to consider the chances of success but with the whole country united behind him, Metaxas plunged into war on Britain's side, making Greece at that time our only ally. The result was that the Italians, a nation of 45 million, were given a sound drubbing by Greece, a nation of 8 million, which is certainly something to celebrate. The Greeks were only defeated when the Germans joined in, in April 1941.

The effect of combining Ochi Day with a yacht festival was that the whole waterfront was lined with large expensive yachts which were, I suspect, what is called Dressed Over All. This I think is what you call it when they hang flags and bits of bunting all over the rigging. Taken together, these two events were celebrated with the making of speeches, the firing of guns, the milling of crowds, the marching of sailors, the broadcasting of pop music and a selection of performances on a raised stage. When I got there a group of schoolgirls were performing rather elementary country dances, solemnly watched by rows of seated dignitaries in blue suits or uniform, who probably enjoyed it about as much as if it had been a school play.

That evening all the yachts were lit up and made a fine sight. There was one which looked like the *Mayflower* and another that I expect should be called a two-masted barque. I felt quite sorry for some of the rich yachtsmen, several of whom obviously owned a boat that in normal circumstances would appear to be pretty grand and should impress their business acquaintances. Here they were obliged to park next to something approaching an ocean-going liner which made theirs look no more than what is commonly called a floating cocktail bar.

The early ferry boats from Poros to Athens on Monday were not early enough for me to be sure of catching my plane, so I moved on to Aegina the next morning. I have fond memories of Aegina because it was there, on an earlier visit, that I found out why Englishmen shout at foreigners. I got a room in a house belonging to a sweet old lady who used to say things to me in Greek in a soft and gentle voice which I never understood. She had, however, a bossy and strident daughter-in-law who used then to shout the same remarks at me, and her I always understood. From this I could see that the habit of shouting at the natives in India was not an unkind thing to do, it was just a way of helping them to get the message. It is surprising that I could not understand the old lady in Trahia better as she shouted like anything, but perhaps she was shouting in dialect.

In Aegina you must visit the magnificent Doric temple of Athene Aphaia, which stands in a remote spot amid pine woods and forms one point of a triangle with the Parthenon at Athens and the temple of Poseidon at Sunium. Outside they have put up a most helpful notice giving the details of Greek temples in general, from which you can understand this one in detail, and are enabled to tell such things as a stylobate from stereobate, or to distinguish a tympanum from an acroterion. I would like to have a small copy for my study, and also want one dealing with Byzantine architecture so that I can be sure of knowing a pendentive from a squinch when I see one.

To anyone who visits Aegina I further warmly recommend a visit to Palaiokhora, which is a peculiar kind of ghost town on the side of a hill. It was built well inland to be away from pirates, a precaution as old as Greece itself. The historian Thucydides says: 'The ancient cities, both in the islands and on the mainland, were built well back from the sea, because piracy was so widespread.'

When latter-day piracy was finally put down in the nineteenth century the people of Palaiokhora dismantled their houses and moved them down to the present town of Aegina. They thought, though, that it would be impious to pull down the churches so they left them behind and you now wander about a deserted town with no houses but twenty or more churches, some going back to the thirteenth century. When my wife and I were there we met a large party of women being shepherded along by two priests. They gave us each some bread, and in one of the churches a man gave us wine, because we had accidentally hit upon a feast day, though we never discovered whose it was.

This time my main purpose in going to Aegina was to catch a boat to get me to the airport on time, and the only one I could rely on to be early enough turned out to be the hydrofoil the *Flying Dolphin*. With some difficulty my bicycle was heaved on and off it, and from Piraeus I set off to ride to the airport.

I had come across a happy Englishman who made a living in Poros by running a sort of paperback exchange, buying used paperbacks from one tourist and selling them to another. On his wall there was a big map from which he showed me that to get from Piraeus to the airport one just had to follow the sea, and, apart from leading me into making one or two abortive plunges into blind alleys, this advice worked very well. The undertaking, though, can seriously damage your health. This is not so much because of the danger of being run over, though that is considerable, but because of the smog and traffic fumes, which are unbearable. On this, the last bicycle ride of the expedition, my eyes were stinging and running and I was constantly coughing. I have never known anything like it. Patras was a pleasure by comparison. Two months later I got flu and a cough that lasted for six months. I have never known anything like that either, and I am inclined to blame it on the preliminary damage done by the Athens smog.

The airport turning was not signposted with the greatest clarity so I managed to overshoot it and thus prolong the discomfort. In spite of this I got to the terminal in good time, at which point a great feeling of relief and self-satisfaction welled up inside me. At the last minute before setting off on such an expedition I am generally assailed by doubts. Would I get food poisoning/be run over/hate it? Will it rain all the time? Will the bicycle be stolen? And all that. But I hadn't and it didn't and it wasn't, and Greece had been at its best, so I felt extremely pleased with myself.

I knew exactly what I should take as a present for my wife – a supply of Apricot Nectar. This wholly delicious fruit juice comes in cardboard cartons. It is found, as far as I know, only in Greece, and if we had an ounce of commercial acumen between us she and I would have got the concession to import it into England and made our fortunes. My wife went so far as to write to the Commercial Attaché at the Greek Embassy pleading that somebody should be encouraged to take it up, but got no reply. Knowing her taste for this amazing delicacy, I turned my back on the airport that I had reached with so much difficulty, and set off in search of a supermarket which stocked Apricot Nectar, and in the space of half an hour returned triumphant with two cartons.

Part II

Epirus and Acarnania

I am also perfectly aware that I have nothing to recommend me as a Companion, which is an additional reason for voyaging alone.

– Byron to Scrope Berdmore Davies, 31 July 1810

Corfu and Parga

A few years later I flew to Corfu, which was a place I did not want to visit in the least. To my mind Corfu had an evil reputation as having been taken over by English football hooligans and lager louts and turned into an imitation of the Costa del Sol. My dislike at the thought of going there was made worse when I found that the only way to do it without changing planes was to go by charter flight leaving at 11.30 p.m. When my flight was delayed and finally left at 1.30 a.m. I was altogether disenchanted with this place that I had never set foot on and did not wish to go to anyway.

Why, you may wonder, was I doing it? Well, Corfu for my purposes was to be no more than a hasty night-stop on the way to a place called Igoumenitsa on the mainland, from where I proposed to start a tour of that part of northern Greece called Epirus, on my bicycle.

I had at the time achieved a sort of minor notoriety by appearing regularly on a television programme called *Watchdog*, which was always seen by seven or eight million people. As there are not many small, bald, old men on television, I found that I had become publicly recognisable to a surprising degree. Sometimes I was mistaken for Bobby Charlton, the famous footballer, but mostly they thought it was me. The first time that the consequences of appearing on *Watchdog* came home to me was when I gave 50p to a beggar in a public lavatory and he said, 'Thank you, Mr Enfield.' Up to that moment I was just an anonymous retired local government officer, but not any more.

I mention this not out of vanity, or not wholly so, but because it may interest readers who have not yet become minor television figures to know how charter airlines treat you if you are one. In the first place, if you arrive to check in with a bicycle, they try to take it away from you. Under normal arrangements the airline staff tell you in a fairly surly way to take the pedals off, turn the handlebars sideways and let the tyres down a bit. Then you have to wheel it to some other part of the airport where, if you are lucky and provided you wait patiently, someone will turn up to accept it. Once, but only once, they made me pay £36 extra. Not so this time. As soon as I arrived a secret signal was given and a man appeared with a huge polythene bag and tried to wrest the cycle from me. I had taken the pedals off at home, so that was all right. I hung on to the bike long enough to let the tyres down. In his hurry to relieve me of any possible further trouble he wanted to dispense with the business of turning the handlebars sideways, but I managed to persuade him that this was essential, and did it. As he was most reluctant to allow me any part in the ceremony of putting the cycle into the polythene bag, I gratified him by letting him do it by himself. Then he carried it off in triumph, leaving me to kick my heels at Gatwick for four hours waiting for the delayed flight.

Beyond giving this kind and anxious treatment to one's bicycle there is not a lot a charter airline can do to enhance one's comfort, but what they could do, they did. There being no Business Class, they could not upgrade me to wallow in champagne and luxury, as my wife and I did when upgraded on a flight to Barbados. Instead, they gave me the best seat on the plane which is 1A, and they left 1B empty, so that I had two seats. The air hostess said that head office had told them that I was coming, and anything I wanted I had but to mention. She interpreted her instructions very well because what I mentioned was that I would like to be left to sleep as much as possible, and so she forbore to wake me up and force me to eat a dinner of baked airline chicken at 2.30 in the morning. She also spread a blanket over me, which was a delicate attention.

I now quite understand how politicians who get up to mischief, like David Mellor or Robin Cook, always get caught. It is the consequence of going on television so that everyone recognises them, which enables other people to make a little money by selling to the newspapers an account of what they have seen going on. Not that I had anything other than the most blameless intentions on this trip, but I was hailed during the flight by various fellow passengers making facetious remarks such as 'Is Anne Robinson with you? Ha, ha!' (Anne Robinson was at the time the senior person on *Watchdog*, which I mention for the sake of posterity, as she is now incredibly famous.) As I was putting the bicycle back together at Corfu airport, a tall, plump, blonde lady in her fifties came up.

'It's Edward, isn't it?'

'Yes, it is.'

'How marvellous! Can I kiss you?'

And she planted a kiss on my cheek willy-nilly. I am tempted to say that I felt like Prince Charles being kissed by a Spice Girl but the comparison would be far-fetched.

In spite of the celebrity treatment given to my bicycle, they had managed to bash it up a bit, as often happens on aeroplanes. The back wheel was out of true and rubbed against the brake once per revolution. It was still possible to ride it, and as I went the short distance from the airport to the town centre I began the process of revising my opinion of Corfu. There is a beautiful bay on your right, with no obese sun-worshippers, skinny-dippers or anything unpleasant of that sort. Ahead is a great Venetian castle. To the left are attractive gardens backed by handsome houses.

I followed the signs to the town centre and booked into the Olympic Hotel. This declared itself to be Category B, a rather grand classification which was at odds with its dilapidated appearance, consequent upon a couple of letters having fallen out of the sign, so it actually called itself the OL PIC HOTEL. The modest charge for a perfectly adequate room also seemed appropriate to a humbler category than B. The manager, as hotel managers do, expressed great admiration for the way that my Greek enabled me to book a room, and furthermore to ask where I could find a mechanic to mend the bicycle. This exercise in Greek was just to give me a bit of practice as he spoke English very well.

The mechanic, whose shop was just round the corner,

said he would have the bike ready in an hour. I went back after an hour and a half to find that he was not so much a mechanic as an artist. The bicycle was upside-down and he appeared to be playing upon the spokes like a harpist preparing for a concert, testing each one and fine-tuning it individually with a little key, until he got the whole to perfect pitch. For this service he charged £4. I may mention that the Greek nation had recently devalued the drachma, a course of action which was greatly to my advantage.

Between taking and fetching the bicycle, I had had a shower and a shave at the Ol pic, shaving under slight difficulty. There was hot water in the shower but however long I ran the tap there was never any in the basin. Luckily the shower pipe could be made to reach the basin, so by this means I managed to shave. Later I discovered that it was merely a matter of eccentric plumbing. Contrary to custom, the tap with the red blob gave out cold water, and the one with the blue blob gave out hot. This further endeared me to the Olympic as it had the charm of novelty.

The bicycle and I were now both in good running order, so I locked the bike away and set off on foot to explore the town, which rose yet further in my good opinion on closer acquaintance. Like most Greek towns of any merit it was built by someone else, in this case the Venetians, and it is most certainly a Venetian sort of town. I came out of a wide street with marble pavements and smart clothing shops into a narrow street with more marble pavements and smart jewellers' shops. The houses on either side had a definite look of Venice, lacking only the waterways. I stopped for coffee in what was undeniably a piazza – unless perhaps it was a *campo*, which is what they tend to be called in Venice – and later emerged into what seemed to be another piazza, or *campo*, with a colonnade down one side, trees on the other, and a cricket green in the middle. Crossing over this, I came to the castle that I had seen on the way from the airport. Outside is a statue of Count Schulemberg erected by the grateful Venetians with a Latin inscription of which I will give the translation:

To Matthew Count Schulemberg
Supreme Commander of the Land Forces
Of the Christian Republic
At the siege of the struggling Corfu
Its stoutest defender
In his lifetime
The Senate [erected this monument]
In the year 1717 on the 12th of the month
of September

The Count is portrayed after the Roman fashion in sandals and a short, metal-plated skirt and vest, but encumbered with a great swirling cloak which must inevitably have tripped him up if he was tempted to move about. He was a soldier of fortune from Saxony, says the Blue Guide, and the hero of 'the celebrated siege of 1716'.

In the belief that the siege of 1716 may not be quite as celebrated as the Blue Guide makes out, I will tell you that in 1714 the Turkish government launched a surprise attack on the Venetian Empire. The Venetians selected Count Schulemberg to command the defence of Corfu, which came under siege in 1716. The new Captain General began by 'exerting himself to the utmost in endeavouring to place the island in an efficient state of defence. The whole of the inhabitants, including even the Jews, were armed and organised.' I am quoting from *The History of the Island of Corfu*, by H. Jervis-White Jervis, 1852.

A siege of seven weeks came to a crisis on 17 August. On that night, as the battle raged round the Fort Neuf, one of the two Venetian citadels,

> Schulemberg, at the head of eight hundred followers, debouched by one of the gates, attacked the enemy with fury in flank, threw them into disorder, drove them from the position they had carried, and forced them to fly to their lines with a loss of two thousand men and twenty standards.

That night there was a terrible storm which convinced the Turks that fate was against them, and next morning their camp was found to be abandoned. So ended the last great attempt of the Turkish government to extend their empire into Christian Europe.

I was treading in the footsteps of Edward Lear, the nonsense writer, landscape painter and traveller, who painted some of his most glorious pictures on the island of Corfu. He arrived in 1848 and his letters include the statements that the city:

'Has little to recommend it – narrow streets and poky houses.'

'Nearest the sea there is the most beautiful esplanade in the world [but] full of exercising troops and endless dogs.'

'On the farther side is the magnificent Palace of the Viceroy, and beyond this the double-crowned citadel – very picturesque.'

To this I reply: perhaps the streets are a little poky, but none the less attractive for all that.

The exercising troops and dogs have gone from the esplanade, which is now the site of the cricket ground. It has a handsome arcade running along one side, built by the French and called the Liston.

The Palace of the Viceroy is now called the Royal Palace. It is a fine, white neo-classical building put up under the supervision of a British Colonel of the Royal Engineers.

The Citadel is one of the two Venetian castles. This one housed the garrison in Lear's time. The other is the New Fortress, or Fort Neuf, from which Count Schulemberg sallied forth with such good effect.

This hotchpotch of multinational buildings came about because Corfu belonged to Venice from 1386 to 1797; briefly to Napoleon; and then to Britain from 1814 to 1864, when we generously gave all the Ionian islands to Greece.

I took a brief turn round the gardens that adjoin Count Schulemberg's statue before going to the Citadel, where they thoughtfully admitted me at half-price because I am so old. You cross a channel connecting two arms of the sea which acts as a moat to the Citadel and a mooring place for a lot of little yachts. There can, I thought, be few worse ways of passing a holiday than being baked like a lobster thermidor in one of these vessels, and in this opinion I am supported by Lear, who tried it and compares it to the sufferings of Victorian ladies in tight stays:

> I have come to the conclusion that yachting does not suit me at all: the nuisance of knocking one's head, and being in a cramped cabin is not repaid by any society in the world. I really believe the liking for yachts is merely a fashion, just as many women will bear the utmost pain in lacing rather than not appear in the mode.

In the Citadel you climb up and up, the way one does in castles everywhere, and are rewarded by increasingly magnificent views of the town. As I looked at Corfu from this eminence I began to wonder if I shouldn't perhaps elevate it to be my favourite Greek city, the position hitherto occupied by another Venetian city, namely Nauplion in the Peloponnese. To put this into perspective, among other places I have been to so far in life, I liked Corfu better than I had liked Verona. If you like Verona I don't see why you shouldn't like Corfu more.

This favourable assessment was confirmed by two excellent and reasonable meals in the open air, a further stroll round some more handsome gardens, and the observation that the horses which pull the hired carriages join in the general cheerfulness. These plump, well-tended animals have an evident zest for their work and set off at a spanking trot whenever they are given the chance. At least, they do this in June – perhaps by the end of the season they may have slowed down a bit.

Next morning I got up early and rode precariously through the crowded city to the harbour. On the ferry to Igoumenitsa I found my way to the saloon, which is what I believe you call that part of a ship, where a disobliging man grumpily sold me a couple of croissants and a cup of coffee. I think the tedium of his life had soured his disposition. I presume that all he did was go to and fro between Corfu and Igoumenitsa selling things like coffee and croissants to people like me, which I readily concede is hardly an inspiring occupation.

Lord Byron the poet, who will figure often in these pages, did not visit Corfu but in 1809 came close to being driven there in a storm.

> Two days ago I was nearly lost in a Turkish ship of war owing to the ignorance of the Captain & crew though the storm was not violent. – Fletcher [his valet] yelled after his wife, the Greeks called on all the Saints, the Mussulmen on Alla, the

> Captain burst into tears & ran below deck telling us to call on God, the sails were split, the mainyard shivered, the wind blowing fresh, the night setting in, & all our chance was to make Corfu which is in possession of the French, or (as Fletcher *pathetically* termed it) "a *watery* grave." I did what I could to console Fletcher but finding him incorrigible wrapped myself up in my Albanian capote (an immense cloak) & lay down on deck to wait the worst, I have learnt to philosophize on my travels, & if I had not, complaint was useless. – Luckily the wind abated & only drove us on the coast of Suli on the main land where we landed & proceeded by the help of the natives to Prevesa again; but I shall not trust Turkish Sailors in future.

Lord Byron, I may say, might not have fared much better with a wholly Greek crew. Although A. W. Kinglake, in 1835, was not in these waters but was making for Cyprus, his account of a Greek crew in a storm is so superb that I have included a slightly shortened version as an appendix. It may introduce new readers to his *Eothen*, which I think is the best travel book ever written.

Any town in Greece that is by the sea will set up to be the ideal spot in which to spend a holiday. I do not wish to be unkind to Igoumenitsa, which may very well have ideas of that sort, but it is really just a place for passing through. Buses arrive from the north and from the south, ferries arrive from here and there, and nearly everyone in Igoumenitsa is, like Joe in *Bleak House*, a mover-on upon the face of the earth. It only came into existence as a significant port in the twentieth century, and earlier travellers landed further south at Preveza.

My plan was as simple as could be: go south, go east, ride north, go west and arrive back at Igoumenitsa. On my bicycle I had a couple of panniers with everything I needed. I had my passport, some Greek money, some English money, and two plastic cards. I turned off the ferry, turned right, and began to pedal in the direction of Parga. It is one of the advantages of the modern age that these things have become as easy as that, compared with the laborious arrangements described by J. C. Hobhouse in 1809, which I will come to in a moment.

John Cam Hobhouse starts his account of his travels in this part of Greece with the words, 'My friend and myself, after many hesitations whether we should bend our steps towards Smyrna or some port of European Turkey, were at last determined in favour of the latter.'

His friend was Lord Byron – the illustrious Lord Byron who was not yet illustrious. He did not become so until 1812, when he published the first two cantos of his poem *Childe Harold's Pilgrimage* and, as he says, awoke to find himself famous. The two were friends from Cambridge days. Byron went travelling because he was fed up with England, unlucky in love, short of money and for a secret reason which was never explained. 'I have no alternative' he wrote to his friend and solicitor John Hanson, 'there are circumstances which render it absolutely indispensable, and quit the country I must immediately.' Hobhouse went because he wanted to write a book. 'Hobhouse' wrote Byron, 'has made woundy preparations for a book on his return; 100 pens, two gallons of japan ink, and several volumes of best blank. I have promised to contribute a chapter on the state of morals, etc. etc.' This is the sanitised version given by Thomas Moore. The original letter says, 'I have promised to contribute a chapter on the state of morals, and a further treatise on the same to be entituled [sic] "Sodomy simplified or Paederasty proved to be praiseworthy from ancient authors and modern practice".'

Hobhouse's book is now quite an obscure rarity, but Byron gathered his materials for the start of *Childe Harold*.

Hobhouse speaks of 'European Turkey' because at that time both Greece and Albania were still part of the Ottoman Empire. Epirus, where I was going to cycle, was regarded as part of Albania in their day and was not ceded to Greece until 1913. When Byron and Hobhouse talked about Albania they meant partly what is Albania today, but mainly what is now Epirus in northern Greece. They were pretty pleased with themselves for going on so adventurous an expedition. Byron later wrote to a friend that, 'Albania I have seen more of than any Englishman (except a Mr Leake), for it is a country rarely visited from the savage nature of the natives, though abounding in more natural beauties than the classical regions of Greece.' The two of them got into present-day Albania as far as Tepelene, about forty miles from today's border with Greece, but otherwise they were in the part which I proposed to explore.

They were both young men, Byron twenty-one and Hobhouse two years older. You are not to think of these two young bucks as travelling in anything like the easy style that was open to me. First of all, they had hired a dragoman, a kind of interpreter and guide, called George. George was more of a nuisance than anything else. 'He never' says Hobhouse, 'lost an opportunity of robbing us. He was very zealous, bustling and talkative; and when we had him, we thought it would be impossible to do without him; when he was gone, we wondered how we had ever done with him.' A. W. Kinglake has an account of a conversation conducted through a dragoman, and I have included the greater part as an appendix, on the same principle that I quoted his description of Greek sailors – that it is so superb. It may well be that Byron and

Hobhouse, Benjamin Disraeli, Edward Lear and others who I will mention, ought to be imagined as having discussions along such lines.

Then there was Fletcher, Lord Byron's valet, who was an even bigger nuisance than George the dragoman. Hobhouse says:

> English servants are rather an incumbrance than a use in the Levant, as they require better accommodation than their masters, and are a perpetual source of blunders, quarrels and delays. Their inaptitude at acquiring any foreign language is, besides, invincible, and seems more stupid in a country where many of the common people speak three, and some four or five languages.

Also there was the baggage, consisting of four large and three smaller leather trunks; a canteen ('quite indispensable'); three beds with bedding and two wooden bedsteads. 'The latter are always serviceable, preserving you from vermin and the damp of mud floors, and possessing advantages which overbalance the evils caused by the delays of half an hour in packing and taking them to pieces.' All of this had to be loaded onto horses each morning, which sparked off a lot of argument among the horse owners, who each wanted his own animal to carry as little as possible, so it often took them two hours to pack up and get going. By comparison with all that complicated performance, there was I, riding along in a carefree manner with a couple of bags and my plastic cash cards.

There is a bit of an up and a down to get out of Igoumenitsa, and thereafter a long, flat valley, sparsely but agreeably sprinkled with houses where there are rooms to let. I don't know why they have rooms to let. There seems to be no reason why anybody should suddenly stop out in the country, nowhere near the sea and some miles from a restaurant, but it was comforting to think that if I pitched head-first over the handlebars I could spend my night in one of them to rest and recuperate. In truth, I would have quite liked to have stayed in one anyway, for the perverse reason that there *was* no reason to do so except that they looked peaceful. But to Parga I was going, so I rode purposefully on.

From time to time there was a garage, which in such circumstances is to be regarded as a source of cold drinks and ice cream. At the beginning of a trip like this it always surprises me that I can pull into a garage and articulate some funny noises which cause them to give me a Coca-Cola. Of course a great many people get all round the world by shouting in English, but my smattering of Greek at least makes me bolder than I otherwise would be in venturing into those parts which tourists more rarely reach.

I once managed to get to a place called Thermon, in a remote part of Aetolia where I went for no other reason than that it sounded nice in the Blue Guide. Thermon has, or had then, a hotel, some ruins and a bank. The people at all three were equally astonished to see me.

The hotel was wide open, with no one anywhere about. I banged on the bell, stamped around, shouted and called, and wandered up and down the corridors looking into bedrooms, but there was no sign of life. At long last a lady appeared from somewhere, and I do not say she thought I was a burglar because I am sure that sort of crime is not known in that part of Greece, but the idea that anyone might want to stay in her hotel was clearly strange to her. My question, 'Have you a room for the night?' was altogether absurd. She had more than a room, she had an entire hotel for the night, if need be. Eventually she became adjusted to the odd idea that I wanted to sleep there, and indulged my strange eccentricity by giving me a key.

The ruins of Thermon consist of some uninteresting rocks watched over by a guardian who sits all day doing nothing. I suppose he draws his stipend for opening the site each morning and closing it each evening, which would be a great convenience for visitors if there were any. No doubt the watchful eye he keeps upon the place would discourage vandalism and enforce good behaviour, if there were any vandals about, or anyone inclined to misbehave. He produced, with something of a flourish, a visitors' book, and from the previous entry to mine I made out that the last visitors had been a honeymooning Greek couple fifteen months before.

I suppose that Thermon has a bank for the use of neighbouring farmers. They certainly did not expect to encounter tourists, and I threw them into confusion by trying to cash a Eurocheque. I gave my card and cheque to the clerk, who had clearly never seen such things before and did not know how to handle them. He called over another man, who I expect was the sub-manager, and they put their heads together but made no further progress. Accordingly they called a third person who was, no doubt, the manager, and the three then grouped themselves around these difficult documents and discussed them volubly in Greek.

The problem, as I understood it, was with the letter H. There is no H in Greek, but there is a similar symbol for a Greek capital E. If they treated it as an E the system did not work. If it was not an E, what was this strange hieroglyphic and what, they asked, should they do about it? While I was very sympathetic to their predicament, I was quite unable to suggest a way out, as trying to explain, in Greek, the phenomenon of the letter H was altogether too difficult. Eventually the manager seized the telephone and had a long conversation with somebody somewhere else, who was more worldly-wise than he. As a result they did something, I don't know what, which enabled them to give me my money, and I left them excitedly chattering over their triumph in encountering an entirely novel set of circumstances and overcoming a difficulty of a quite unprecedented nature.

But back to me and my bicycle in Epirus. The valley between Igoumenitsa and Parga by an optical illusion appeared to be going up but from the way the bicycle behaved it was evidently going gently down. Then what looked like a steepish rise made its appearance so I thought, 'Now I shall have to pay for all that easy pedalling,' but there was nothing much to it, and I was rewarded by a long run down immediately afterwards, with my sunhat tugging at the chinstrap in the breeze.

I turned off the main road at lunchtime to buy a sandwich in a village called Margariti. George Ferguson Bowen Esq. M.A. passed this way in 1849 with obvious feelings of discomfort at being in what was then a Mahommedan country. Quoting *Childe Harold*, he says:

> We descended into a broad, fertile valley, leaving on our right the large village of Margariti, where
>
> 'the pale crescent sparkling in the glen,
> Through many a cypress grove'
>
> showed that the inhabitants are Moslems. We made our mid-day halt in a small Mahommedan hamlet, there being no Christians near. Neither my servant nor our guide seemed to relish much throwing themselves on the hospitality of an

> infidel, but I felt so hungry that I would hear of no such fears or scruples. So I rode up to the first peasant I saw, and asked leave for us to go into his cottage to boil my coffee at his fire. He readily consented, after making me wait for a few minutes while he extemporised a harem, by removing his wife behind a loose partition of planks, through the chinks of which I could, however, see her black eyes watching us as we lay by the hearth.

Bowen's book was first published as a series of papers in the *Colonial Church Chronicle*, and the profits he donated to the Fund for Colonial Bishoprics, a devout proceeding which explains his hesitation in trusting himself under the roof of an infidel. At Margariti the crescent sparkles in the glen no more and instead they have a church with a wide, cool portico, on the marble floor of which I was able to doze for twenty minutes after lunch.

After Margariti one follows the road towards Preveza, which is not at all busy and is made very picturesque by the hills on either side. A little before the turning to Parga you come upon a pretty sight in the shape of something between a marsh and a lake on your right. Then there is a right turn and a sharpish climb followed by a downhill run to Parga, which seems ominously long if you mean, as I did, to retrace your steps next morning. It was altogether a mysterious feature of the day that though I started at sea level at Igoumenitsa and ended at sea level at Parga, in the intervening 30 miles there seemed to me to be a lot more going down than going up.

It is difficult to think of a more pleasant place wholly devoted to tourism than Parga. It has a castle, a reasonable beach, and very old houses in very narrow streets. In anything with pretensions to being a main road, by which I mean anything eight feet wide or more, pretty well every house is equipped to sell you something. There are a few alleys under eight feet wide where, on the whole, no attempts at trade are made, but even in these you may stumble upon a shop or find that it leads to a restaurant. Much of the stuff for sale consists of things like beach balls and sun cream, but I had the impression that a reasonable person could actually buy something quite good in Parga, such as a cotton sweater or even conceivably a rug. The town is largely pedestrianised; there are bars and restaurants everywhere; they never ever hassle you, and if I were required to spend a fortnight in a recognised seaside resort I should choose Parga.

If it helps you to form a judgement as to whether you ought to go on your own account, I can tell you that Parga is very popular with Swedes. There was a tour advertised to the nearby mouth of the River Acheron, with guides speaking German or Swedish. In a bookshop I found a guidebook to Epirus available in German or Swedish but not in English, and in the bank there was a group of fair-haired women jabbering in a strange tongue which I took to be the language of Sweden. This Swedish interest is something which, in all my travels in Greece over the best part of twenty years, I have never come across before, but I think a liking for Parga does the Swedes credit.

There is a small islet just offshore, so close that even I could have swum to it, with a pretty white chapel that is floodlit at night. I did not swim to it, but I chose a restaurant from which I could see it while I drank superior up-market retsina which I know was superior because it came in a smaller bottle than the ordinary stuff and cost more.

Another merit of Parga was that in spite of signs saying 'Full English Breakfast' and due perhaps to the prevalence of Swedes, there appeared to be few English people. At least, if there were, they did not watch *Watchdog*, so nobody asked facetiously if Anne Robinson was with me and no large elderly women wanted to kiss me.

Rather to my surprise there seemed to be no mention anywhere of Byron. If there was a Hotel Byron or a sign advertising 'Happy Hour in the Lord Byron Bar', I missed them. Why should there be, you may ask. Well, Parga is mentioned in some of his most famous lines:

Fill high the bowl with Samian wine!
On Suli's rock, and Parga's shore
Exists the remnant of a line
Such as the Doric mothers bore.

Byron was not considered to be anything of a classical scholar by his contemporaries – 'Of the classics' he wrote, 'I know about as much as most schoolboys after a discipline of 13 years.' However, 13 years is a good long time to give to Latin and Greek, and the discipline with which learning was enforced upon schoolboys of the time was pretty ferocious. Certainly he could toss off a learned allusion at a moment's notice, as he does here. By 'Doric mothers' he refers to the women of Sparta, the tradition being that the Dorians originated from Epirus and nearby parts. They migrated south and overran the Peloponnese, where the Spartans became the leading power and were also, of course, the finest foot soldiers of Greece.

The hills of Suli lie to the east of Parga and 'Suli's rock' I meant to visit the next day. In his travels Byron conceived a great admiration for the heroism of the people of this area and says in a note to *Childe Harold*:

> Five thousand Suliotes, among the rocks and in the castle of Suli, withstood 30,000 Albanians for eighteen years: the castle

> was at last taken by bribery. In this contest there were several acts performed not unworthy of the better days of Greece.

Hence his encouraging belief that Spartan blood still flowed in the veins of the people of Parga's shore and Suli's rock, and his poetical aspiration that they might one day restore the liberty of Greece.

I have at this point, with great regret, to tell you that in 1819 we the British played the Christian community of Parga a sorry trick, because we faced them with the choice of being handed over to Muslim Albanians or evacuating the town altogether. Parga had long been coveted by Ali Pasha, the Albanian warlord who, by a mixture of cunning, ferocity, duplicity, cruelty and courage, had made himself master of southern Albania, Epirus and, through his sons, parts of the Peloponnese. He was nominally subject to the Turkish government, which also made him Governor of Trikkala in Thessaly 'with the rank of Pasha with two tails', by which is meant that he had the honour of having two horses' tails carried in front of him when he travelled about.

Byron conceived a sort of liking for the man, who later received him with the utmost politeness:

> His manner is very kind and at the same time he possesses that dignity which I find universal among the Turks. He has the appearance of anything but his real character, for he is a remorseless tyrant, guilty of the most horrible cruelties. He has been a mighty warrior, but is as barbarous as he is successful, roasting rebels, etc. etc.

No one in his right mind would get into Ali Pasha's clutches if it could possibly be avoided, and certainly not the people of Parga.

Parga had always gone with Corfu. When Venice ruled

Corfu they ruled Parga as well; when the French got Corfu they also ruled Parga. When the British dispossessed the French, it was assumed that Parga would be part of the British Protectorate, but for complicated diplomatic reasons the British government decided to cede Parga to the Sultan of Turkey. In the words of George Ferguson Bowen:

> … the Parguinotes were commanded, early in 1819, either to submit to the Turks, or to quit their country for ever, an asylum being offered them in the Seven Islands, and the Lord High Commissioner promising to procure for them full compensation for all the private property they should abandon. They chose the latter alternative for they knew that, though nominally ceded to the Sultan, they would really be given over to Ali Pasha, who was their bitter enemy, both as being the last Christians in Epirus who had successfully opposed his power, and because they had assisted the Suliotes in their wars against him.
>
> When at length it was signified to the unhappy Parguinotes that the fated day of their expulsion, the 10th May 1819, was arrived, and that numerous bands of the Infidels were crowding the hills around eager to seize on their territory, they solemnly declared that if a single Turk should pass their borders before they all had a fair opportunity of quitting their country, they would instantly put their wives and children to death, and defend themselves against any force, British or Turkish, to the last extremity.
>
> This was no idle menace; the history of Greece affords numerous instances of such self-devotion. Notice of their determination was sent to the Lord High Commissioner, who immediately dispatched some British officers to expostulate with them. They found the Parguinotes digging up the bones of their ancestors, and burning or burying them in secret places, to prevent their profanation by the Turks; still it was declared that the meditated sacrifice would be perpetrated, unless the advance of the Albanians, who had already got close

> to the frontier line, could be stopped. On the arrival of an English frigate, means were found to effect this object. Then the embarkation began, after the whole people had solemnly knelt down to kiss, for the last time, the land which gave them birth, and had watered it with their tears; some of them carried away a handful of the soil to comfort their exile; others, a small portion of those sacred ashes which had once been animated by their forefathers. When the bands of Ali Pasha reached the walls, all was silence and solitude; 'the city', as it has been observed, 'received its infidel garrison as Palmyra salutes the traveller in the desert; nothing breathed; nothing moved; the houses were desolate, the nation was extinct; the bones of the dead were almost consumed to ashes; while the only signs that living creatures had been there was the smoke slowly ascending from the funeral piles.'

Bowen concludes:

> No Englishman can wander among the ruined houses and deserted gardens of this beautiful spot, without a feeling of shame and regret that his country should have abandoned to the Infidels a gallant Christian community, which had defended against them for four hundred years its liberty and religion.

In case any reader should be put off from visiting Parga by this unhappy tale, let me assure you that none of the latter-day Parguinotes appear to hold the slightest grudge against visiting Englishmen. Furthermore, I stayed in what I regard as an ideal room. It was in a house about twenty yards from the beach, custom-built for the letting of rooms, away from any noise from the town, with a shaded balcony overlooking greenery at the back. It was clean and cool and, unlike the Ol pic, the hot water was reliable. Also, the landlady indulged in the common practice of cheating herself.

This I have found to be very widespread among hoteliers and landladies in Greece. Not long ago my wife and I went into a very superior hotel in Ioannina, beautifully situated and delightfully furnished.

'Have you a double room?' I asked.

'But of course,' said the lady at the desk.

'How much would it be?'

'Twenty thousand drachmas,' came the reply.

I was just opening my mouth to say, 'That will be fine,' when she added, 'But we will give you a special price: sixteen thousand drachmas.'

To this I was about to reply, 'Thank you very much,' but she was too quick for me. 'With breakfast,' she added.

'Thank you,' I managed at last, but then she added, 'But not until Friday. We are completely full; only on Friday do we have a room.'

We booked in for Friday. The room was delightful and had, as always, a notice on the door giving the proper price, which was 20,000 drachmas without breakfast. The breakfast was delicious, with fresh orange juice, fresh rolls and fresh coffee. The hotel on Friday was, as I expect it always is, completely full and they were turning people away. There was no reason for them to reduce their price by so much as a drachma, but such is the nature of Greek hospitality, and it also afflicted the lady in Parga who considerably undercharged me for my excellent room.

Suli and Zalongo

Somewhere near Parga there were two important places that I wanted to visit, each of them a scene of brave endeavour and heroic action. One was called Suli and the other Zalongo, but where exactly were they and how to get to them? A lady in the Greek Tourist Office in London was frankly misleading in a well-intentioned sort of way. I told her that I wanted to go to Suli.

'I have been there,' she said. 'It is wonderful.'

'I want to see the castle.'

'There is no castle. I do not remember a castle. There is a monastery but it is at Zalongo. Zalongo is the place you want,' and she snatched up a copy of a leaflet with a map of Epirus, and drew a black circle round the word 'Zalongo'.

This was a facer. She had been there, so she must know. But there certainly had once been a castle. Edward Lear had visited it; Edward Lear had painted it; there is a lithograph of it in his book *Travels in Albania*. Had it been destroyed, and if so where had it been while it still existed?

Furthermore, the Zalongo she had marked seemed to be much further north than the scene of the famous deeds in which I was interested. Eventually I discovered from diligently poring over maps that there are two Zalongos, and she had drawn her circle round the wrong one. At least, it was wrong from my point of view, but perhaps she had been to the right one from hers. But then again perhaps she had been to the right one for me but had circled the wrong one by mistake. Whichever it was, according to her the ride to Zalongo in a jeep had been perfectly terrifying, a matter of sliding along a gravel track beside a precipice without daring to look down. The idea that it could be reached by bicycle was absurd; preposterous; unthinkable. On this point she was emphatic.

My reference books at home were a little more helpful. While the *Rough Guide to Greece* is altogether silent on the subject, the Blue Guide says that the River Akherontos (otherwise Acheron)

> flows through a deep and gloomy ravine with precipitous sides, suggesting the terrors of Hades. At Gliki it enters the wide plane of Phanari. A track leads through the gorge and after one hour turns north and enters by a narrow pass into the region of Suli. The scenery is grand and impressive. The Castle of Suli stands on an isolated hill near the ruined villages of the same name, 1,200 feet above the Acheron.

So that is what I had to go on. If I got to Gliki, then somewhere nearby was to be found the Acheron, a gloomy ravine, a track, a narrow pass and a 1,200-foot climb with the castle at the top. By yet more diligent study I found Gliki on the map and it looked to be quite some way from Zalongo. But never mind. Situated as I now was at Parga, I knew how to get as far as Gliki because I had noticed on the left of the highway a road clearly marked 'Gliki'.

So far, so good. There is, as I mentioned, a steep hill down to Parga, and as I had no wish to climb it on two successive days, I booked out of my excellent room in Parga next morning, struggled up to the village of Agia Katerini at the top, and booked into a house for that night. There I left my bags and set off for Gliki carrying only first-aid equipment for myself and bicycle, plus a full water bottle.

Up. That is how you go to Gliki. The only sign of life is an occasional lorry going to or from a quarry, otherwise you just push or ride upwards in solitude with just the scenery for company. The signs to Gliki quickly become a thing of the past, but my map seemed to suggest that I should aim for the Springs of Acheron. These were signposted as a left turn, and after that it was down, down, down. When the road flattens out you are riding through a lovely rich and fertile valley with corn and vegetables on either side. The irrigation system by the road was working vigorously, and in my first encounter with the River of Hades I was well soaked by a sprinkler. This was quite acceptable, being an invigorating experience in the heat. There were no signs pointing to anywhere at all in the valley, but by now there were occasional people from whom to ask directions, and they kept telling me to go straight ahead. It was a lovely ride.

Once you reach Gliki by this route there is no means of knowing that you have got there. There is no sign to announce that this is it, but you arrive at a T-junction which looks promising, so you ask at the Café River, so called, if this is Gliki, and they say it is. You may perhaps be curious to know exactly what fascination drew me to this spot, and the Acheron itself was part of it. Milton, describing the underworld rivers in *Paradise Lost* speaks of:

> Abhorred Styx, the flood of deadly hate;
> Sad Acheron of sorrow black and deep;
> Cocytus named of lamentation loud
> Heard on the rueful stream.

Greek mythology is not generally logical or consistent, but the usual river across which the dead were ferried by the boatman Charon was the Styx, which is somewhere in Arcadia in the Peloponnese. The Acheron, with its tributary the Cocytus (whose name means 'river of wailing') was the other principal river of the underworld, and as far as I was concerned it would be something to have done what Milton and the thousands of poets and classical scholars and schoolboys who wrote about it had never done, namely to visit it.

At Gliki the Springs of Acheron are clearly marked and you come upon the river at once. I cycled along the bank until the track got too rough, then I left the bike and walked among plane trees and shrubs. The Acheron here is neither black nor deep as per Milton, but grey-blue, shallow and wide. After a bit you find there are springs everywhere, sometimes little ones bubbling up on the path, sometimes in the form of bigger streams and tributaries from minor sources, and finally, in my case, a proper cavern with a great gush of water pouring out. Clearly I was looking at an entrance to the underworld. I reached this point by scrambling over stepping stones and by taking off my shoes and wading. To go further it seemed to me you had to wade a lot, and I didn't fancy this in bare feet on the stones but I think it must be the proper thing to do. On my way back I came upon a large party of (probably) Swedes, wearing shorts and shod with trainers, wading boldly along behind their guide. I got one of the younger waders to fill my bottle with Acheron water, which was cool and delicious.

I feel obliged to say that the Springs of Acheron remain to me a bit of a mystery. The word 'springs', whether in English or Greek, suggests that here the Acheron starts, and that here are to be seen the sources, the fountain heads, the very starting point of the river. Not so. It is clear from the map that the Acheron is going strong to the east and north long before it reaches Gliki, and why it is bubbling out of the ground at this point, as well as flowing in a continuous stream, is a question which I have been unable to resolve.

At Parga, whenever I mentioned that I wished to visit Gliki the locals met the idea with nods of approval. When I said I wanted to see the castle at Suli they gave me much the same treatment as I had had from the lady in the tourist office in London.

'By bicycle it is impossible!' they cried, throwing up their hands in horror. 'By jeep only it is possible.'

'What about with my feet?'

'No, no, no. It is very much too far.'

I have to say that in their assessment of the situation as it affected me personally they were quite correct, but I managed to do it in spite of them. In a moment I will tell you how it was done, but first I must say why the castle of Suli was an even bigger attraction than the Acheron.

'The mountains of Suli extend 30 miles from north to

south, and about the same length transversely.' So says Hobhouse. In respect of the inhabitants, the words of George Ferguson Bowen echo those of Byron that I quoted earlier:

> The Suliotes contested this ground inch by inch, and during several years, against Ali Pasha, performing deeds of heroism worthy of the best days of Greece. They were a tribe of Christian Epirotes, mustering perhaps 4,000 fighting men, nominally subjects of the Sultan; but as really independent of the supreme Government until finally reduced in 1803, as were the Scotch Highlanders until after the suppression of the insurrection of 1745. The stories told of their speed in running over mountains to us impassable, of their skill as marksmen, of their keenness of sight, of their vigilance and sagacity, of their ability in planning, and activity in executing the most refined stratagems of their desultory warfare, of their powers of voice, remarkable even among the βοὴυ ἀγαθός ['good at the war cry' – a phrase from Homer] mountaineers of Greece, and by which they were enabled to exchange signals at immense distances, in short, their prodigies of strength, skill and valour against overwhelming odds, would, in some instances, exceed belief, if they were not so universally attested by their enemies.

Hobhouse and Byron, Bowen and Lear all thought it important to visit the territory of these heroic people, and so did I.

It took Ali Pasha, with an army of 20,000, eleven years to overcome the Suliotes. According to R. A. Davenport, who wrote a life of Ali Pasha, they treated him with a refreshing and unusual contempt. On one occasion

> he was under the mortifying necessity of desiring a short truce, that he might ransom the dead, the wounded, and the prisoners. The Suliotes manifested their scorn of the enemy

> by the value which they set upon them in exchange. An ass belonging to them having strayed into the Turkish camp, they sent a flag of truce to request that it might be returned. The captors complied with the request, upon condition of receiving an equivalent. The Suliotes sent back an Aga, and a message, stating that, if he were not deemed an adequate compensation, they were willing to give something to boot.

Davenport continues:

> Of all the leaders of the Suliotes the most singular character was undoubtedly the monk Samuel. No one knew his country or his origin, or whence he came; and the mystery which this threw round him increased the effect which was produced by his bravery, his activity, and his enthusiastic language. By turns a consoler, an orator, a preacher, and a soldier, he exercised a boundless influence over the Suliotes. Sometimes laden with chaplets, relics and images, he made sudden visits to the neighbouring towns to exchange his consecrated burden for provisions; at others, disguised as a beggar, he ventured into the camps of the Turks to ascertain their numbers, and procure a knowledge of their designs. The palikars [warriors], and even the women, followed him to battle with that implicit confidence which a belief in his doctrine was calculated to inspire. Loss of life was, he told them, nothing more than the road leading to a future, where astonished death and nature should see the creature reborn in imperishable glory.

Eventually the Suliotes were blockaded into their mountain fort, and compelled by thirst and hunger to negotiate a surrender. But:

> There was one Suliot who had taken no part in the negotiation, he having resolved not to survive his country; this was Samuel the monk. He saw unmoved the Mahometans advance to take possession of the fort of Kunghi, and when

> they intimated that he had much to fear from the anger of the vizier, he replied, 'he who holds life as cheap as I do, has no fear of viziers.' He then set fire to the powder, and blew into the air the fortress and all that it contained. It is said that Ali had sworn, if he took him, to flay him alive, and stuff his skin.

The terms of the surrender gave the Suliotes an absolute right to go in safety wherever they wanted. Veli Pasha, the local commander, 'invoked on his head the worst earthly disgrace and the vengeance of Heaven, should he ever violate the treaty'. The treaty was immediately violated.

> The Suliotes had not proceeded far on their march before they were furiously attacked by the troops of the vizier. The largest column of the Suliotes, about two thousand in number, under Foto Tzavella and Dimo Draco, took its way towards Parga, whence it was to pass over to Corfu. It was pursued by four thousand Albanians, who came up with it not far from Parga. Sending forward the main body which formed a hollow square containing the women and children, Foto Tzavella with a feeble rear-guard kept the enemy at bay, and succeeded in covering the retreat with no other loss than a small portion of the baggage.

Ali's behaviour after his final victory was consistent with the rest of his conduct.

> To massacres on a great scale succeeded a series of executions and cruelties which made humanity shudder. When his thirst for blood was somewhat slaked, Ali turned his attention to the securing of his difficult and dearly-purchased conquest. He repaired the forts, and built a strong fortress on a lofty insulated cliff in the vicinity of Kiaffa, in which he placed a large garrison of his trustiest Albanians.

Although the name Kiaffa has disappeared from all maps, atlases and guidebooks as far as I can make out, this is the fortress that the Blue Guide calls the castle of Suli, and the one to which I wanted to go.

Now, if you too want to visit this allegedly inaccessible place, I can tell you one way of doing it. Fall into conversation with a man who is sitting around at the Café River in Gliki. He will tell you that the castle exists, which is comforting. He adds that it is a two-hour walk each way, very steep and difficult, on the far side of the river. He lets this idea sink in for a little and then adds that it can be reached by taxi. Once you have digested that, he lets slip that he himself happens to be a taxi driver and by coincidence his taxi is at hand. This conversation is carried on in Greek, so if you think that is beyond you, you had better arrive with an appropriate written note of your requirements.

I considered the matter. On the one hand, having got so far by bicycle it seemed a bit feeble to take a taxi. On the other hand, with a stiff ride back to follow, I could not feel enthusiastic about a steep four-hour walk. To be scrambling about alone on a rocky mountain could be considered foolhardy. Also, even if I neither sprained an ankle nor got seriously lost and stranded on the mountain, I might miss the path and give up in despair without reaching the castle at all.

'How much would the taxi be?'

'Four thousand drachmas,' which was then about £8.

So we struck a bargain, and after I had explored the Acheron and he had finished a game of cards, we set off. The taxi could only be so called on a most generous interpretation. The word 'taxi' was indeed painted on its side, but this to my mind was no more than a courtesy title. It was an old, beaten-up German affair with slashed seats and no seat belts. The meter had long since ceased to function. When the road went up we went at a furious speed, as I think the taxi man wished to keep up momentum without having to change gear, as he had little faith in the gearbox. The descents he tackled more sedately in a low gear, not liking to ask too much of the brakes, which were in a similar condition to the gears. At one moment I thought we were on fire as the interior seemed to be filling with smoke, but it was only dust from the road coming up through the holes in the floorboards.

The drive was stupendous. Nobody with any tendency to vertigo should attempt it. A little way out of Gliki we turned through an archway saying 'Suli Villages' and began dashing upwards. The road was very well made, a triumph of engineering in the form of an excellent surface with terrifying drops on the right-hand side of the ascent. We reached a summit where the driver declared what is called a 'photo opportunity' in certain circles, and here he photographed me crouching nervously on the edge of a precipice. The distances were prodigious. We went up to huge heights and we plunged down to immense depths, then we circled back and we rose yet again, and I could not think how all this could cost as little as £8. Finally we reached the village of Suli, where the road ran out. At least, the good road came to an end and thereafter there was a slippery gravel track. Ahead, to my enormous pleasure, I could see the castle of Suli looking much as I thought I remembered it in the Edward Lear lithograph. The idea of little short-sighted Lear somehow struggling up here on horseback at a maximum of three miles an hour was wholly delightful.

'I will walk from here,' said I, taking account of the state of the road.

'No, it would take two hours,' was the answer, and accordingly we plunged down the gravel track with a fine disregard for anything whatever except a determination to arrive at a spot below the castle, where the driver would let me off. When we got there he parked the car under one of two ample plane trees, told me not to hurry, opened all the doors of the taxi and went to sleep on the back seat.

I began the ascent. Apart from the sleeping driver there was total solitude, with nothing to be seen but mountains and nothing to be heard but an occasional bird. The castle rose majestically above me, perched on the summit of a hill that was steep to the point of being almost sheer. There was nothing resembling a path except occasional glimpses of what might have been a goat track, or here and there a water-course. The surface was a mixture of rocks and shale, studded with what I took to be wild sage and some prickly plants of different sorts. Slipping and sliding, proceeding as best I could from rock to rock and certainly obeying the driver's instruction not to hurry, I made my way up, feeling increasingly nervous as the taxi and the two trees got to be further and further below. Finally, trembling rather, I reached the wall of the castle at the top.

The gate was locked and all inside was a ruin, but never mind. Ali Pasha had built it, but earlier it had been one of the centres of Suliot resistance. In 1792, according to Hobhouse, 'Ali made several attacks on Kiaffa and Trypa but was obliged to retreat with loss, and was followed by two thousand Suliotes, even into the plains of Ioannina.' Davenport further says that by September 1803 'Kiaffa and the fort of Kunghi were the only positions which the Suliotes retained.' So, you see, it was all right – I had reached a spot from which the brave Suliotes had defied Ali Pasha to do his worst. As far as I could make out nobody ever visits it anymore, and even the taxi driver later said that he had never been higher than the trees beneath which he slept. To be there was an undeniable triumph, and I sat under the wall for a quarter of an hour to savour it.

Then there was the matter of getting down. Going up was difficult; coming down was treacherous. The shale, as is its way, slipped from under my feet. The rocks were generally more reliable, but now and again one on which I had built my faith took on the nature of shale and went bounding off. Where the rocks were sparse and shale predominant I got hold of a root of sage and hoped for the best, sometimes slithering down on my bottom. My thoughts as I came down were these:

1. I must at all costs survive, and therefore must not hurry.
2. How can anybody build a castle in such a situation? The act of building seems an impossibility and requires the mentality of an eagle.
3. How can anybody be fool enough to attack a castle in such a situation?
4. What a dreadful thing it would be if my wife, or worse still my son, were somehow to find themselves transported to this castle. My wife has a poor head for heights, but if her life depended on it she would get down by some means or other, if only for the sake of her children or grandchildren. My son, on the other hand, is even worse and would probably prefer to curl up and die at the summit.

The fact that this book exists is proof positive that I got down alive, and indeed unscathed, to find the taxi man snoring on the back seat. I wandered about trying to hit upon the exact spot where Edward Lear settled down to sketch. Then I woke the taxi man up.

The gravel track reverts to metalled road at the village of Suli, where we stopped for a few minutes on the return journey. There are a few seemingly unoccupied houses and an official-looking building with a lawn, a brass cannon or two, and two magnificent bronze busts. One is of the monk Samuel and the other of Foto Tzavella who commanded the retreat to Parga. His heroic exploits in the long war against Ali Pasha were such that, according to Davenport 'so brilliantly was his valour displayed that to swear by his sword became a custom of his countrymen.' Accordingly I gazed upon his countenance with respectful admiration.

At Suli there are forty wells. This the driver told me, and stopped expressly to let me verify the fact. On a wide expanse of grass are dotted about a great number (I did not count them) of stone well-heads. Each has a metal lid hinged across the middle, and if you heave one side up you look down and see water. The ways of water are wonderful; what was water doing at such a height? But most of all it seemed to me strangely touching. There in this apparently deserted village was a silent relic of a community which by ingenuity and determination had created not one or two but forty sources of water, enough to support a substantial population, nearly all of whom had disappeared.

The driver spoke no English, and this restricted the conversation. He had a habit of saying 'Po-po-po' about anything he disapproved of, such as the Albanians, who were not far away across the border, or his personal pension rights. It seemed to me that his pension would only amount to £100 per month, so I was quite on his side about that and would have been ready to go 'Po-po-po' in unison if it hadn't sounded silly. This pension, such as it was, would be his on his sixtieth birthday in ten days' time. If I understood correctly he was going to give up the taxi, but it seemed to me that it would be a close-run thing as to whether he gave up the taxi before the taxi gave up on him. It was not very generous of me, perhaps, but when we got back to Gliki I increased the fare from £8 to £10 in consideration of the length of the journey, the poverty of his pension prospects, and his very obliging conduct. He went off contented to a fresh game of cards, and I hope he didn't lose the fare.

Which brings me to the question of how a visit to the castle can be made now that my taxi friend has gone into retirement. Anyone with a hired car, steady nerve, and a positive liking for hairpin bends could drive to Suli with its forty wells. The road surface is excellent up to that point and the mountain scenery exhilarating in the extreme. From the village to the castle would be a pleasant walk of a couple of miles each way. Whether you climb up to the castle is something which I leave to you, merely saying that it was done by a man of 69 with no skill or experience of any special sort. Otherwise Gliki, although it does not figure much in guidebooks, is on a good main road and I expect it could be reached by bus from Preveza or Ioannina, either of which are likely places for travellers to find themselves. If you reach Gliki, who knows? A successor taxi driver to mine may possibly have arisen to drive you over my route.

About this castle there is, I have to say, like the Acheron and its sources, a certain mystery. When I got back to England I looked again at the lithograph in Edward Lear's book, and he appeared to have approached and painted it from a different angle.

Also, my little scramble up to the castle was as nothing compared to what Lear had to overcome:

> I shall not soon forget the labour it cost to convey our horses through this frightful gorge. In many places the rains had carried away even what little footing there had originally been, and nothing remained but a bed of powdered rock sloping off to the frightful gulf below; and all our efforts could hardly induce or enable each horse to cross singly. The muleteer cried, and called on all the saints in the Greek calendar; and all four of us united our strength to prevent the trembling beast from rolling downwards.
>
> At sunset we reached the only approach on this side of 'the blood-stained Suli' – an ascent of stairs winding up the sides of the great rocks below Avariko – and very glad was I to have accomplished this last and most dangerous part of the journey.
>
> At the summit of the rock, Ali Pasha built a castle, and within its walls I hoped to pass the night. I reached it at nearly two hours after sunset, the bright moon showing me the Albanian governor and his twenty or thirty Palikari sitting on the threshold of the gate. But as unluckily I had not procured any letter from the Turkish authorities at Prevyza, the rough old gentleman was obdurate, and would not hear of my entering the fortress. 'Yok,' said he, frowning fiercely, 'yok, yok.' And had it not been for the good nature of a Turkish officer of engineers who had arrived from Ioannina on a visit of inspection, I must have passed the night supperless and shelterless. Thanks to him, men and horses were at length admitted to the interior of the fort.
>
> I gazed on the strange, noiseless figures about me, bright in the moonlight, which tipped with silver the solemn lofty mountains around. For years those hills had rarely ceased to echo the cries of animosity, despair, and agony; now all is silent as the actors in that dreadful drama. Few schemes can compete in my memory with the wildness of this at the castle of Kiaffa, or Suli-Kastro; and excepting in the desert of the

> peninsula of Sinai, I have gazed on none more picturesque and strange.

Picturesque and strange I certainly found my castle to be, but different from Lear's – not so big, not approached by stairs, not looking like the picture in his book. I think perhaps his castle has disappeared from the peak of some neighbouring mountain.

After parting from my taxi-driver friend I went spinning back along the Acheron Valley, managed the first climb without difficulty, plunged down the first descent, struggled up to the top of a long hill and had an encounter with a dog. A line of black goats was crossing the road. Between them and me, on the verge, was a dog which at first barked; then crouched, snarling, like a lion about to spring, with hair standing up along its back; and finally rushed at me gnashing its teeth. The goats made a solid phalanx across the road ahead but I was on a downhill slope so I pedalled at full speed straight for the goats, cursing the dog at the top of my voice. The goats divided to left and right, I shot through the gap, and after 30 yards or so the dog gave up, not liking to carry on the chase at about 25 miles per hour. These things happen. Near here Bowen says he was 'attacked, with more than even their usual ferocity, by a pack of the descendants of the far-famed Molossian dogs, huge hairy brutes, looking like a cross between an English Mastiff and a sheepdog.' The Molossi were the main tribe of Epirus, so I expect mine was also a Molossian descendent.

Bedbugs, which were the bane of early travellers, have been eradicated from Greece but mosquitoes have not. My room at Agia Kiriaki, at the top of the hill from Parga, had a lovely view but was infested with these whining creatures, and my so-called repellent was altogether useless.

Byron, before he reached Greece, reported that he had 'got a diarrhoea and bites from the mosquitoes but what of that? Comfort must not be expected by folks that go a-pleasuring', but I am not so easygoing. Mosquitoes seem to me to be the most malevolent, useless and unnecessary creatures that nature has ever dreamt up. On a general principle of live and let live I might not grudge a drop or two of blood if all they did was bite me now and again. If mosquitoes fed on me, and the swallows fed on them, that would all be part of the general merry-go-round of life. The mosquito, though, feels obliged to inject me with a poison which leaves me with an itching toe or arm or face, and this I regard as an act of mere ill-nature. Luckily I had with me, because I always keep it in my bicycle bag, a tube of Anthisan, so that if any bee, wasp, hornet, midge, mosquito or other insect bit me I could slap it on at once. Never be parted from your Anthisan is my advice to travellers everywhere.

Mosquitoes apart, staying at Agia Kiriaki was a good idea because I made an early start next day and got over the first hill on the road toward Preveza before the real heat began. After that it was a matter of free-wheeling happily down with the Acherousian plain, a continuation of that at Gliki, spread out below.

The oleanders were white, dark pink, medium pink, a very faint blush-colour and occasionally almost apricot. There was broome in flower everywhere. Bougainvillea was climbing all over the place. Hibiscus was flowering, by English standards well ahead of the proper season. Now and again I got a strong scent of thyme or a powerful whiff of honeysuckle. From time to time a green lizard with a yellow belly would dart into the road in front of me and stop dead, evidently petrified with stage fright. These are the sort of things you admire from a bicycle.

At the bottom of the hill was a sign to the Nekromanteion, the oracle where people went to consult the spirits of the dead, which could be summoned from nearby Acheron. I rode up to the site, clambered over the great stone blocks of which the temple is made, studied the plan on the noticeboard, and climbed down a steep metal ladder into a sort of arched crypt. This was the scene of the action. After rites of purification and preparation, including a special hallucinatory diet of beans and lupins, the pilgrims were taken to the crypt and the interview with the departed took place, aided by a bit of jiggery-pokery from the priests. The pilgrims were then made to leave by a different road from that by which they had come, so that they could not spill the beans, as it were, to new arrivals. They were anyway sworn to silence about what they had seen on pain of offending the gods of the underworld. It is only a little place, well preserved and helpfully signed, and the crypt is impressive.

This deviation was a little sideshow in a day with a more serious purpose. Of the two places I most wanted to visit in this part of Epirus, the castle of Suli was one, and the other was Zalongo. You may perhaps remember that the Greek lady in the tourist office in London had told me to go to Zalongo when I asked directions for Suli, and while she seemed to be in a bit of a muddle on the whole subject, I had since discovered that Zalongo was a place of great importance.

When Ali Pasha finally overcame the Suliotes, Foto Tzavella, he whose monument was by the wells of Suli, got through to Parga with a column of two thousand people. But, says Davenport:

> A second Suliot column, of about a thousand individuals, which designed to proceed to Arta to embark for Santa Maura [the former name for Levkas], was less fortunate than the first column. It was overtaken at Zalongo, and threw itself into the monastery of that place, where it was soon invested by the enemy. About sixty women, with their children, were cut off from the rest, and fled towards a steep rock. There, seeing no hope of escape, the despairing mothers fondly kissed their babes, averted their faces from them, and threw them down the precipice. Then, joining in a frantic dance, they successively approached the edge of the cliff, and leaped after their mangled offspring.

The scene of this heroic action was what I wanted to see. I had been to Suli, the place from which they had started, and I needed to go to Zalongo which was the place where they finished. My Blue Guide said there was a 'passable dirt road' leading to the scene, and a huge sculpture to commemorate the heroism of the Suliot women. That, in England, was all I could discover. At Corfu I had tried, with a total lack of success, to find a detailed map of Epirus, but subsequently things had looked up. In the tourist office at Parga they gave me exactly what I wanted: a simple map with Zalongo boldly marked. It clearly implied that a reasonable man might aspire to go there. There were roads leading to Zalongo from the east, the west and the south. Dirt roads or not, they existed. In spite of this, everyone that I spoke to continued to cast doubt on the idea, Zalongo being, they thought, too steep, too remote and too inaccessible to be reached by an elderly man on a bicycle.

The second thing that this map showed – and it was a revelation of overwhelming importance – was that, unknown to anyone in the Greek Tourist Board or elsewhere in the civilised world beyond Epirus, there had grown up along the coast a series of resorts. Like the *Book of Common Prayer* with its Choirs and Places Where They Sing, the coast now abounded with Hotels and Places Where They Stay. My original plan had been to cycle all the way to Preveza, book into a hotel, get instructions on how to find Zalongo and make an expedition there next day. This would have involved overshooting Zalongo and coming back, but my new map disposed of this idea at a stroke. I could see that if I found the right spot at which to stay on the coast, I could reach Zalongo next day by stopping short of Preveza and going across country.

At a place called Ligia I descended from the high road to the coast and discussed my new plan with the owner of a *cafeneion* and his solitary customer. They came up trumps, there is no other word for it. Certainly I should go to Zalongo, they saw nothing odd in the idea and they had a sure-fire formula for achieving it. I should stay somewhere on the coast near to the turning where the road to Arta branched off from the main road. I should leave my bags at whatever hotel I chose and next morning I should ride to Archangelos. From there I should take a taxi to Zalongo. I should have to use my feet to climb about 500 metres to the cliff-top, but the taxi would wait and would not charge a lot – about two or three thousand drachmas, say, about £5. The idea of dispensing with the taxi and going all the way by bicycle they greeted, as usual, with scorn and derision.

We all three pored over my map. The nearest resort to the Arta turning looked to be Kanali Beach, so for there, by mutual consent, I set off. The *cafeneion* owner insisted on giving me my coffee for nothing, he being a practitioner of what Bowen calls 'the barbarous virtue of hospitality'. This, Bowen adds, had in his day been rather lost among the higher classes but was 'still practised by the peasants to a degree which could hardly be expected from their poverty'. The *cafeneion* did not seem a very thriving undertaking and it may well have been poverty that inspired the owner to be so generous, but I have to say that I have always found the Greeks to be a most hospitable nation, especially in places like Epirus when you are well outside the established tourist spots.

Everything went nicely. Almost immediately after the turning to Arta, and before I reached Kanali Beach, there was a sign to what I took to be a previously unknown resort called Kastrosikion. 'Perhaps,' I thought, 'these places are springing up with a speed which has outstripped that of the mapmakers.' Anyway, the sign said that if I turned off I should find the Poseidon Hotel, so turn I did and found instead a gravel track. If I went along it I should come, said the next sign, to Elena's Fish Restaurant which had rooms to let. Along I went and found instead the Golden Beach Hotel, into which I booked.

Before I describe the soaring merits of the Golden Beach Hotel, let me deal with the word 'resort'. You are not to conjure up a picture of a beach swarming with sun-worshippers, the females either exposing their persons or hastily scrabbling for a towel when they feel my eye upon them. There is a Latin phrase much delighted in by eighteenth-century English writers, who liked to talk of a *lucus a non lucendo*. This is impossible to translate but means roughly that the name for the thing in question is totally illogical. In this sense the resorts along this coast are called resorts because no one resorts to them.

Such at least was the state of affairs that June. At the Golden Beach Hotel I was the only occupant of the eight rooms. The beach was indeed golden, and I shared it with three Greek couples and their children who arrived from somewhere else and fairly soon returned to the place from whence they came. I was the only person eating in the restaurant, where they gave me a delicious meal. In my clean white bedroom there were three different devices by which you could separate the room from the balcony. One was a sliding plate-glass window; one was a sliding shutter, and one, marvellous to relate, was a sliding mosquito net. But these are all minor and incidental merits to the great moment when the landlady leading me to my room paused for a moment on the open landing, pointed to a distant spot and said, 'There is Zalongo.'

There it was! I could see the monastery, apparently perched in a sort of col. Above it was the towering cliff over which the women threw their children and afterwards themselves. At the top was the shining white monument, built indeed upon the monumental scale, clearly depicting a group of women dancing hand in hand. It was almost too much for me. Yesterday I had reached the castle at Suli and today I had the clearest possible view of the precipice at Zalongo. If you could picture a man capering and exclaiming with delight, something like an aged football supporter when his team has scored a vital goal, you will not be much wide of the mark.

Next morning I rose early for the assault upon the summit. Bearing in mind the frightening picture painted by the lady in the Greek Tourist Office and the adamant way that yesterday's *cafeneion* owner had insisted that I take a taxi from Archangelos, I thought that getting from Kastrosikion to Zalongo would be at least as difficult as getting to the castle at Suli. Not a bit of it. Few things could be more simple. I rode to Archangelos as directed, where the *cafeneion* beside the garage was doing brisk business. I opened discussions with the owner, and then a taxi driver joined us at the bar. Neither of them expressed the least surprise at my wanting to go on by bicycle. The taxi driver said Zalongo was ten kilometres away, the first four kilometres being level road, followed by a clearly marked right turn and a climb. He dropped not the slightest hint that I might need his services.

So I set off by bike. They know a thing or two, these taxi drivers. It was exactly as he said. The four kilometres sloped very slightly upwards, which was encouraging as it brought me nearer to the summit without any great exertion. Along the way I was sustained by a vision of women dancing hand-in-hand on the brink of a precipice, which was not the product of an overheated imagination but a clear view of the monument itself. This is stylised somewhat in the Henry Moore manner and conveys exactly what it intends, set high up and visible for miles.

After the right turn forecast by the taxi driver I pushed my bicycle steadily upwards to the halfway village of Kamarina, where I left it and walked on. The road is not a dirt road by any means, but is excellently paved and there is a bus park at the top. A bus drew up as I arrived, which alarmed me at first as I thought it might contain a load of foreign tourists but they were Greek, fully entitled to visit their own monasteries and monuments.

The sister at the monastery (which I think must actually be a nunnery) let me in in my shorts and did not insist on my wrapping myself in a skirt. She allowed me to visit the beautiful chapel with peeling frescoes dating, she said, from 1600. I bought a booklet and a postcard and admired the clean, peaceful calm which always seems to characterise such places. Then I went on up to the top.

Anyone could do it. In utter contrast to the hazardous and solitary scramble at Suli, the ascent is by a stone staircase with a reassuring low wall on either side. The steps come seven or eight at a time, then a little landing follows. I met old Greek ladies coming down on the arms of old Greek gentlemen, and they greeted me cheerily and seemed to have made nothing of the climb.

Halfway up there is a Greek inscription set in the rock which can be translated as:

Farewell sweet life!
The women of Suli do not live
without freedom.
On 18th December 1803
they fell, dancing from the cliff
in order not to bend
beneath the yoke of the tyrant
Ali Pasha

You look up and the rock is towering above, then you look down at the sickening drop below, and you have no difficulty in imagining the scene.

The monument itself is at the cliff top, quite close to the edge, and assuming this to be the spot from which the women jumped, I lay on my stomach and crawled towards the brink, trying to nerve myself to look over, but my courage failed. Then a French girl arrived and I asked her to take my photograph at the monument. She took up her position between me and the cliff, looked through the viewfinder and, as is the way with photographers, took a step backwards to get a better view. I shouted at her in terror, thinking that she might at any moment go the way of the Suliot women, and insisted that she come round to the safety of the other side, which she did with a merry laugh.

When she had gone I went back to the cliff, crawled forward again and tried stretching my arms out with my camera in my hands to photograph the drop without having to look over the edge myself. In this I failed again as I could not bring myself to get close enough even for such a photograph. I do not have an especially bad head for heights, but the whole story was so vivid in my mind, the situation so magnificent, the precipice so sheer and the rocks below so jagged that I felt a kind of sympathetic horror. A chill runs down my spine as I write about it now.

On the way down, between Zalongo and Kamarina where my bicycle was, lies the ruined city of Kassope. I approached through pleasant pinewoods, there was no other visitor when I arrived, and it is more interesting than at first it seems. Kassope, says a notice, was founded about 360 BC. Its prime was from 232 to 168, when it was 'an important member of the Epirote league', this being an association of cities under republican governments. In 167 BC Kassope was destroyed by Roman troops in retribution for their having sided with Perseus of Macedon in his war with Rome. R. A. Davenport says:

> The Roman Senate determined to take a terrible vengeance upon the Epirotes, and the task of exacting it was entrusted to Paulus Aemilius. As the valour and despair of the Epirotes, had they been aware of what was intended, might have been productive of fatal consequences, the high-souled Romans stooped to mask their design under a fraud. Pretending that it was meant to withdraw all the garrisons, Paulus sent small bodies of troops into the cities, and distributed the remainder of his army in such a manner that it might be able to act simultaneously. At the same hour the work of pillage and destruction was commenced throughout the country, and the people thus taken by surprise were unable to offer any

> resistance. A hundred and fifty thousand persons were made captive and sold into slavery; the principal persons were sent to Rome, where most of them were condemned to death, and the walls of no less than seventy cities were levelled with the ground.

They were a nasty lot in many ways, the Romans, and I don't think that 'high-souled' is at all a proper adjective to apply to them.

Kassope was subsequently rebuilt, but after the Battle of Actium (in 31 BC – the defeat of Antony and Cleopatra) the Emperor Augustus decreed that all citizens should abandon the town and resettle at Nicopolis, after which Kassope went to ruin.

The horseshoe shape of the hills behind Kassope, with the sea below, provide, as always in Greece, a spectacular situation. There is a recognisable theatre in poor repair and what the guidebook told me was an ancient hotel with the remains of a colonnade. The whole was built of enormous stone blocks which I would have thought an unpractical material. Between 232 and 168 BC surely they would have worked out how to use small stone blocks or even bricks and mortar? Just when an archaeologist was needed to deal with this question, one appeared in the shape of a young Texan, brought up in Canada, married to a girl from Coventry and living in Athens, whose name was Bruce. According to Bruce the people at that time understood bricks and mortar perfectly well, but they were building 'to last'. Huge interlocking stone blocks held together by gravity gave them a feeling of permanence which, up to a point, had worked.

Bruce was busy photographing bits of masonry with a superior camera on a tripod. This, he explained, was for a course that he would be running next year. He would 'digitise' the photographs, feed them into a computer and create 'virtual reality' for his students.

'I suppose that will save them the trouble of coming here,' I said, but I had got that wrong – it was supposed to make them keen on coming.

Bruce was attached to the American School of Archaeology at Athens. Some of the courses they ran involved the students tramping over every inch of a classical site all day, hurrying to the next site on the next day and doing the same thing again. 'They are like boot camps,' Bruce said.

Bruce and I had lunch together at the place where my bicycle was parked. I mentioned that I was going on to Arta, and he volunteered that there was a recently discovered inscription at Arta, exactly a hundred feet long in old Greek feet and therefore precisely corresponding to the length of the funeral pyre of Patroclus described by Homer in the *Iliad*. (I meant to ask him why this measurement was significant, as you might think plenty of things could be a hundred feet long, but I forgot as I got interested in what followed.) The trouble with ancient inscriptions, according to Bruce, is that the letters follow one another without a break and a lot of the words are abbreviated anyway, which makes for great uncertainty. The job of deciphering the Arta inscription had been given to a female scholar who had retired with it into a sort of purdah from which she emerged some years later to publish the text and her translation. Immediately, other scholars pounced upon it and upon her, all intent on showing that they were cleverer than she was, by trying to prove in their different ways that she had got it wrong. One Frenchman in particular was most violent, saying that she had entirely misunderstood the breaks between words, had misinterpreted the abbreviations and had generally made a mess of it. Such it seems are the trials of a scholarly life, which consists not of a quiet and cloistered calm, but a raging sea of petty jealousies.

Bruce's final observation was that trying to get anything done in Greece was 'like wading through sludge', whereas if you try to do something in America 'you felt you had the wind behind you'. This jaundiced view of the host country was brought on by his recent experience in clearing the new tripod for his camera through Customs. He had started with one piece of paper, ended with thirteen and it all took five hours. I said that I thought it was his own fault. 'There are people called Customs Agents who make a living by clearing things like tripods through Customs. If some buccaneering Canadian-Texan like you starts doing it himself, the Customs men are bound to close ranks against you in a spirit of solidarity with the Agents.'

I think a fellow archaeologist would have shown more sympathy but he took it well. It is very rare for me to talk to someone who is an archaeologist, and I think it was rare for Bruce to talk to someone who wasn't. I was glad to have met him, and we parted cordially. Then having so triumphantly accomplished my visit to Zalongo, to finish the day I thought I would go to Victory City, otherwise Nicopolis, which was the place to which the people of Kassope were forcibly transferred.

There is nothing to tell you how to get to Nicopolis from the main Parga-Preveza road, but I can reveal that it is the next turning signposted to Arta after Kastrosikion. A short way along that road you come upon some Roman walls with holes in them, and if you turn right off the Arta road you will find an entrance through a chain-link fence. Inside there is a plan of the site which is hard to follow, and a museum nearby which was shut when I visited. If you try very hard you can find the odeon, or brick-built Roman theatre, which is about the most interesting feature of the place. If you go back to the Arta road you will come upon the much bigger and more dilapidated theatre, and if you follow one of the very rare signs to the top of the hill you come to some excavations described as the Monument of Augustus. This too was closed, so I could not discover much about it.

There is a good view of the Ambracian Gulf, at the very mouth of which the future of the Roman Empire was settled. On one side was Octavian, later the Emperor Augustus, and his brilliant admiral Marcus Vipsanius Agrippa, whom I have seen described as 'the great Roman naval tactician'. On the other side was Marc Antony, he who in Shakespeare's play came to bury Caesar, not to praise him. Antony had raised a fleet and army to invade Italy, and with him was Cleopatra with sixty Egyptian ships.

Modern historians like to argue about what actually happened, but the version followed by Shakespeare is that at the height of the battle Cleopatra's ships suddenly hoisted sail and took flight, and Antony, in a fit of cowardice brought on by his devotion to the Egyptian queen, deserted the rest of his fleet and followed after her.

In Byron's *Childe Harold*, the scene appears as follows:

Ambracia's Gulf behold, where once was lost
A world for woman, lovely, harmless thing!
In yonder rippling bay, their naval host
Did many a Roman chief and Asian king
To doubtful conflict, certain slaughter bring.

Byron does not explain why Cleopatra was to be regarded

as a harmless thing, but he does add, in a note about the Asian Kings: 'It is said that on the day previous to the battle of Actium, Antony had thirteen kings at his levee.'

The city of Nicopolis was built at the site where Augustus was encamped before the battle. It is very big, very sprawling, very badly signed and not awfully interesting. I did not like it much, but Hobhouse found 'a certain melancholy grandeur' in the remains. Whole provinces had once been stripped to fill this artificial monument to the emperor's vanity, but now Hobhouse found a solitary shepherd to be the only inhabitant, while 'the bleating of the sheep, the tinkling of their bells and the croaking of the frogs were the only sounds to be heard.'

Bishop Wordsworth, the geographer Bishop of Lincoln, disapproved of Nicopolis in principle:

> It was erected to commemorate a victory on a Grecian sea by a Roman conqueror; and was intended by him to prove and consolidate his power over the inhabitants of the Hellenic soil; it was, if we may be allowed the comparison, a great Zoological Garden, into which Greeks were brought from their native hills, in order to be trained in the arts of civilisation and caged like prisoners by Imperial Rome.
>
> We cannot forbear from sympathising with these wild mountaineers when, uprooted from their own free villages, they quitted the massive walls and castellated gates by which those villages were defended, and came to live under the protection of the red brick ramparts which surrounded this City of Victory. They descended from their healthy hills into this low and swampy plain, and exchanged the clear native fountains which gushed from beneath the rocks of their own citadels for water drawn from lead pipes and a stuccoed aqueduct – they sacrificed the natural pleasures of the field and of the chase in order to come and sit through their long days under an awning on the seats of one of these Theatres, filled with courtly gentlemen and Romans.

So you see it is not a place at which you are required to fall into ecstasies of admiration, but to do it justice, it was empty. You can roam all over it undisturbed, and you might come across some sheep but are unlikely to be troubled by people. Round the Roman odeon I found a chain-link fence with a locked gate, so I lay on my stomach and wriggled under it like a snake. This is not necessary. Keep walking and you will find another gate, wide open.

Then, with my head spinning with tales of heroic Suliot women, ravaged cities, lost battles, classical references and Byronic versifications I went back to the Golden Beach a bit tired after a long day and fell asleep at quarter to seven. Luckily I woke up in time for another excellent fish dinner.

Arta and Ioannina

The distance from the Golden Beach Hotel to Arta was a mere 24 miles. There was no hill to speak of, and having left at 8.30 I was there by 11.00 after stopping on the way at Louros, where I bought two bananas. I had noticed that bananas are eaten by Wimbledon players to keep themselves going through a hard-fought match, and perhaps it was the bananas that got me to Arta so quickly. I also tried to buy a pen at a shop selling magazines, but the lady said she did not sell pens so she gave me one instead and would not take any money.

At Arta I could not find the ambiguous 100-foot inscription that Bruce had told me about. There is a

Byzantine museum, which was shut, a castle turned into a hotel, which it was too hot to climb to, and a famous bridge. This is a Turkish packhorse bridge and it is a well-known fact that the mason who built it also built his wife into the foundations to give it strength. Such was, it seems, fairly common practice at the time. The ancient Greeks would think nothing of sacrificing a horse or an ox to a river in order to propitiate it, and the Albanians rated a woman somewhat lower in the scale, as recorded by Edward Lear. He came across

> some eighty or one hundred women laden as never women were elsewhere – their male relatives taking it easy up the mountain. 'Heavens!' said I, surprised out of my wonted philosophy of travel, which ought not to exclaim at anything, 'how can you make your women such slaves?' 'To you as a stranger' [came the reply] 'it must seem extraordinary; but the fact is we have no mules, that is the reason why we employ a creature so inferior in strength as a woman; but there is no remedy, for mules there are none and women are next best to mules.'

As for the building of the bridge at Arta, there is a folk song about it which can be found with a prose translation as number 255 in the *Penguin Book of Greek Verse*. It seemed to me to be the stuff of which ballads are made, so I have tried to turn it into that form. What follows is a free, but I believe faithful, version, and I hope it gives a kind of vividness to the scene.

The Ballad of Arta Bridge

Five and forty masons skilled
Forgathered once at Arta,
With sixty lads to help them build
A bridge across the water.

Men and boys right hard worked they,
And strove with all their might,
But everything they built by day
Was washed away by night.

For very rage the masons wept,
'Alas,' the young lads cried,
'Our daily labours all are swept
From off the river's side.'

Then on a tree a little bird
Alighted near the throng
And from its tiny beak was heard
A passing wondrous song.

No thrush-like singing did they hear
Nor yet a swallow's note.
A human voice came forth full clear
From out its speckled throat.

'To build the bridge, there's one must die'
(Such was the song it sang)
'Whose bones beneath the bridge must lie
Whose ghost shall guard the span!

'High is the price; no sacrifice
Of man from foreign land,
Or orphan child, would e'en suffice
To make the bridge to stand.

'The master mason's lovely wife
Who cometh day by day
To see the bridge, she with her life
To build the bridge must pay!'

The master mason loud did groan,
The tears flowed from his eye,
And he did make such piteous moan
That he was like to die.

A nightingale was singing near
Aloft upon a tree.
'Fly, nightingale, and to my dear
This message take,' said he.

Say 'Late do thou arise this day
And slow a meal prepare
And to thy husband make thy way
But slowly come thou there.'

But Oh! the nightingale misheard
Aloft upon the tree.
With this false message flew the bird
As fast as fast could be:

'Early do thou arise this day
And swift a meal prepare
And to thy husband haste away –
Right swiftly come thou there!'

And so she hastened, as she deemed
At her good man's behest,
But when he saw her, then it seemed
His heart died in his breast.

'Good health to you, my masters all!'
But then she cried, aghast,
'What evil, husband, doth befall?
Why art thou so downcast?'

'From off his hand his ring of gold
Did fall,' the men replied,
'Nor is there anyone so bold
Will plunge into the tide.'

'Master mason grieve not so
For I will have no fear
And in the river I will go
To find thy ring, my dear.'

She searched along the river bed
A rope around her tied.
'No ring lies here, my dear,' she said,
'Now pull me to the side.'

Then down cement and lime they threw
And pity showed her none,
Until at last her husband too
Threw down a mighty stone.

'Alas,' she cried, 'for I am slain
Who was the last of three.
That fate that took my sisters twain
Is now reserved for me.

'The Danube bridge the first of these
Doth lie entombed below.
The bridge across the Euphrates
The second claimed also.

'And I who was the last of three
Am now to live no more,
For Arta's bridge must builded be
So I must die therefore!

'But weak as any flower tall
I pray this bridge may be,
And they who cross it, may they fall
Like leaves from any tree.'

The masons cried, 'Do thou forbear,
And that fell curse unsay!
Thou hast a brother may come here
To cross the bridge some day!'

The mason's wife did then amend
Her curse, and thus she spake:
'Firm stand the bridge from end to end
Until the mountains shake.

'Naught but the fall of mountains tall
Shall sound the bridge's knell;
Across the bridge pass safely all
Till wild birds fall as well.

'For it may be my brother here
May chance to come some day,
Then safely cross, my brother dear,
Go safe upon thy way!'

This famous, this amazing, this tragic bridge crosses the Arachthos River with one large and three smaller arches. The stone surface is highly polished and very slippery; only pedestrians, cyclists and I suppose packhorses may use it; there is another bridge for the internal combustion traffic. The river below is beautiful, with gardens on either bank, and there are hills towering in the background. The bridge takes on a mellow glow in the evening light, at which time the frogs start chattering; BRE-ke-ke-kex-koax-koax, exactly like the chorus in the play of Aristophanes. I have heard many frogs in my time, but never any so classically correct.

On one bank there is an enormous plane tree with a restaurant underneath. This tree is a tree of trees. Its branches have spread so far that they have to be propped up with wooden supports, and children who climb among its hospitable limbs can disappear into the hollows of its gigantic trunk. Rarely if ever have I seen such a tree, and as I sat under it that evening looking at the bridge, which by now was floodlit, I speculated on a matter which I suggest you might start as a dinner party topic should the conversation lag. 'In the entire world,' you should ask, 'which is your favourite bridge?' This will set them thinking, and it is probably not a matter on which they have ever thought before. I have not seen the Sydney Harbour Bridge, nor yet the famous Golden Gate Bridge at San Francisco. I have a great affection for a little stone bridge which is itself a packhorse bridge near Fittleworth in Sussex. I have a confused and not too favourable recollection of the Ponte Vecchio in Florence, and was not greatly struck with the Bridge of Sighs in Venice. I must have seen many other bridges which impressed me at the time, but they do not seem to have stuck in my memory, and taking bridges for all in all I do not recall one that I liked better than the Turkish packhorse bridge at Arta.

The waiter at the restaurant under the plane tree chose to conduct the discussion in English, which was fine by me as I had had enough Greek for one day. There was aubergine on the menu, fried in something that I did not recognise, and for which he did not know the English word.

'Never mind,' I said. 'I will have it anyway.'

When it came, 'Ah ha!' said I. 'The word is "batter".'

'No, not butter,' said he.

'Batter,' said I firmly, but he was equally firm.

'Not butter,' he insisted.

'Indeed not butter, but *batter*. You spell it with an "a".'

Possibly this exchange enlarged his English vocabulary, but it didn't have that effect on my Greek as I have by now forgotten the word he used in the first place.

In Arta I stayed at the Cronos Hotel, which has a fine bronze statue of King Pyrrhus of Epirus outside. This is he of the 'Pyrrhic victory' who routed the Romans in 279 BC at such cost to his own army that he exclaimed, 'One more such victory and we are undone.' It was near a bank, and second to building churches, the Greeks like to build banks. The idea in England now is to have as few banks as possible, to close down all the branches they can and to do as much as possible by remote control. By contrast, any Greek town of any size will have not one but several banks, and in the smallest and scruffiest of places, if there is a bank at all, it will stand out as a marble palace of coolness and tranquillity. The people who work in banks are conscious of their superior status, like people who live in great houses, and so tend to be supercilious in their treatment of customers. Eurocheques are now in the past but I used to find that if I presented a Eurocheque they appeared to assume that I was probably a cheat and a forger, and gave me my money with ill-concealed reluctance.

The bank at Arta was like that, but as I sat patiently waiting the calm was broken by one of the female cashiers crashing to the floor. Everyone but me thought this was very interesting and exciting, and crowded round to get a better view, whereas I stayed where I was, giving my stolid impersonation of an imperturbable Englishman. The cashier rose from the floor after a minute and retired, white-faced, from the scene. She did not reappear; I hope she came to no harm.

Arta is now a big, bustling place, but it wasn't when Benjamin Disraeli, later to be Prime Minister, arrived in 1830 at the age of 26. He found it 'in ruins, whole streets razed to the ground and scarcely a tenement not a shell'. This was the result of the Turkish government reasserting its authority over the rebellious Albanian chieftains, having disposed of the wicked Ali Pasha nearly nine years earlier. Disraeli was travelling mostly by yacht ('I like a sailor's life much, though it destroys the toilette, and one never feels, or is indeed, clean.'), and with his friends Meredith and Clay made various expeditions inland.

At Arta they paid a courtesy visit to Kalio Bey, the Governor. 'I cannot describe to you' says Disraeli, 'the curious feelings with which for the first time in my life, I found myself squatting on the right hand of a Bey, smoking an amber-mouthed chibouque, drinking coffee and paying him compliments through an interpreter.'

This exchange of compliments took rather longer than they wanted, but finally they set off for Ioannina. Among the party was Clay's valet Giovanni, of whom Disraeli says that 'Byron died in his arms, and his mustachios touched the earth. Withal mild as a lamb, though he has two daggers always about his person.' To Byron he was known as Tita, which was an abbreviation of Battista, his full name being Giovanni Battista Falcieri. He had been Byron's gondolier in Venice, a position of great trust in view of his Lordship's escapades in that city. He came with Byron on his final expedition to Greece, and was with him to the end. Disraeli eventually took him back to England and made him the steward of his family home in Buckingham.

Their first night after leaving Arta en route for Ioannina was spent like this:

> Two hours before sunset, having completed only half our course in spite of all our exertions, we found ourselves at a vast but dilapidated khan [an inn] as big as a Gothic castle, situated on a high range, and built as a sort of halfway house for travellers by Ali Pasha. This khan had now been turned into a military post; and here we found a young Bey, to whom Kalio had given us a letter. He was a man of very pleasing exterior, but unluckily could not understand Giovanni's Greek, and had no interpreter. What was to be done? We could not go on, as there was not an inhabited place before Yanina; and here were we sitting before sunset on the same divan with our host, who had entered the place to receive us and would not leave the room, while we were there without the power of communicating an idea. We were in despair, and we were also very hungry, and could not therefore in the course of an hour or two plead fatigue as an excuse for sleep, for we were ravenous and anxious to know what prospect of food existed in this wild and desolate mansion. So we smoked. It is a great resource, but this wore out, and it was so ludicrous smoking, and looking at each other, and dying to talk, and then exchanging pipes by way of compliment, and then pressing our hand to our heart by way of thanks.
>
> The Bey sat in a corner, I unfortunately next, so I had the onus of mute attention; and Clay next to me, so he and M. could at least have an occasional joke, though of course we were too well-bred to exceed an occasional and irresistible observation. Clay wanted to play écarté, and with a grave face, as if we were at our devotions; but just as we were about commencing, it occurred to us that we had some brandy, and that we would offer our host a glass, as it might be a hint for what should follow to so vehement a schnaps. Mashallah! Had the effect only taken place 1830 years ago, instead of in

> the present age of scepticism, it would have been instantly voted a first-rate miracle. Our mild friend smacked his lips and instantly asked for another cup; we drank it in coffee cups. By the time that Meredith had returned, who had left the house on pretence of shooting, Clay, our host, and myself had despatched a bottle of brandy in quicker time and fairer proportions than I ever did a bottle of Burgundy, and were extremely gay. Then he would drink again with Meredith and ordered some figs, talking I must tell you all the time, indulging in the most graceful pantomime, examining our pistols, offering us his own golden ones for our inspection, and finally making out Giovanni's Greek enough to misunderstand most ludicrously every observation we communicated. But all was taken in good part, and I never met such a jolly fellow in the course of my life.
>
> In the meantime we were ravenous, for the dry, round, unsugary fig is a great whetter. At last we insisted upon Giovanni's communicating our wants and asking for bread. The Bey gravely bowed and said 'Leave it to me; take no thought' and nothing more occurred. We prepared ourselves for hungry dreams, when to our great delight a most capital supper was brought in, accompanied, to our great horror, by – wine. We ate, we drank, we ate with our fingers, we drank in a manner I never recollect. The wine was not bad, but if it had been poison we must drink; it was such a compliment for a Moslemin; we quaffed it in rivers. The Bey called for the brandy; he drank it all. The room turned round; the wild attendants who sat at our feet seemed dancing in strange and fantastic whirls; the Bey shook hands with me; he shouted English – I Greek. 'Very good' he had caught up from us. 'Kalo, kalo' was my rejoinder. He roared; I smacked him on the back. I remember no more.

Future Prime Ministers did things well in those days. There is nothing half so dashing as that in Mr Major's memoirs, and I don't suppose Mr Blair was ever up to anything so stylish.

Unlike Disraeli and his party I was not restricted to the standard packhorse pace of three miles per hour, so I proposed to get to Ioannina in one day. At first the road is fairly flat, and you have the best of it by going towards Ioannina rather than away, because, riding on the right, the rushing waters of the River Louros are beside you, making a cooling noise, with plane trees on the bank giving intermittent shade. Still, there were several very hot and strenuous patches. By about half past twelve I arrived panting at a little settlement of one garage and three *cafeneia* where I lunched most gratefully on Coca-Cola and tomato salad, trying to wave the flies off the bread as I ate. Opposite there was a grove of plane trees with the Louros dashing through the middle.

I crossed the river on an old, rusty, springy metal suspension bridge which bounced about in an alarming manner, and a strange man appeared who considered himself to be a friend of mine. He compelled me to shake his hand, and demanded that I take his photograph on the bridge. I held the camera up and pretended to click the button, after which he invited me to write down his name and address on a piece of paper so that I could send him the supposed photograph. I have no idea who he was or what the fuss was about, but finally and mercifully he went away and I went to sleep under the trees till three o'clock. Then I set off again, thinking that perhaps by now the heat had abated.

It hadn't, or if it had it must have been an inferno before. After a couple of miles I came to a sign saying 'Sources of the Louros', and that was the last I saw of the river. 'Now I am for it,' I thought, 'there is bound to be a hill after this,' and there was. It was enormous and seemingly unending. There was no shade, in fact there was the reverse of shade because the rocks at the side reflected the heat straight back at me. I took copious drinks of now-warm water from my water bottle; the sweat ran off in rivulets; I rode a little, pushed a little, rested a little, and slogged on.

Bruce the archaeologist had a theory about heatstroke, which went like this:

Rule 1: To avoid heatstroke, you must drink a lot.
Rule 2: If you get it, do not drink but lie in the shade until the palpitations stop. Then drink.

Palpitations? What are palpitations? How do you tell a genuine palpitation from a heart that is racing with exertion like mine? Anyway, there was no shade to lie in, so all I could do was struggle on until at last I found a meagre little fig tree that cast a sparse shadow on a patch of prickly scrub. With some difficulty I got into a tolerable position under it and waited till my heart got back to a normal rate, which took about half an hour. I don't suppose heatstroke was at all imminent but it would have been inconvenient to expire just there and just then, so I thought it best to be safe.

Then I set off again and at last I saw ahead, like a traveller in the desert, what was either an oasis or a mirage, in the shape of a garage. If it was an oasis it would be open and have soft drinks and chairs and shade. If it was a mirage it would be shut, and as there was no sign of life I braced myself to bear it if it was. But no, it was open. I drank cold water from its drinking fountain and Coca-Cola under a sun-shade, luxuriating in the breeze which had sprung up by then.

By the time I went on from there the heat had eased off quite a lot and the crest of the mountain turned out not to be far away. Once over the top it was an easy run to Ioannina which I reached at six thirty p.m., having started at eight thirty a.m. I should think I was resting for four of the ten hours so my average speed when moving was about 8 miles per hour, more than twice as fast as a packhorse. All in all, I think it was quite good going.

Ioannina seems to me to be two places. There is the mainland town, and there is the island on Lake Pambotis. The town is noisy, bustling, and at first sight not very interesting, but it repays study and the place to start is the castle.

This is a very fine castle. It was once the headquarters of the great and dreadful Ali Pasha. Within the outer wall, at the north corner, you find cannons and cannon balls lying around, and a former mosque called the Cami of Aslan Pasha. You realise at once that this was for centuries Muslim Albanian-Turkish territory which does not feel Greek, and only became part of Greece in 1913. Opposite the entrance to the mosque is a long, low Turkish-looking building, which was once a seminary for Muslim students. The mosque itself now houses an exhibition of Greek, Muslim and Hebrew objects (there having once been a thriving Jewish community here), and it has one of the two surviving minarets in Ioannina. The guidebook says there is a fine view from the top of the minaret, so I asked a very pleasant and English-speaking young lady at the desk if I could go up it.

'Unfortunately it is closed.'

'That is a great pity. Why is it closed?'

'Because it is dangerous.'

'In what way dangerous?'

'The stairs are very narrow and difficult.'

'I do not mind narrow and difficult stairs.'

'In that case you may go up it,' and she summoned a man with a key who unlocked the door at the bottom.

As I don't suppose many readers will have climbed up a minaret, I will tell you that it is like going up the inside of a very fat pencil. You are turning sharply to the right all the time, with nothing much to hold on to, up worn stone steps. It is intended for a single imam to ascend and call the faithful to prayer, so it would be madness to open it to the public at large as the people going down could hardly get past the people going up, and there would be panic, confusion, claustrophobia and death. At the top you emerge onto an extremely narrow circular platform meant for the single imam aforementioned, which feels as if it would collapse if two such imams stood on it. As there was a high wind blowing at the time, it felt as if the whole thing might collapse anyway. Still, if you venture to look over the alarmingly low parapet that runs round the platform, you certainly get a magnificent view of the town, the lake, the mountains and the other minaret in what they call the Fortress.

You will find, when you come down, that the spirit of Ali Pasha broods over Ioannina and you will be reminded of him at every turn, particularly by the sellers of postcards. There is a popular one of Ali Pasha being cuddled by his favourite wife, and another of him personally supervising the drowning of fifteen ladies accused of adultery. This card is rather cryptically entitled 'Kira Frosinis Drown', and shows a wild-eyed Albanian about to throw a sad-looking lady into the lake by moonlight. She has a stone round her ankles and her hands and feet are tied together, while the ferocious vizier watches from a nearby rock. Phrosini was a Greek girl 'celebrated', says R. A. Davenport, 'for the beauty of her person, and no less so for the graces and accomplishments of her mind'. Unluckily she became involved in an affair with Ali's son Mouctar, having, it is said, rejected the advances of Ali himself. Mouctar's wife complained to Ali, who accordingly rounded up Phrosini and fourteen others accused of similar frailty, and had them drowned in the lake. Mouctar's brother Veli sent him a letter with the news, and Mouctar, true to type, shot the messenger.

When Byron and Hobhouse arrived Ioannina was in a flourishing state:

> A gleam of sunshine afforded us an opportunity of contemplating the fine prospect of the city and its neighbourhood. The houses, domes, and minarets glittering through gardens of orange and lemon trees, and from groves of cypress – the lake spreading its smooth expanse at the foot of the city – the mountains arising abruptly from the banks of the lake – all these burst at once upon us.

They got rather a surprise though as they entered the town:

> As we passed a large tree on our left, opposite a butcher's shop, I saw something hanging from the boughs, which at a little distance seemed to be meat exposed for sale; but on coming nearer, I suddenly discovered it to be a man's arm, with a part of the side torn from the body, and hanging by a bit of string round one of the fingers. We learnt that the arm was part of a robber who had been beheaded five days before, and whose remaining quarters were exposed in other parts of Ioannina.

Ali had left a message, says Hobhouse, that he 'was sorry to be obliged to leave his capital to finish a little war – *une petite guerre* – in which he was engaged'. They encountered him later in Albania proper, where, says Byron

> he received me standing, a wonderful compliment from a Mussulman. He said he was certain I was a man of birth, because I had small ears, curling hair and little white hands. He told me to consider him as a father, and said he looked on me as his son. Indeed, he treated me like a child, sending me almonds and sugared sherbet, fruit and sweetmeats, twenty times a day. He begged me to visit him often, and at night, when he was at leisure.

That was sinister enough. Then Hobhouse noticed that Ali seemed to know a lot about an Albanian they had taken on, called Vassily.

> 'Yes,' said Vassily, 'he ought to be well acquainted with me; for I have come down with the men of our village, and broken his windows with shot, when he did not dare stir out of Tepellene.'
> 'Well and what did Ali do to the men of your village?'
> 'Nothing at all, he made friends with our chief man, persuaded him to come to Tepellene, and there roasted him on a spit; after which we submitted.'

In spite of all this, Byron was impressed by the Vizier's kind and dignified manner, and is thought to have made him the model for the pirate father of Haidée in *Don Juan*:

> He was the mildest mannered man
> That ever scuttled ship or cut a throat;
> With such true breeding of a gentleman
> You never could define his real thought.
> Pity he loved adventurous life's variety,
> He was so great a loss to good society.

The prosperous city of Ioannina was later destroyed by Ali himself, in his last desperate resistance when the Sultan of Turkey determined to bring his rebellious subject to heel. As a result of this, and subsequent steps by the Turkish government to regain control of the area, Disraeli and his party found 'a vast scene of destruction. Ruined houses, mosques with their tower only standing, streets utterly razed – these are nothing.'

As visiting 'Myllorts Ingles', Disraeli and his party were granted an audience with the new vizier – a man who, according to the Austrian Consul, had in the previous three months put 4,000 people to death:

> Suddenly we are summoned to the awful presence of the pillar of the Turkish Empire, the man who has the reputation of being the mainspring of the new system of regeneration, the renowned Redschid, an approved warrior, a consummate politician, unrivalled as a dissembler in a country where dissimulation is the principal portion of the moral code. I bowed with all the nonchalance of St. James's Street to a little ferocious-looking, shrivelled, care-worn man, plainly dressed, with a brow covered with wrinkles and a countenance clouded with anxiety and thought.
>
> I seated myself on the divan of the Grand Vizier with the self-possession of a morning call. Some compliments passed between us, and pipes and coffee were brought; then His Highness waved his hand, and in an instant the chamber was cleared. We congratulated him on the pacification of Albania. He rejoined that the peace of the world was his only object, and the happiness of mankind his only wish.

The town of Ioannina slopes down towards the lake and you can sit by the lake, walk by the lake or cycle by the lake. If you take an evening spin along the shore under the plane trees you come to a Gypsy encampment where the lorries are piled high with plastic tables and chairs. The principal source of Gypsy revenue is, according to my researches, to go about in pick-up trucks with deafening loud speakers touting garden furniture throughout the villages, where you meet them all the time.

Ioannina is one of those places, I should warn you, where they like to keep things secret, so I will tell you how to find the archaeological museum. This modern, cool, marble structure, better even than a bank, is concealed beside a pleasant garden, which they do not wish you to know about, in the general area of the clock tower, and tucked in behind the Ethnic Bank of Greece. The museum has much that is very good, in particular marvellous bronzes such as bowls, statuettes of warriors, animals, a couple of boys playing – things that you might actually like to have about the house, rather than the busted-up stuff that comprises much of the relics of antiquity. Perfectly fascinating are the relics of Dodona, which I will come to in a later chapter. You definitely should not miss the museum, and nearby, at the top of the semi-secret garden, is a vast terrace with a staggering view across the lake and the city. There is an enormous café-restaurant, which looks as if it ought to be the smart place to go of an evening and which was, at mid-morning, deserted.

I will also tell you that, provided it is still going, there is a brilliant Italian restaurant called Arnaldos. If you should, by the time you reach Ioannina, feel that a change from Greek food would be welcome, that is the place to go. The road divides at the bottom of the hill, with the castle on the right, shortly before the lake, which at this point is in sight. Take the left fork. Keep a sharp look-out on your left and you will see an unobtrusive doorway with 'Arnaldos' written above it. From there a passage leads to a pretty walled garden set with tables, very peaceful. In it there was a waiter with an unfortunate resemblance to the actor Martin Clunes, and a slender, attractive waitress in a miniskirt, which became her very well – a rare enough sight in Greece.

Ambience is not a word I care for, but Arnaldos has a very good one, a sort of leisurely elegance that you do not find in your average slap-dash, rough-and-ready taverna. They brought me hot rolls in a little basket, and as it grew dark they put a little paraffin lamp upon the table, while unobtrusive lights came on in the stone walls. The long-legged and desirable waitress, when she arrived to take my order, leant forward and rested her elbows on the table, clasped her hands together, gazed into my eyes and asked me what I wanted. Most of all I wanted to elope with her, but Martin Clunes was hovering nearby so I did not dare propose it. Instead I asked her whether I could possibly have a bottle of wine from nearby Zitsa, which I had heard was very good, and which was on the wine list. 'No,' she said emphatically. It was, she said, too expensive. Then she drew herself up, disappeared and came back with two glasses, one with a little red wine, the other with a little white for me to sample. I preferred the white, which she assured me was very much cheaper than that from Zitsa. Did I want a glass or half a litre? I would have half a litre, and it came in an Italian carafe.

The food was excellent, though there was rather too much of it. I didn't know what to expect of Eggplant Al Forno, which proved to be aubergines baked in a cheese sauce, and would have been enough for two. There was an expensive feel about the place, so I prepared myself with the equivalent of £20 at the ready, but they only wanted £10. Neither Martin Clunes nor she of the lovely legs were

Italian, nor, she told me, did they speak Italian. The Italian element is supplied entirely by Arnaldo, who labours in the kitchen and owns the place.

Ferries buzz across Lake Pambotis to and from the island all the time. Once there, you can take a pleasant walk above the lake leading to St Nicholas's Monastery, where a girl of twelve gave me a guided tour of the tiny establishment, speaking in difficult English. The frescoes, she said, were of the sixteenth century and the oldest on the island, but were badly damaged by the Turks, particularly about the eyes. This was useful information because when I later got into the next monastery, there being several to see, I noticed that here too the saints and heroes had been knocked about in the same way. Apparently the Muslim dislike of pictures and graven images extended particularly to the eyes. I was sorry the paintings had been mutilated, but the painters had gone in for frescoes of especially gruesome martyrdoms which I did not care for, so I did not mind the mutilation as much as I might have done.

By slipping and sliding along narrow cobbled streets you get to the monastery of Panteleimon where Ali Pasha was killed. He had retired there in the belief that he had negotiated a settlement with the Turkish government and was either treacherously stabbed or treacherously shot. The bullet holes in the floor support the latter theory. Davenport writes that:

> The body of the vizier was buried in the tomb of his wife Emina, with all the honours due to his rank; the head was enclosed in a silver box, and sent to Constantinople, where, placed in a dish, it was exposed to the popular gaze, before the gate of the Seraglio. Appended to it was the yaptha, or statement of the crimes which had brought down on its owner the penalty of death.

There is at the monastery of Panteleimon, among other mementoes, an awe-inspiring picture of the head of Ali Pasha being presented on a golden dish to the gloating Sultan Mahmoud. When you get back to the mainland you should certainly visit Ali Pasha's grave, where he is buried with his wife but without his head, within the fortress which houses the Byzantine Museum. The wrought-iron cage over the grave is a reproduction, as the Germans took the original during the war.

The islanders of Ioannina keep their fish fresh by keeping them alive. The first thing you see as you step off the ferry is a big tank of fish with unhappy looks on their faces, swimming round and round their cramped apartment, the bottom of which is covered by a heap of eels. On the way to the Ali Pasha Museum I passed a fishmonger who had not only living fish and eels but also frogs, crabs, a couple of tortoises and two baby ducks, which he said had been caught on the lake. It was all rather horrible – the sort of thing that makes a man feel he should live the rest of his life on a diet of Marmite sandwiches and macaroni cheese.

Silversmithing is the great industry at Ioannina, and the five hundred or so people who live on the island spend their time either trying to feed you on fishy food or sitting around hoping to sell you silver. Everything that could be made of silver has been made of silver. There are plates and dishes; corkscrews and bottle-openers; clocks, cutlery and candlesticks, plus a variety of jewellery, but I never saw anybody buying any of it. The Ioannina silver business is one of the mysteries of life. They have a huge amount of money tied up in stock, and none of it seems to sell.

I spent a day wandering about the town and the island, recovered from the close encounter with heatstroke of the day before, and next morning rode to Dodona, which is 13 miles from Ioannina.

Dodona, Zitsa, Corfu

There are three utterly compelling reasons to go to Dodona – historical, archaeological and scenic.

Historically speaking, Dodona was the site of the oldest oracle in Greece, and was Egyptian in origin. So says the historian Herodotus. Uniquely in Greece, it was an oracle of Zeus, the king of the gods no less, who nowhere else condescended to act in an oracular capacity. The god spoke out of an oak tree and was served by priests called Selloi who slept on the ground and never washed their feet. So says Homer.

As well as fragmentary ruins of the temples of Zeus and Aphrodite, and of some public buildings, Dodona has a theatre of the utmost magnificence, a jewel in the setting of Mount Tomaros. Its undoubted splendour is enhanced by the fact that unless something is going on by way of a dramatic festival, very few people go there, so for a lot of the time you have it almost to yourself. Edward Lear passed that way in 1849 and says that 'in spite of the driving rain it was impossible not to be greatly struck with the magnificent size and position of the great theatre, which ranks in dimension with the largest ones of Greece'. Just so.

Dodona was, for a long time, lost. People knew of the site, but they did not know it was Dodona so they speculated as to where Dodona might be. Thus Byron:

> Oh! where Dodona! Is thine aged grove,
> Prophetic fount, and oracle divine?
> What valley echo'd the response of Jove?
> What trace remaineth of the thunderer's shrine?
> All, all forgotten –

Byron had no inkling that he and Hobhouse had been there. They had visited some ancient remains 'in the neighbourhood' says Hobhouse, 'of a village called Chercovista. The amphitheatre, which soon presents itself, is indeed magnificent and, for a ruin, very entire.' It remained for Christopher Wordsworth, scholar, topographer and Bishop of Lincoln, to point out that these were the ruins of Dodona. He says:

> To ascertain the site of DODONA would seem now to require a response from the ORACLE itself. The former dwelling of the spirit, which once guided half the world, is lost. For many generations Kings, Generals and Statesmen came from the extreme coasts of Greece to consult the Oracle,

> but now none can point to its place. Still even the uncertainty of its site is not without its interest, and we do not believe that the search for it is hopeless.

If you visit the site, as you certainly should, you can follow his arguments with the greatest ease. They are:
1. The remains 'stand in a *plain*. The selection of such a spot shows a remarkable confidence in the inherent resources of the city; for if there is one particular attribute of an ordinary Hellenic town, it is this – that its citadel is placed upon a *hill*. A Greek city was always full of suspicions.'
2. The surrounding city was very small. 'The strength of its population could never have compensated for the weakness of its position.'
3. The remains are very big. 'The existence of so grand a theatre, in so insignificant a place is without parallel in the whole of Greece. Between it and the gate of the lower city, are vestiges of two temples; of the more distant of the two, fourteen columns, or at least the fragments of them, are still standing. There are not, we believe, fourteen other columns remaining together in the whole of Epirus.'

From this the Bishop concludes that 'considering these circumstances, and the inferences to be deduced from them, we feel disposed to enquire whether, when contemplating these ruins, we are not treading the soil once hallowed by the presence of DODONA?' Quite right, and the observations and deductions of the Bishop were confirmed in 1875 by excavations at the site by a Greek archaeologist, Constantin Carapanos.

The first and only other time that I went to Dodona I had had to make an early start from Ioannina. There were two buses a day, and the first one left at 6 a.m. with no one but me on board. It dropped me off at Dodona, filled up with people going to work in Ioannina, and disappeared until the evening when it brought them back to Dodona and returned me to Ioannina. On arrival at Dodona I got off at the theatre, which seemed the proper thing to do, and there was absolutely no one around. This mattered only because I was hungry, so I walked up to the village where a sweet old lady gave me a delicious breakfast of coffee, bread and two fried eggs, which I ate with the hens that laid them clucking around my feet.

The rest of that day I divided between the theatre and the *cafeneion*. At one moment when I was drinking coffee a hot and dusty workman arrived from a nearby building site.

'Hello, how are you?' he asked in Greek.

'Very well, thank you – and you?' I replied in my best Berlitz Greek for Travellers.

'Ow,' he said in broadest Australian, 'yer niver well when yer workin'.'

He had spent years in Melbourne, which I believe has the largest Greek population of any city in the world except for Athens, and had now come home to build a house and grow nuts. (To cultivate nut trees I mean, not to become gradually demented.)

Much of the rest of that day I spent climbing over the ruins or dozing under the trees. Just as I completed my exploration of the theatre a man arrived with high boots on his legs and a scythe in his hand. '*Fee-thes*,' he said, or something like it.

'*Fee-thes*?' I repeated. The word was not familiar.

'*Fee-thes, fee-thes*,' he said emphatically, making wriggling movements with his left hand. 'Oh, *fee-thes*,' I replied, recognising this as a modern version of the word which I would, had I been translating Homer, have rendered as serpents.

The conversation then lurched along in a mixture of dumbshow and Greek, in which I could identify the words for 'twenty minutes' and 'death'. I think the substance of our discussion was that in the long grass, which it was his business to cut, there were serpents lurking which if they bit me, would kill me in twenty minutes. I was glad to have met him after my explorations and not before.

Coming to Dodona by bicycle this time was a straightforward but strenuous affair. The turning off the Ioannina–Arta road is clearly marked, and you go along the flat until you are seven kilometres from Ioannina. Then you turn right at another sign which tells you that Dodoni, as it is now called, is eleven kilometres away, and you start to climb. The theatre being low down, you go right to the top of a high hill and right down the other side, and there it is at the very bottom of a valley with Mount Tomaros towering above it.

The theatre is indeed, as the Bishop said, grand and the place insignificant, but the situation superb. Bruce the archaeologist said that he had been there in the 'fall' and the colours were wonderful, which I can well believe. It was a sad thought that Dodona in autumn was a sight that I should probably never see, because it would be a long way to come just for that and at my time of life one feels that the sands are running out. All the same there was plenty for me to savour for the present. There had been a vast variety of mountain scenery on this trip but there is something special about Mount Tomaros. The River Acheron has character, but Tomaros has majesty. It is wooded to a great height and divided into little ridges and clefts so that light and shadow alternate all along, especially in the evening.

The grass at the theatre this time had been cut short, and anyway Bruce the archaeologist had said that he had never heard of poisonous snakes in Greece, so I approached without anxiety. At the centre of the orchestra was a stone that looked like the one at Epidaurus from which the lightest whisper can be heard in every seat. There was an English couple two-thirds of the way up above me, so I said in a quiet undertone, 'Can you hear me pretty well up there?'

'Absolutely clearly,' they replied.

You can be certain that from that spot your voice will carry to every one of the 18,000 seats, but this stone is in the orchestra, where the chorus were. The actors, on the other hand, were further back on the stage, and I wondered if they needed to shout a bit to get their lines across. Having thought thus far, I made a test with the help of a Greek-American undergraduate and his wholly Greek aunt, and found that I could be heard perfectly well from the actors' position. I then thought that if all the seats were full, 18,000 people might cushion the reverberations and make it necessary to speak up, but this couldn't be tested as there weren't ten people there altogether, let alone 18,000. I was on the right lines though. Greek actors wore masks and some say that these had a mouthpiece, which, according to a writer called Aulus Gellius, acted as a megaphone. Also it says in Dr Smith's *Dictionary of Greek and Roman Antiquities* that 'we know that all circumstances united to compel the tragic actor to acquire a loud and sonorous voice.' I hope they don't cheat nowadays and have microphones when they put on a performance.

The Blue Guide says there are no oaks at Dodona now,

but there are, with one exactly where it ought to be in the temple of Zeus. They only need to hang up a whip and some brass pots to clatter in the wind, this being one of the ways that oracles were delivered, and it would be ready to give out marriage guidance and forecast the movements of the stock exchange. These were the sort of questions that were put to the oracle, except that the Greeks had no stock exchange. They have found some little lead strips at Dodona with questions on them, which they keep in the museum at Ioannina, and they go like this:

'Ariston asks whether it is wise and possible for him to sail for Syracuse later on.'
'To which God should I pray for my fortune, my children and my wife?'
'Timodanos asks Zeus if he should engage in trade by land and sea with money from his silver mine.'
'Shall I take another wife?'
'Has Pistos stolen the wool from the mattress?'
'Am I her children's father?'

Such is a fair selection of the questions to which Zeus was expected to supply the answers.

On my previous visit I had wanted to stay overnight but could not because there was no hotel, nor any rooms to let. There is now the Andromache Hotel, which overlooks the archaeological site and has a restaurant. There had been a trickle of cars and one bus during the day, but by 6.30 p.m. they had all gone. As a result of sitting on the balcony of the Andromache Hotel while the shadows lengthened on the mountain and sunset dwindled into night, I can tell you three things which you will find in no other book:

Mount Tomaros goes pink in the evening light.

The bells of returning sheep amount to a positive carillon.

The streetlights in the village above the theatre come on like so many candles on a cake.

It is to relish such things that I like to pass the night at the place I have come to see.

The ride back to Ioannina next morning seemed somehow shorter than the ride out. This is partly because you come at the hill fresh without a preliminary eleven kilometres on the flat; partly because there is a place some way up the hill at which you can get coffee and a croissant to recharge your batteries; and partly because the rocks cast a lot of shadow from the early sun, so you don't get so hot. Altogether it was easy enough to do, and having got to Ioannina I spent some time in the museum, dined once more at the excellent Arnaldos, and made an early start next morning for Zitsa.

Why Zitsa? Because of Byron, of course:

> Monastic Zitsa, from thy shady brow,
> Thou small, but favour'd spot of holy ground!
> Where'er we gaze, around, above, below,
> What rainbow tints, what magic charms are found.

That sounded pretty promising, and furthermore in 1809 Byron wrote to his mother that 'I went over the mountains through Zitsa, a village with a Greek monastery (where I slept on my return), in the most beautiful situation (always excepting Cintra in Portugal) I ever beheld.'

I write as a man who has been to Cintra in Portugal and Zitsa in Greece, and there is no comparison. Cintra has become a great tourist trap, swarming with people who have come to gaze at buildings, many of which were put up after Byron's visit. Zitsa, on the other hand, remains a spot of rainbow tints and magic charms. Everybody goes to Cintra and almost nobody goes to Zitsa, except for the wine festival in August to celebrate the wines which the waitress at Arnaldo's would not let me have. I loved Zitsa, and if I ever get a mad fantasy that I will run away from England and hide from the world, I think of myself as snugly holed up among the magnificent surroundings of Zitsa.

On the way to Zitsa Byron got lost, much to the distress of Fletcher, his English servant. Byron wrote to his mother:

> We were one night lost for *nine* hours in the mountains in a *thunder* storm. Fletcher was sorely bewildered from apprehensions of famine and banditti. His eyes were a little hurt by the lightning or crying (I don't know which) but are now recovered.

Hobhouse had gone ahead with some of the party and on this, the outward trip to see Ali Pasha, they did not stay in the monastery but found 'a miserable hovel' prepared for their reception. 'The room was half full of maize in the stalk; the floor was of mud; and there was no outlet for the smoke but through the door.' When the storm got going the roof shook, the thunder never stopped, the distant hills, which they could see through the cracks of the cabin, appeared to be in a perpetual blaze. Then, says Hobhouse:

> A little after midnight a man, panting and pale, and drenched with rain, rushed into the room, and, between crying and roaring, with a profusion of action, communicated something of which I understood only – that they had all fallen down. I

> learnt, however, that no accident had happened, except the falling of the luggage horses, and losing their way, and that they were now waiting for fresh horses and guides. Ten were immediately sent to them, together with several men with pine torches; but it was not till two o'clock in the morning that we heard they were approaching, and my friend did not enter our hut before three.

Byron's difficulty had been made worse by George the dragoman, who got in such a rage with the guides that he threatened to shoot them. They then ran away, whereupon George fired off both his pistols, which caused Fletcher the valet to scream in terror as he thought they were being attacked by robbers. In the midst of all this Byron was calmly composing a poem of eighteen verses which is headed 'Composed October 11th 1809, during the night, in a thunder storm, when the guides had lost the road to Zitsa, near the range of mountains formerly called Pindus, in Albania.'

It starts:

> Chill and mirk is the nightly blast
> Where Pindus' mountains rise
> And angry clouds are pouring fast
> The vengeance of the sky.

Fletcher comes in at verse four:

> Through sounds of foaming waterfalls
> I hear a voice exclaim –
> My way-worn countryman, who calls
> On distant England's name.

From verse nine onwards it is addressed to Mrs Spencer

Smith, with whom Byron had fallen in love with in Malta a few weeks earlier and who was now in Spain:

Clouds burst, skies flash, oh dreadful hour!
More fiercely pours the storm!
Yet here one thought has still the power
To keep my bosom warm.

While wandering through each broken path,
O'er brake and craggy brow;
While elements exhaust their wrath,
Sweet Florence, where art thou?

I dare say that if you are inclined that way there is nothing like versification to keep the bosom warm in a thunderstorm. I have given an example of my own poetical powers in my version of the *Ballad of Arta Bridge*, but otherwise I rarely get beyond a couplet, and that never in the rain. I sometimes used to pass the time on a bus by composing little verses on the names of Greek towns, which I then sent home on postcards. As, for instance:

Into a crowded bus they tightly packed us
And drove along until we reached Naupactus,
Which formerly they used to call Lepanto –
Perhaps you still can if you really want to.

Even that I think would have been beyond me if I were soaked to the skin. But anyway, one is not likely now to get lost en route to Zitsa, though the start of the ride from Ioannina is not inspiring. You plug along the road towards Igoumenitsa, go past a big industrial area, toil up a long hill and after twelve kilometres reach a right turn marked to Zitsa. Things look up from that point. You pass through one or two villages set among hills and as you get closer to your objective you become aware of vines, and then you round a corner and you are there.

Not having any idea what to expect but having established from a tourist leaflet that there was a pension in Zitsa, I had had a telephone conversation with a lady from whose high-speed Greek I got the impression that I had managed to dial the right number and that there would be a room available. She seemed to ask what time I should get there, and I said eleven o'clock. When I arrived sharp at eleven I found a huge white building facing me which did not say it was the pension but looked as if it might be. A sign outside said: Coffe Bar – Grill Room. Local Wines Zitsa.

It was Saturday morning, and Saturday in Zitsa is apparently kept as a general holiday. As I went into the white building the whole place was humming with men drinking and playing cards, drinking and playing dominoes, or just drinking and shouting. This was not hard drinking, mind you – indeed a lot of it was coffee drinking, but it had the same effect as regards noise. From all this a large man with a huge stomach emerged and said 'Welcome' in English. It was indeed the pension, and I was expected. On which side would I like a room? The side with the better view. (By this time his source of English had dried up so we lapsed into Greek.) He led the way upstairs, opened a door, ushered me in to quite the most palatial room of the trip, flung back the curtains to reveal quite the finest bedroom view of the trip, and proposed to charge me about £10 for the night.

I felt pretty good about all that, although I will admit that my first, and entirely wrong, feeling about Zitsa had been one of slight disappointment. I had imagined a village of old stone houses such as the tourist leaflets say are to be found in Epirus, but it has been rebuilt. If you walk about you find bits of old cobbled streets but the houses are new. Never mind, the situation, ringed around with hills on every side, is perfectly superb, and the reason houses have been rebuilt must be that the village is prosperous, which is a pleasant thing. This prosperity I believe to be built on the wine trade and not on tourism, which is yet another pleasant thing, especially for people like me who dislike other tourists. My luxurious pension was for the accommodation of wine buyers and any other knowing visitors who came for the festival.

On arrival I had asked the large landlord how far it was to the monastery. 'Five hundred metres,' he said. As soon as I came downstairs he led me outside, pointed to a high hill and said I must go up it. I should go past the *plateia*, turn right and follow the *strada* he'd said, having lapsed into Italian for the moment. These instructions were puzzling because, almost exactly where we stood, was a sign pointing in the opposite direction saying 'Monastery of the Holy Fathers'. Why did he insist that I climb that hill when what I wanted was to visit the monastery? His answer, as far as I could make out, was that I might go the other way in the afternoon if I so wished, or even tomorrow, but now I must climb the hill.

In these matters I am of an accommodating disposition, and so I walked obediently past the *plateia* and up the *strada*, which led towards some woods. Then I came upon a sign saying 'Winery Monastiri Zitsa' that pointed down a gravel track, so I went along and found a big modern building.

'This,' I thought, 'is clearly a modern monastery built to replace an old one and here the monks live by making wine, as Benedictines live by concocting Benedictine.' One of the gates was latched but not locked so I went in and wandered about, hoping to find a monk to tell me more, but it was deserted. I found heaps of bottles but no people.

'Well,' I thought, 'I suppose this is what the landlord meant me to see. I shall tell him it was shut.' Then I photographed it respectfully and went to cool off under the trees.

At that point a party of four people and a dog went striding past going further up the hill. They looked neither left nor right, and there was something so purposeful about their progress that I thought they must know something that I did not. So, at a distance of some fifty yards, I followed.

The road became a track through cool pinewoods and led to an old, solitary and derelict-looking stone building. On it was a sign saying 'Monastery of Prophitis Ilias'. In the wall was a plaque with an inscription in Greek which, literally translated, reads:

In this Monastery there stayed
on the 12 and 13th of October 1809
Lord Byron

Then in English under that:

Monastic Zitsa, from thy shady brow
Thou small but favoured spot of holy ground.

How wise the landlord had been! This was exactly what I had come to Zitsa to see. How right to deflect me from the monastery of the Holy Fathers which had nothing to do with Byron, to the monastery of Prophitis Ilias, which had everything to do with him. It became one of those occasions when a shivering thrill of excitement runs down the spine. I wanted to dance and sing, but I cannot sing and am no good at dancing, so more soberly I entered into discussion with the party that I had been following.

This consisted of a middle-aged couple who were German, two young men who were Greek, and a dog who was Alsatian, but Greek with it. The young men spoke excellent English and were most helpful, as follows:

1. The building I had photographed was not a modern monastery but was the local wine co-operative. They call it the Monastic Winery merely to give it a name.

2. The monastery of Prophitis Ilias was abandoned and shut, so we could not go in. We could peep through a crack at an overgrown garden (which we took it in turns to do). The door was opened once a year during the wine festival, but that was all.

3. The considerable building works going on nearby were to do with the wine festival. A big marble platform was the base of the bandstand from which the band would play. An arched ecclesiastical-looking structure was the place from which wine would in future be dispensed. Some rather tumbledown wooden sheds which had served for this purpose up to now were to be swept away and the whole thing brought up to date.

After they had told me all this they went their way but I stayed there. I was deeply thrilled and moved. There was a pair of huge old oak trees that must have been there in 1809, and I thought of Byron riding between them and then hobbling about on his poor lame club foot. His friend E. J. Trelawny thus describes

> the peculiarity of his gait. He entered a room with a sort of run, as if he could not stop, then planted his best leg well forward, throwing back his body to keep his balance. In early life whilst his frame was light and elastic, with the aid of a

> stick he might have tottered along for a mile or two; but after he had waxed heavier he seldom attempted to walk more than a few hundred yards without squatting down or leaning against the first wall, bank, rock or tree at hand.

At the time of his visit to Zitsa Byron was 21 years old, so I suppose that his frame was still light and elastic, and he was up to tottering a mile or two.

Anyway, what Byron saw then I was seeing now, except for the inside of the monastery. Then, to my great delight, I *did* succeed in getting inside. After strolling through the woods I thought I should walk as far round the outer wall of the monastery as possible, and found that on one side there was a big gap. There were signs of restoration work going on, and the builders had simply knocked a hole in the wall for the convenience of getting their materials in and out. All I had to do was to scramble over a few blocks of marble and a pile of cement and there I was, walking in the garden where Byron and Hobhouse had walked, and climbing the stairs which they had climbed. There was no one to tell me to stop it, so of course I photographed it all very freely to prove the point, and came away delighted.

The peace and prosperity of Zitsa is something new. Hobhouse writes:

> We went into the monastery, after some parley with one of the monks, through a small door plated with iron, on which the marks of violence were very apparent, and which, before the country had been tranquillised under the powerful government of Ali, had been frequently battered in vain by the troops of robbers, then by turns infesting every district.

This tranquillity was obtained at a price. The village priest complained to Hobhouse in the most unhappy terms about the exorbitant taxes demanded from them.

> The annual sum of 13,000 piastres being paid, they had hardly sufficient remaining out of the produce of their labour, to support themselves and their children. Employed in the cultivation of a rich soil, and in the tending of numerous flocks, their wine, their corn, their meat, their fleeces and skins, and even the milk of their sheep and goats, all were to be sold to raise so exorbitant a tax; they were starving in the midst of abundance; their labour was without reward, their rest without recreation; even the festivals of their church were passed over uncelebrated, for they had neither the spirits nor the means for merriment.

This pathetic description entirely reconciles me to the current opulence of Zitsa and the lack of anything picturesque in the housing line.

As for me, that night there was the matter of dinner to be dealt with. On the terrace of the pension there was a grill where they were fiddling about with the bottled gas. Once they had got that arranged to their liking they would, I gathered, be ready to cook. The next step was to choose a table where I should be able to see the sun dip behind the mountains without it shining directly in my eyes. This I achieved by trial and error, and then a young waiter drew up a chair, sat down, and said in excellent English: 'Mr Enfield, what would you like for your dinner?'

This may not seem surprising, but in terms of my visit to Epirus the waiter at Arta spoke in such terms, but no one else. Without difficulty we settled upon grilled fillet of veal and fried peppers, and moved on to the wine.

'The wine of Zitsa is famous,' said I, 'so what do you recommend?'

'We have a home-made wine,' came the reply.

That was an unforeseen complication. I had intended to throw economy to the winds and sample one of the finer vintages of the monastic winery.

'Is it white or red?' I asked, thinking that whichever it was, I should say I wanted the other and get out of it that way.

'Rosé,' he replied, so there I was caught, as you might say, upon the horns of a compromise. I had an indistinct idea that under the rules of Greek hospitality it would be ungracious to resist, so I surrendered.

'Fine,' I said. 'Can I have a bottle now?'

Away he went and came back with a paper tablecloth, a glass of water, a wineglass and a bottle of beer. Or so it looked.

'That isn't wine,' I said. 'It is beer.'

'No, it's not.'

'You're joking?'

'No,' he said, and added helpfully, 'we wash the bottles first.'

So he snapped the top off what was to all appearances a bottle of Heineken lager complete with label, and poured out a little pink liquid, which frothed and bubbled in the glass. There was nothing wrong with it, in fact it was quite pleasant, and had I drunk it blindfolded I might have thought it was a dry cider. It had an agreeable effect, did me no harm, and made me wonder how many Health and Safety, Food Labelling and Trading Standards regulations would have been broken in England by a public restaurant that served home-made wine out of a beer bottle labelled Heineken.

By the time I had finished my dinner the large landlord had appeared in order to take over the grill, which seemed to require his personal attention. I tried to pay him for my dinner, but, 'Tomorrow,' he said emphatically, drawing heavily on his reserves of English. When it came to tomorrow the total bill for room and dinner was 8,000 drachmas, which made the price of the dinner about £6. I cannot say whether the home-brew was charged for or was just a present, because he did not bother with any paperwork but waved his hands about and plucked the figure of 8,000 drachmas out of the air in the manner of a conjuror.

As I was so thoroughly well satisfied with every aspect of my Zitsa visit, I should perhaps warn you that Edward Lear said 'the view from Zitsa, to speak plainly, disappointed me.' Only a thorough soaking he had suffered in a violent storm could have brought on such a heretical perspective, and Byron of course rose above it. After dinner I retired to my balcony to watch the mountains glowing pink in the twilight. They were spread out in succeeding eminences one behind the other, and I counted seven different ranges at receding distances, or there might have been eight if what I took to be cloud on the furthest horizon was actually yet more mountains. Either way, disappointment was out of the question.

The issue now was how to get back to Igoumenitsa in order to get back to Corfu in order to get home. The distance from Zitsa to Igoumenitsa was perhaps a little over 50 miles, and thinking back on the journey from Arta I did not relish the thought. It was as hot now as it had been then, if not hotter. The road looked very hilly on the map. There was no charitable river to smooth my path through the mountains. There was no hotel between here and there, or so the Ioannina Tourist Office had assured me, and there was nothing I particularly wanted to see en route. After balancing all these arguments against the simple desire to complete the whole circuit by bicycle and no other means, I came to the conclusion that this was again a case for an easy way out. So I rode from Zitsa back to Ioannina and went to Igoumenitsa by bus, taking the bicycle with me.

At the time I did not regret this decision. I felt a bit feeble at first because there was nothing daunting about the first twelve miles or so, but then the road turned upwards with a vengeance. Just as the sun reached its zenith and the world reached boiling point I should have been toiling up a seemingly interminable climb with the prospect of plunging down the other side and then doing it again. Possibly I was right but I am not entirely sure. It is a funny thing, but hills always seem worse from a bus than they do from a bicycle. I have often gone by bus over ground that I have traversed before by bike and marvelled how I did it, though at the time it didn't seem too bad. I shall never know whether I was right or wrong.

At Igoumenitsa the ferry was waiting and in a couple of hours I was back at the Ol pic Hotel in a different room, this time with hot water coming out of the tap on the left with the red blob. Then I set about exploring Corfu further, and it grew on me still more. I climbed over the New Fortress, so called, in spite of its having been built in 1577, to distinguish it from the Old Fort or Citadel. The day was Sunday and the town very quiet so the various chambers, stairways and outlooks of the New Fortress were, apart from me, deserted. I came down into the Esplanade and found they were playing cricket. Such cricket! They were most fearfully sporting. They clapped every run and every neat bit of fielding. The bowler took the batsman's middle stump out and the entire fielding side enquired politely of the umpire 'How's that?' and did not leap about, punch the air or kiss each other. One batsman absolutely walked on an LBW appeal, an example of gentlemanly conduct which I think has quite gone out in the rest of the world, though it could possibly survive on the playing fields of Simla and Peshawar. The area of grass was rather small, and one side of the out-field was a car park, with a couple of fielders stationed on the tarmac, one of them leaning on a parked car. I watched entranced for quite some time, then wandered on. I strolled among tiny alleys, climbed steps, found churches and might have been in Venice if there had been canals and no hills. Then, as it was now evening, I went in search of the wine of Zitsa.

Somewhere among the many restaurants in the many alleys was one which called itself a Wine Restaurant, so I went in.

Had they got wine from Zitsa?

No they had not!

Did they know where I might find it?

No they did not.

For me this was becoming an obsession. I had been put off by the miniskirt in Ioannina; I had been fobbed off with home-brew in Zitsa; in Corfu it seemed to be unobtainable. Then I applied to a restaurant in a square close to the town hall. On their wine list they had Cuvée de Balthazar from Zitsa at the staggering price of about £9 the bottle. So I had it, and very good it seemed to be – certainly a great advance on the rosé from the Heineken beer bottle in Zitsa itself. I am no wine-bibber, no connoisseur of whatever degree of affectation, unable to trot out the sort of phrases that are commonplace among wine writers. I cannot tell you that the wine of Zitsa had a complex nose of apple, pear and damson, followed through with melon and dough flavours and a spectacular chewy finish. All I say is that I have had bottles of white wine in Greece often enough, and this was a long way in advance of the rest. I did not finish the bottle so they carried it off, promising to write my name on it and keep it carefully in the hope and expectation that I would be back to drink the rest of it.

I shouldn't be surprised if I had hit upon the swishest place in Corfu. The meal of olives, tsatsiki and something they described as 'melange of fish' came to the unheard of total of 9,500 drachmas, or about £19. The exchange rates being what they were, a man who awarded himself a dinner costing £19 could only be regarded as a rake, reprobate and roué, so I felt rather ashamed.

All through this trip I had been keeping a sort of mental inventory or score sheet of places that my wife would like to visit with me on another occasion, on the lines of 'Corfu – yes; Parga – yes; Ioannina – maybe; scrambling up the castle at Suli – not likely!' Thinking that a proper reconnaissance would include some scouting among seaside aspects of Corfu, I set off next morning for a place called Palaiokastritsa. This I had chosen because it was said to be a possible site for the twin ports of the Phaeacians and the Gardens of Alcinous in the *Odyssey*. For those who don't know the story, Odysseus, having made a raft and sailed away from the amorous embraces of the nymph Calypso, is washed up on the shore of the Island of the Phaeacians, which is nowadays taken to be Corfu. He is discovered by Nausicaa, the daughter of King Alcinous, taken to her father's palace and later sent on his way back to his home in Ithaca. If there were any physical features or other resemblances to the descriptions of Homer of this episode, a wise man would try to visit them.

On the way to Palaiokastritsa I passed through a Corfu which was more like the one I had originally envisaged. Beside the road there were uninviting hotels, put there for no sensible reason that one could detect. There were some hot, tired people walking to supermarkets and other hot, tired people sitting at bus stops, and they did not look as if they were enjoying themselves at all. Nor should I, in their place.

Palaiokastritsa turned out to be potentially lovely and actually pretty awful. The sea views are superb, the beaches rocky or stony, the water clean and clear. I got a pleasant room overlooking all this, above a taverna. That is the up-side. The down-side is that all along the road one taverna jostles up against the next, with an occasional hotel interposed. The road itself swarmed with mopeds – people riding mopeds, people pushing broken-down mopeds, pick-up trucks retrieving disconsolate people with hopelessly out-of-action mopeds. When I went to look for dinner, every taverna was crammed with English people who spoke loudly, perhaps to make themselves heard above the piped music. They all appeared to be intimate friends of the waiters, with whom they exchanged unceasing badinage, and they all seemed to watch *Watchdog*. They did not kiss me, but they shook my hand and asked facetiously where I had hidden Anne Robinson.

In the time between my arrival and the eating of as good a dinner as was ever spoiled by blaring music, I swam three times and made a conscientious effort to see what the guidebook meant about the Phaeacians. Above Palaiokastritsa, it says, is a village called Lakones from which it is alleged that you get a superb view and can see what may have been the twin ports of the Phaeacians and the site of the Gardens of Alcinous. No doubt I could have got such a view if I could have found Lakones, but there were no signs to it and nobody had ever heard of it. I went up a hill above Palaiokastritsa but I never came to Lakones. I saw lots of little inlets which might once have been ports, and nothing to suggest a garden.

Bishop Wordsworth, he who found Dodona, gives it up, saying 'the topographer will not find it an easy task to discover the natural objects connected in the *Odyssey* with the city of Alcinous.' Quite so; my experience exactly.

The next day the last part of the ride back to Corfu was hot, dusty and nasty so I got back in a disagreeable mood, having observed at close quarters the corrupting effects of tourism. All that was put right that evening. I went back to drink the rest of my expensive wine and to try to keep the bill down to a more reasonable figure. As I was eating I noticed the sound of music but did not take much notice. Then as I was walking away past the town hall, properly called the Demarcheion, a Greek lady announced that the next part of the evening's entertainment would be traditional Corfiot dances. On the whole I don't like traditional dances. I don't like morris dancers, and these dancers looked very much that way inclined, but I did them an injustice. My doubt about morris dancing is that it always seems a bit bogus, but this somehow was entirely genuine, in spite of the antique costumes.

The young ladies of the troupe wore rather Alpine-looking dresses and linked themselves together with red handkerchiefs. They circled and stamped gravely and sedately, and I thought of Zalongo and the women on the cliff, so I quite enjoyed their performance. Then five men took over, and they were something different altogether. Each wore black trousers, a red shirt, black waistcoat, black cap and a red or white sash. Each had a silver watch in his pocket and a silver watch-chain across his waistcoat. They leapt, they capered, they slapped the soles of their feet, they circled, they crouched, they snapped their fingers. They laid their arms together at shoulder height and swayed to and fro in intricate steps. They danced with such vigour and uninhibited enthusiasm that we cheered. We could not help it, the crowd just had to cheer. Old men cry easily and the tears were running down my cheeks for a reason which will sound strange, but their dancing seemed to embody the spirit of a nation which never signed a treaty with the Turks, which fought the Italians to a standstill and which kept up a heroic resistance to the Germans in spite of the most savage reprisals. It quite wiped away the unhappy impression left by tourist-ridden Palaiokastritsa.

The name of the square where this takes place must be written up somewhere but I could not find it. It can be found by turning up from Eugenios Voulgaris Street and is, as I have said, at the back of the Demarcheion. There is said to be a cultural performance every Tuesday evening in the summer, and a choir came on after the dancers but I did not stay to listen, fearing it might be an anticlimax.

I had a little more time to spend in Corfu, and the more time I spent, the more I became confirmed in the idea that it is my favourite Greek town. Those who have been on holiday at some coastal villa and made no more than a day trip to the capital have not had enough time to realise its full merits. The great attraction of Corfu is that there is nothing *difficult* about it. You can easily walk everywhere. Walking through the Venetian streets is a pleasure in itself, and strolling through eucalyptus groves beside the sea is a delight. There are, furthermore, no difficult paintings in Corfu – neither exhausting collections of Holy Families and Saint Sebastians, as in Siena, nor miles of Post

Impressionists, as in Paris. There is, on the other hand, a little gallery rather cleverly concealed behind the Palace of Saint Michael and Saint George, with a simple collection of pictures by Corfiot artists, all very pleasant to look at and including several fine portraits and one or two history pictures.

The Palace houses a collection of Asiatic Art, and if you have any interest in Asiatic Art you should visit it; if you have no interest you should visit it anyway, as to my mind the building is better than the exhibition. It has splendid spacious State Rooms befitting the dignity of former British High Commissioners, with wonderful floors and ceilings and pillars and staircases.

Corfu is also well supplied with statues, and I think statues are a kind of barometer of the level of civilisation. The many noble bronzes to be found in English cities are a sign of what we once were, and those examples of municipal art which are springing up now are a sign of what we have become. The Corfu statues are, at the very least, interesting. Outside the Palace stands Sir Frederick Adam, veteran of Waterloo and the second High Commissioner. Private William Wheeler, who served under his command, describes him as 'very passionate'. When a wrong command was given on parade, 'he discharged a volley of oaths at the Sergeant, then threw his gold snuff box at him.' In a garden near to the Old Fort you will find Lord Guilford, an extremely eccentric classical scholar who founded the university and went around dressed as Socrates, as his statue shows. You will also find a statue of John Capodistrias, the first President of Greece, but for a real feast of sculpture you need to go to the Achilleion.

This is a palace built in 1890 for Empress Elizabeth of Austria. To sneer at the Achilleion is, or was, the fashion, but what with the rehabilitation of Art Nouveau and Art Deco and all that, I think the fashion is due for a change. Henry Moore called it 'an abomination in the face of nature' and Lawrence Durrell 'a monstrous building surrounded by gimcrack sculptures' but I thought it was great. There are beautiful gardens, a handsome semi-neo-classical white building, huge rooms, statues everywhere, superb views. It is now a casino and enough money spills over from the gaming tables to keep it all in tip-top condition. The set-piece picture of Achilles dragging the dead Hector around is a bit over the top, but if I had been Kaiser Wilhelm II, I would have done as he did and come for a holiday every year.

On the way home to England, greatly to my disappointment, nothing of any interest happened. I got no special treatment at the airport. Nobody made a fuss over me on the aeroplane. My bicycle was obliged to rough it just as much as I. It occurred to me, as I sat squashed up in my aisle seat with a stewardess banging into me every few minutes, that throughout the whole of this expedition to Epirus I had not met another cyclist. You might think that we cyclists have a sort of Freemasonry among ourselves and exchange tips and information, like tramps. There may be such a feeling in some quarters, but I do not share it. I am the sort of tourist who likes to go where there are no other tourists, and to cycle where cyclists are a rarity.

In all my travels in Greece, France, Ireland, Poland and Germany the only one other cyclist with whom I have exchanged more than a few words is the Australian Pate (short for Pater). He and I had actually had dinner together, and our acquaintance must have extended over at least eight hours, but otherwise I go alone in order to enjoy solitude. Lord Byron has come into these pages from time to time, and I am very much of his mind when he wrote, 'I only go out to get me a fresh appetite for being alone.'

I put this before you as an added merit of Epirus. Although you will see plenty of tourists at Igoumenitsa and Parga, they seem to be a comparative rarity elsewhere, and none of them were on wheels.

The Road to Mesolongi

The BBC then took a hand and suggested that I should make three half-hour radio programmes. I was to go round Epirus again, but this time would I also please follow Byron and Hobhouse southwards as far as Mesolongi. 'Very well,' I said, or words to that effect, and set off.

Their journey through Acarnania started at Vonitza on the southern shore of the Ambracian Gulf. 'Vonitza' says Hobhouse, 'is a small town inhabited by Greeks, whose chief trade consists in Boutaraga, or the roes of fish, salted and pressed into rolls like sausages. The fortress is garrisoned by a small body of Albanians.' The trade in fish-roe sausages seems to have lapsed, but the fortress is still there, and an old gentleman who was drinking coffee advised me to go to the town hall and ask if it was open. There a young lady who said her name was Nancy insisted that I meet the mayor, and took me along to be introduced.

His Worship, if that is what you should call a Greek mayor, immediately and with some ferocity demanded the return of the Elgin Marbles. This was a situation which might have led to unpleasantness, but I am equipped to deal with it. Should it happen to you, just say 'Symphony'. Don't say anything else, just say 'Symphony' (like Beethoven's Fifth Symphony) over and over again, whether or not you believe that the marbles should be here or there. It is like Alan Bennett's advice to anyone going backstage to visit an actor after a performance – you should just keep saying 'Marvellous'. Don't say anything else or you may get into hot water, just keep saying 'Marvellous'. In the same way you will find that if you just say 'Symphony', which expresses complete agreement with whatever the other party may be saying, you will defuse the situation without the need for discussion or argument.

It calmed the mayor down wonderfully. The castle was open and at my disposal. He hoped the BBC would publicise Vonitza as a desirable holiday resort. He denied absolutely that Byron had ever been there, but said at Mesolongi Byron had many mistresses to whom he wrote passionate letters, which were still extant. He spoke almost as if he had these letters in his pocket, or at least in his desk drawer, but when I expressed great interest in such letters he became less certain. Under close examination by means of Nancy, who spoke excellent English, he gave a general indication that they were at Mesolongi. I am afraid that I do not believe in these letters, which I think were invented in a fit of overanxiety to be helpful because of the sound position I had taken up on the matter of the Elgin Marbles.

The Venetian fortress was delightfully empty. Poppies were blooming freely inside, and there were no workmen, no attendants at the gate, certainly no visitors. It has a fine view over the town and the walls are in very good shape. That is about the best I can do to gratify the mayor by publicising Vonitza as a tourist spot. All right for a night stop, but not a place to linger, I would say.

The next point on the route was to be Loutraki, which Hobhouse called Utraikee. This involved a brief and fairly level ride with glimpses of the Ambracian Gulf coming and going on the left. Here Byron and his party, which now included a guard of 37 soldiers, spent the night:

> At Utraikee there was only a custom-house and a barrack for soldiers, both of stone, close to each other, and surrounded on every side, except to the water, by a high wall. In the evening the gates were secured, and preparations were made for feeding our Albanians. A goat was killed, and roasted whole, and four fires were kindled in the yard, round which the soldiers seated themselves in parties. After eating and drinking, the greater part of them assembled round the largest of the fires, and whilst ourselves and the elders of the party were seated on the ground, danced round the blaze to their own songs, with astonishing energy. All their songs were relations of some robbing exploits. One of them, which detained them more than an hour, began thus –
>
> 'When we set out from Parga, there were 60 of us,'
>
> then came the burden of the verse,
>
> 'Robbers all at Parga!
> Robbers all at Parga!'

> and as they roared out this stave, they whirled round the fire, dropped, and rebounded from their knees, and again whirled round as the chorus was again repeated. The rippling of the waves on the pebbly margin where we were seated, filled up the pauses of the song with a milder, and not more monotonous music.

Three verses of *Childe Harold* are devoted to this scene, with lines like:

> For ere night's midmost stillest hour was past,
> The native revels of the troop began;
> Each Palikar his sabre from him cast,
> And bounding hand in hand, man link'd to man,
> Yelling their uncouth dirge, long danced the kirtled clan.

A Palikar, as Byron helpfully explains in the note, is 'A general name for a soldier amongst the Greeks and Albanese.'

Loutraki is not now a place you either arrive at or pass through; you have to turn off the main road to get at it, and time has passed it by. There are a few more houses than Hobhouse says, but not many. There is a tap for public use out of which no water comes. The only people to appear were a shepherd who said he was Albanian and spoke no Greek; an old lady who had never heard of Lord Byron but complained about the tap, perhaps thinking I was from the water board; and a farmer who vehemently denied that Byron had ever been there. He was wrong. There is a wall, a crumbling and neglected wall, but still a wall which obviously once enclosed the custom house and barrack on three sides. I passed through the gateway and gazed at a patch of scrub where once the goat was roasted and the Albanians drank and danced, then I paused to record for the BBC 'the rippling of the waves upon the pebbly margin' where the travellers sat.

From Loutraki I struck inland to Katouna, on a road which looked from the map as if it might be uncomfortably hilly, but was not. Hobhouse says they travelled 'amongst thick forests' but these have disappeared and given way to a mixture of scrub and tobacco fields. Katouna, which was a place of twenty houses in 1809, is a lot bigger now, and prosperous because of the tobacco farming.

I had supposed that their next stopping place, which Hobhouse calls Makala, had become that place marked on the map as Machairas, but this did not exactly correspond with Hobhouse's description. He said it was four hours' ride from Katouna, which makes it twelve miles, but on the map Machairas looked much further. I asked a lady at Katouna if she knew where Makala might be, and she said, 'Further on.' So I went further on and arrived at a sizeable village called Phyties.

'Where,' I asked, 'is Makala?'

'Here,' they replied. 'This is it!'

'Then why is it called Phyties?'

'That is the Greek name. Makala is the old Turkish name.'

For no very good reason the fact that I had found Makala in spite of the name change felt like a little triumph, as if I had solved a difficult clue in the *Daily Telegraph* crossword. In terms of triumph though it was as nothing compared to what took place subsequently.

You are to picture me, if you will, sitting outside a *cafeneion* surrounded by a small group of sheep, goat and tobacco farmers. I had said, 'Good day,' in my taped Greek, and received a curt acknowledgement.

Nervously I raised the subject of Lord Byron. Did they

know anything about Lord Byron, the English poet and philhellene?

'No, we do not. Our business is with sheep, not with literature.' (*Provata* not *Grammata* – it has a good ring to it in Greek.)

'You would not then be aware that he came this way in 1809?'

'No.' But one of them then said grudgingly that if I wished to know about Byron I should go to Mesolongi.

Seizing upon this admission of at least some knowledge, I persevered. 'He definitely came here in 1809. It says so in this book. As you can see, it is a very old book,' and taking up my copy of Hobhouse I gave an impromptu rendition into Greek of the passage in question, skipping lightly over such words as were beyond my vocabulary. It came out something like this: 'Makala is a well-built stone village containing about forty houses. The houses we saw were much better than any we had seen in the villages of Albania.' (I think they liked that bit.) 'The one we slept in at Makala had very much the appearance of one of those large houses that are to be met with in England.' (Hobhouse actually says 'One of those mansion houses that are to be met with in the bottom of the Wiltshire Downs' but that would have been too difficult for all parties.) 'The whole,' I continued, 'was surrounded by a very high wall, which was perfectly necessary in a country frequently overrun by large bands of robbers.' Mashallah! as Disraeli would have put it. A first-rate miracle took place, the ice melted in a moment; they smiled broadly. 'Of course we know about *that*! If that is what you want to see, we will gladly show you. The house you have described belongs to this man here. We will take you to see it.'

We walked. Acarnanian tobacco farmers walk in a manner

reminiscent of gun-slingers in a spaghetti Western, with a great deal of style and movement of the hips, but not a lot of forward progress. This is not because they have been watching too much television, but is an inheritance. It is the Albanian walk of their northern neighbours, as exactly described by Byron in a note to *Childe Harold*: 'Their manner of walking is truly theatrical; but this strut is probably the effect of the capote, or cloak, depending from one shoulder.' They have discontinued the capote but kept the strut.

In this leisurely manner we advanced. We found almost precisely what Hobhouse described, although in a ruinous state. We clambered among thistles and nettles into a dilapidated stone-built mansion, no doubt similar to those found in the Wiltshire Downs. All round were the remains of a stone-built wall. 'He with whom we lodged' Hobhouse wrote, 'was a grave important gentleman, calling himself a merchant and keeping a secretary.' This was clearly a merchant's house where I was standing, because it answered exactly to Hobhouse's description of such houses in Ioannina: 'Large and well-built, containing a courtyard, and having warehouses or stables on the ground, with an open gallery and the apartments of the family above.' This one had contained two courtyards, and even in its derelict state it had the rickety remains of the gallery and family apartments above. The warehouse or stables below are now used to house goats, but nevertheless it deserves to have a plaque put upon it like the one at Zitsa. If anyone from the Byron Society would like to get in touch with me I shall be pleased to give them any help I can.

As we were making our stately way back to the *cafeneion*, a priest was decanted from the passenger seat of a pick-up truck. Word had reached him that something was going on, and he had come to see about it. He was a man of immense learning who had been a headmaster but was now quartered in this little village, I suppose being semi-retired. In this situation I fear that his learning was rather a burden to him, and as he can have had little scope to unload it onto men whose business was with sheep and not books, he seized the opportunity of discharging it onto me. He talked rapidly, volubly, incessantly, and I had little idea of what it was all about, although it was clearly very friendly and intended to be helpful. At one point I summoned all my powers of concentration and seemed to make out that he was telling me that some time after the Battle of the Granicus in 334 BC Alexander the Great had caught a cold from plunging into the river Cydnus and would have died but for the skill of his physician, who came (he seemed to say) from Phyties, or Makala, as you prefer. That, I may say, emerged quite late on in his lecture so possibly he had started further back, even perhaps at the Trojan Wars. I was rapidly reduced to nodding and smiling while he continued his harangue over the coffee, which I had proposed that we take but for which he insisted on paying. The tobacco farmers accepted this cheerfully, saying that the money came from God.

In the *cafeneion* there was one man who spoke a little English. As a way of reciprocating the flattery commonly paid to my Greek, I complimented him on the elegant fluency with which he used our language.

'Where did you learn your English?'

'I was for many years in South Africa.'

'What were you doing in South Africa?'

'I had a restaurant. It was very successful, and I made a lot of money.'

'Did you like South Africa?'

'Very much – better than Greece.'

'Why did you come back?'

'Because I became a smuggler and was caught. They did not put me in prison, but they took my business and all my money and sent me out of the country.'

'What were you smuggling?'

'Diamonds.'

He told me this with the air and manner of a man who had made some investments on the Stock Exchange which had turned out badly through no fault of his own.

He was now living in Makala and, he said, helping his brother, by which he must have meant he was helping him to wait for the tobacco to grow. Patience, it seems to me, is the primary requirement for successful tobacco farming. At planting and harvest times there must be a burst of activity, but otherwise the principal requirement is that you should sit in a *cafeneion* all day waiting for it to grow. Only once did I find a farmer anywhere near his tobacco, and that was at nine o'clock in the morning and he was on his way home. I suppose he had made something like a quick social call upon it before retiring to drink coffee. He was very pleased, he said, with his tobacco. The men of Brussels and the EU gave him a handsome subsidy for the production of the weed, which afforded him great satisfaction. They also, of course, give similar pleasure to advertising agents by handing out parallel subsidies for campaigns to stop people smoking the stuff.

From Makala Byron's party passed through forest and

> lighted upon three new-made graves, which, as our Albanians passed, they pointed at, crying out 'Sir, the robbers!' and not long after this on something being seen in the gloom of the woods, they rushed amongst the trees to practise their manoeuvres, but found nothing to attack.

Such robbers were no joke. Hobhouse continues:

> They lie patiently and in dead silence, perhaps for hours, behind stones, in the water-courses, or in the thickets on each side of the road. They suffer their prey to get into the midst of them, when they fire upon them suddenly without rising. The prisoners are gagged and bound and plundered; and if there is amongst them a man of consequence the robbers make him write to his friends for a ransom. If the money arrives they release him; if not they cut off his head.

However, they got safely on to Gouria, and to reach Gouria I had to make a loop, crossing the River Achelous, by a bridge at Katokhi. Hobhouse appends to his text an odd quotation from Colonel Leake, the great topographer. The river here, he says, 'may be compared to the Thames at Staines'. Not at Henley; nor yet at Marlow, you understand, but precisely at Staines. About Gouria itself, Hobhouse says no more than that they passed the night there, but when I arrived there were enormous preparations being made for a wedding. This greatly disgusted a pair of storks whose nest was on the church tower. From time to time they became airborne and flew in circles gnashing their beaks in fury at all the bustle below. The bridegroom came in good time; the bride arrived like an American president in a motorcade with all horns blaring; half the congregation went inside for the service, and half stayed outside chatting, lounging and smoking – at all of which the storks became even more worked up, though I would have thought that by now they should have been used to it. After all, if you choose to make your nest on top of a Greek church, you must expect some measure of disturbance.

The next stop for Byron's party was Natoliko (now Etoliko) and to reach it you cross a lagoon, which they did in punts and I by bridge. They were treated in rather a cavalier fashion by the Albanian governor, who was disinclined to exert himself to find lodgings for them and their soldiers, but they were struck 'by the civility of a Jew physician who told us that he was honoured by our partaking of his little misery.' To be in Etoliko now is not a source of misery in the least. It is a pleasant, unassuming little town, full of agreeable people, with a good and reasonable hotel on the waterfront. The proper thing to do on a Sunday morning, I discovered, is to buy fish and go to church, which is what everyone was doing. 'The water flows through many of the streets, which have wooden causeways on piles,' says Hobhouse, but this problem has been attended to and the roads are perfectly dry.

Some years after Byron's visit, Etoliko was the scene of an episode that illustrates the odd way in which some of the Greek War of Independence was carried on. In 1823 a general by the name of Mustai Pasha assembled an army of about eleven thousand Albanian tribesmen, invaded western Greece and proceeded to lay siege to Etoliko. According to W. Alison Phillips:

> The place was garrisoned by some 600 men, and entirely unfortified. It had, however, a small battery of 6 old-fashioned cannon commanded by William Martin, an English seaman who had deserted from some ship of war, and who succeeded with these in dismounting the only Turkish gun. The Pasha now could do nothing but bombard the place with a couple of mortars, which did but little damage, the garrison, in fact, suffering much more from thirst than from the Ottoman shells. In this strait, the Angel Michael came to their assistance. A bomb from the Turkish mortars fell into the church of the Archangel, shattering the pavement; and lo! from the hole thus made there bubbled up a plentiful spring

> of pure water. Encouraged by this miracle, the Greeks made so stout a resistance that Mustai raised the siege.

I am greatly taken with William Martin, who deserted from some ship or other at some time or other and by some means or other found his way to Etoliko to organise this heroic and gallant resistance. He seems to flash across the pages of history and to disappear, leaving no trace or explanation of how, presumably without a word of Greek, he managed to be there at the right time and take it into his head to put himself in charge and to issue his instructions with such startling success.

There is no monument to the gallant deserter, but as I cycled along by the lagoon I came to a wide expanse of empty gravel with a pillar in the middle. On top was a stained and weather-beaten bronze bust, which to my delight proved to be a memorial to Frank Abney Hastings, one of the great English philhellenes. In his day, men and boys were made of sterner stuff than now, and Frank Abney Hastings (who always seems to be referred to by his three names in full) had fought at the Battle of Trafalgar at the age of 11. He pursued his colourful career by getting himself dismissed from the Navy for challenging a Flag Captain to a duel, and came dashing over to join the Greeks at the beginning of the War of Independence. He endeared himself very much to the Greeks by volunteering to join their naval forces, where he was one of the few foreign philhellenes actually to be of some help, but he was mortally wounded in an unsuccessful attack on Etoliko in 1828.

I was moved to find that this great man had been properly recognised at the place of his last gallant exploit, but his memorial is in a lonely, almost neglected situation on what looks suspiciously like wasteland. One comes across it by accident; it is not mentioned in the Blue Guide; I hope the people of Etoliko are fully aware of its importance.

From Etoliko Byron and Hobhouse sent their baggage by punt to Mesolongi and rode after it on horseback. Once you get to the seaside at Mesolongi you find it all as Hobhouse described it – a wide lagoon, shallow water, fisheries, rows of stakes, remnants of huts on stilts in the water. I will come back to the town itself, but on 23 November 1809, says Hobhouse, 'we left Messalonge having dismissed all our Albanians except one, who was taken into service as a companion to Vassily. His name was Dervish-Tacheere; he was a Turk.'

These two, who Byron calls Basili and Dervish, appear in a note to *Childe Harold*:

> When in 1810, after the departure of my friend Mr H. for England, I was seized with a severe fever in the Morea, these men saved my life by frightening away my physician, whose throat they threatened to cut if I was not cured within a given time. To this consolatory assurance of posthumous retribution, and a resolute refusal of Dr Romanelli's prescription, I attributed my recovery.

If only they had still been in his service when he came back to Mesolongi thirteen years later, they might then have used the same means to save his life a second time.

This was my second visit to Mesolongi. I had been there about fifteen years before, after which I sent a postcard home with the following immortal couplet:

Someone told me Mesolongi was
Not worth a visit. Well how jolly wrong he was!

To this sentiment I strenuously adhere, more so even than the last time, when I made an unaccountably short visit. I then got off the bus and wandered a little way into town, when some small boys accosted me. 'Spiti Vironos!' they cried. 'Spiti Vironos – Byron's house,' and led me to the place where his house once was, but is no more. Next I found my way to the museum, where a schoolmaster was conducting a party around the exhibits, excitedly explaining the many pictures of heroes of the War of Independence. Then, after a quick look at the lagoon, I went and caught another bus, and had been brooding ever since on my folly in not staying longer.

This time I did better – much better – but also I was better prepared. I knew more about Byron and about the War of Independence. Not everybody may wish to share in my enthusiasm for these matters, and a full description might bring on an attack of historical overload. I have therefore consigned to an appendix an account of Byron's later experiences in Greece, from the time he crossed from Mesolongi in November 1809, until he returned there to die in 1824. It is all there if you wish to read it.

All I will say now is that I went again to the site of his house, I lingered ecstatically in the museum, and I discovered the wonderful Garden of the Heroes, dedicated to many of the great men of the War of Independence. Then, having done all the BBC required, I went, with a certain sense of achievement, to the airport and home, with the aid of a car most kindly supplied by the aforesaid BBC.

When I went to hand my bicycle to the airline people, they would not accept it until I had let every last puff of air out of the tyres. I remonstrated with them as best I could, pointing out that the tyres could not possibly burst if they were half – or even three-quarters – inflated, but to no avail. They were in a position to dictate terms, and the result of this act of folly on their part was that when I got back to Gatwick the front tyre would not inflate, owing, I later found, to having a great hole in it.

But this did not matter very much. My wife was there with the car and the bicycle rack to take me home. On the way back I didn't much want to talk about Greece – that could wait – I wanted to know about the children and the phone calls and the letters and whether the man had been to paint the window frames, and that sort of thing. She told me all that and when we got home there was a chicken in the lavatory.

I mention this because it is unusual, as we do not generally keep a chicken in the lavatory. When I went away we had four chickens, but on the night before I got back a fox got in so when my wife went to feed them next morning she found one in shock cowering in the nesting box; two dead; and what she thought was a third corpse till she picked it up, whereupon it flapped feebly. Accordingly she got a box of hay and put the chicken in it on the floor of the lavatory to be snug and warm and on the spot for her to nurse it back to health. She was a good deal annoyed that this had happened, as everything else was in the apple-pie order that she manages to maintain when I am away. The chicken, you will be glad to know, survived and the loss of the other two was the only serious blemish on the whole episode of my absence.

Envoi

There came upon me a delicious sense of peace, a fullness of contentment which I do not believe can be felt by any but those who have spent days consecutively on horseback or at any rate in the open air.

– Samuel Butler, *Erewhon*

Exactly so. Whenever I spend days consecutively in the saddle, though of a bicycle rather than a horse, I get that feeling entirely. If this gives any reader a new thought, and if this book has cast any fresh light on the Greece that was and is, I shall be greatly pleased.

Appendices

Appendix I

'Greek Sailors' from A. W. Kinglake's *Eothen*

Our mate was a Hydriot, a native of that island rock which grows nothing but mariners, and mariners' wives. His character seemed to be exactly that which is generally attributed to the Hydriot race, he was fierce and gloomy, and lonely in his ways. One of his principal duties seemed to be that of acting as counter-captain, or leader of the opposition, denouncing the first symptoms of tyranny, and protecting even the cabin boy from oppression. Besides this when things went smoothly, he would begin to prognosticate evil, in order that his more light-hearted comrades might not be puffed up with the seeming good fortune of the moment.

The wind had been gradually freshening; it now blew hard, and there was a heavy sea running. As the grounds for alarm arose, the crew gathered together in one close group; they stood pale, and grim under their hooded capotes like monks awaiting a massacre, anxiously looking by turns along the pathway of the storm, and then upon each other, and then upon the eye of the captain who stood by the helmsman. Presently the Hydriot came aft, more moody than ever, the bearer of fierce remonstrance against the continuing of the struggle; he received a resolute answer, and still we held our course. Soon there came a heavy sea, that caught the bow of the Brigantine as she lay jammed in betwixt the waves; she bowed her head low under the waters, and gently shuddered through all her timbers – then gallantly stood up again over the striving sea with bowsprit entire.

But where was the crew? It was a crew no longer, but

rather a gathering of Greek citizens; the shout of the seamen was changed for the murmuring of the people – the spirit of the old Demos was alive. The men came aft in a body, and loudly asked that the vessel should be put about, and the storm be no longer tempted. Now, then, for speeches: The captain, his eyes flashing fire, his frame all quivering with emotion – wielding his every limb, like another, and a louder voice, pours forth the eloquent torrent of his threats, and his reasons, his commands, and his prayers; he promises, he vows, he swears that there is safety in holding on – safety, *if Greeks will be brave!* The men hear and are moved; but the gale rouses itself once more, and again the raging sea comes trampling over the timbers that are the life of all. The fierce Hydriot advances one step more near to the captain, and the angry growl of the people goes floating down the wind, but they listen; they waver once more, and once more resolve, then waver again, thus doubtfully hanging between the terrors of the storm, and the persuasion of glorious speech.

Brave thoughts winged on Grecian words gained their natural mastery over terror; the Brigantine held her on her course, and reached smooth water at last.

Appendix II

'A Conversation through a Dragoman' from A. W. Kinglake's *Eothen*

A traveller may write and say that "the Pasha of So-and-So was particularly interested in the vast progress which has been made in the application of steam, and appeared to understand the structure of our machinery – that he remarked upon the gigantic results of our manufacturing industry – shewed that he possessed considerable knowledge of our Indian affairs, and of the constitution of the Company, and expresses a lively admiration of the many sterling qualities for which the people of England are distinguished." But the heap of common-places thus quietly attributed to the Pasha, will have been founded perhaps on some such talking as this:-

Pasha. – The Englishman is welcome; most blessed among hours is this, the hour of his coming.

Dragoman (to the Traveller). – The Pasha pays you his compliments.

Traveller. – Give him my best compliments in return, and say I'm delighted to have the honour of seeing him.

Dragoman (to the Pasha). – His Lordship, this Englishman, Lord of London, Scorner of Ireland, Suppressor of France, has quitted his governments, and left his enemies to breathe for a moment and has crossed the broad waters in strict disguise, with a small but eternally faithful retinue of followers, in order that he might look upon the bright countenance of the Pasha among Pashas – the Pasha of the everlasting Pashalik of Karagholookoldour.

Pasha. – The end of his honours is more distant than the

ends of the Earth, and the catalogue of his glorious deeds is brighter than the firmament of Heaven!
Dragoman (to the Traveller). – The Pasha congratulates your Excellency.
Traveller. – I want to get at his views, in relation to the present state of the Ottoman Empire. Tell him the Houses of Parliament have met, and that there has been a Speech from the throne, pledging England to preserve the integrity of the Sultan's dominion.
Dragoman (to the Pasha). – In England the talking houses have met and the integrity of the Sultan's dominions has been assured for ever and ever, by a speech from the velvet chair.
Pasha. – Wonderful chair! Wonderful houses! – whirr! whirr! all by wheels! – whiz! whiz! all by steam! – wonderful chair! wonderful houses! wonderful people! – whirr! whirr! all by wheels! – whiz! whiz! all by steam!
Traveller (to the Dragoman). – What does the Pasha mean by that whizzing? He does not mean to say, does he, that our Government will ever abandon their pledges to the Sultan?
Dragoman. – No, your Excellency; but he says the English talk by wheels, and by steam.
Traveller. – That's an exaggeration; but say that the English really have carried machinery to great perfection; tell the Pasha (he'll be struck with that) that whenever we have any disturbances to put down, even at two or three hundred miles from London, we can send troops by the thousand to the scene of action in a few hours.
Dragoman. – His Excellency observes to your Highness, that whenever the Irish, or the French, or the Indians rebel against the English, whole armies of soldiers, and brigades of artillery, are dropped into a mighty chasm called Euston

Square, and in the biting of a cartridge they arise up again in Manchester, or Dublin, or Paris, or Delhi, and utterly exterminate the enemies of England from the face of the earth.

Pasha. – I know it – I know all – the particulars have been faithfully related to me, and my mind comprehends locomotives. The armies of the English ride upon vapours of boiling cauldrons, and their horses are flaming coals! – whirr! whirr! all by wheels! – whiz! whiz! all by steam!

Traveller (to his Dragoman). – I wish to have the opinion of an unprejudiced Ottoman gentleman, as to the prospects of our English commerce and manufactures; just ask the Pasha to give me his views on the subject.

Pasha (after having received the communication of the Dragoman). – The ships of the English swarm like flies; their printed calicoes cover the whole earth, and by the side of their swords the blades of Damascus are blades of grass. All India is but an item in the ledger-books of the merchants, whose lumber-rooms are filled with ancient thrones! – whirr! whirr! all by wheels! – whiz! whiz! all by steam!

Traveller. – You can explain that we are a truth-telling people, and, like the Osmanlees, are faithful in the performance of our promises.

Pasha (after hearing the Dragoman). – It is true, it is true:- through all Feringhistan the English are foremost, and best; for the Russians are drilled swine, and the Germans are sleeping babes, and the Italians are the servants of Songs, and the French are the sons of Newspapers, and the Greeks they are weavers of lies, but the English, and the Osmanlees are brothers together in righteousness; for the Osmanlees believe in only one God, and cleave to the Koran, and destroy idols, so do the English worship one God, and abominate graven images, and tell the truth, and believe in a book, and though they drink the juice of the grape, yet to say that they worship their prophet as God, or to say that they are eaters of pork, these are lies, – lies born of Greeks, and nursed by Jews!

Dragoman. – The Pasha compliments the English.

Traveller (rising). – Well, I've had enough of this. Tell the Pasha, I am greatly obliged to him for his hospitality, and still more for his kindness on furnishing me with horses, and say that now I must be off.

Pasha (after hearing the Dragoman, and standing up on his Divan). – Proud are the sires, and blessed are the dams of the horses, that shall carry his Excellency to the end of his prosperous journey. May the saddle beneath him glide down to the gates of the happy city, like a boat swimming on the third river of Paradise. May he sleep the sleep of a child, when his friends are around him, and the while his enemies are abroad, may his eyes flame red through the darkness – more red than the eyes of ten tigers! Farewell!

Dragoman. – The Pasha wishes your Excellency a pleasant journey.

So ends the visit.

Appendix III

Byron and Mesolongi

There is a letter from the Roman writer Pliny in which he says 'The lucky people are those to whom it has been given by the Gods either to do something worth writing about, or to write something worth reading; and the luckiest of all have done both.' Byron was one of the few. He died at the age of 36 leaving behind an international reputation as perhaps the most famous English writer of his time. His poetry occupies eleven volumes on my bookshelf, and his altogether brilliant letters run to another twelve. There was more, in the form of memoirs, but these were destroyed. And yet he wrote once to Thomas Moore saying:

> If I live 10 years longer you will see that it is not all over with me. I don't mean in literature, for that is nothing – and it may seem odd, I do not think it my vocation. But you will see that I will do something or other – the times and fortune permitting.

He certainly did. In Athens you will find, at the edge of the National Gardens, a statue of Byron with a Byron bus stop to go with it. At the Benaki Museum they have his pistols, his travelling desk and much else besides. In the Historical Museum you can see his strange Homeric helmet and his sword. At the National Gallery there is a fine canvas depicting his arrival at Mesolongi. There is a Byron Street running off Shelley Street, but they have difficulty in turning the names from English to Greek and back again, so they appear as Vironos and Sellei streets on the signs. To understand how the lordly English poet became a national hero to the Greek nation you have to have details – some brief, some ample – of the time between his first and second visits to Mesolongi.

Leaving Mesolongi, Byron and Hobhouse went on together to Patras, to Delphi, to Thebes and to Athens, where they arrived on Christmas Day 1809. They stayed till March 1810, exploring Attica and Athens. Byron had a fixed aversion to any displays of enthusiasm and, according to Samuel Rogers, 'When he and Hobhouse were standing before the Parthenon, the latter said "Well, this is surely very grand." Byron replied, "Very like the Mansion House."'

One day at Athens, says Hobhouse, they were 'insulted by a renegade Spaniard, of whom we complained to the Waiwode [from 'voivode', the leader of the army]. Our Spanish friend thereupon was bastinadoed with about fifty strokes on his feet. Whatever I may think of it at home, abroad autocracy has its advantages.'

From Athens they went to Smyrna, where they stayed with a Mr Werry. 'Mrs Werry actually cut off a lock of Byron's hair on parting and shed a good many tears. Pretty well for 56 years at least.' They sailed to the Dardanelles where Byron swam the Hellespont from Sestos to Abydos in imitation of the legendary Leander – something he boasted about forever. At Constantinople they called on 'Mr Canning, a pleasant young man with a bad voice', who was then Secretary to the British Minister, and who was later to play a great part in negotiating the terms of Greek independence. They returned to Athens, and on 17 July 1810 they parted, having been constantly together for just over a year. 'Took leave' says Hobhouse in his diary, '*non sine lacrymis* [not without tears] of this singular young person, on a little stone terrace at the end of the bay, dividing with him a little nosegay of flowers.'

Byron wrote rather differently to his friend Scrope Berdmore Davies:

> sojourned at Constantinople, went into the Black Sea, and got rid of Hobhouse. I determined after one year's purgatory to part with that amiable soul, for though I like him, and always shall, though I give him almost as much credit for his good qualities as he does himself, there is something in his manner etc. in short he will never be anything but the 'Sow's Ear'.

He wrote very differently in the generous dedication of the fourth canto of *Childe Harold* some eight years later where he describes Hobhouse as 'one whom I have known long, and accompanied far, whom I have found wakeful over my sickness and kind in my sorrow, glad in my prosperity and firm in my adversity, true in counsel and trusty in peril – a friend often tried and never found wanting.' Consistency was not something that Byron bothered about, and I have no doubt that both sentiments were entirely genuine.

Byron stayed on in Greece from July 1810 until June 1811. He made a tour of the Peloponnese and caught the fever through which his Albanians nursed him. The winter of 1810/11 he spent in Athens, living in the Franciscan convent, now destroyed. He is supposed to have written some part of *Childe Harold* in the Choragic Monument of Lysicrates, which is still there.

He became, as he says, a 'Tolerable master of the Italian and Modern Greek languages, which last I am also studying with a master'. Then, says Moore, he 'employed himself in collecting materials for those notices on the state of Modern Greece which he has appended to the second Canto of *Childe Harold*.' These seem to me to be remarkable in many ways, not least for their length. In my edition, the poetical part of this Canto occupies 33 pages, but the notes 93. There is an immense appendix on the state of Modern Greek literature, of which the large part is in Greek, sometimes with a translation but often without.

There are also appendices on the general state of Greece as he found it. On the vexed question of whether the latter-day inhabitants were actually Greeks or just a degenerate mongrel race he wrote this:

> The poor Greeks do not so much abound in the good things of this world, as to render even their claims to antiquity an object of envy; it is very cruel to disturb them in the possession of all that time has left them; viz. their pedigree of which they are the more tenacious, as it is all they can call their own.

To this he adds:

> At present, like the Catholics of Ireland and the Jews throughout the world, and such other cudgelled and heterodox people, they suffer all the moral and physical ills that can afflict humanity. Their life is a struggle against truth; they are vicious in their own defence. They are so unused to kindness, that when they occasionally meet with it they look upon it with suspicion, as a dog often beaten snaps at your fingers if you attempt to caress him. 'They are ungrateful, notoriously, abominably ungrateful!' – this is the general cry. Now in the name of Nemesis! For what are they to be grateful? Where is the human being that ever conferred a benefit on Greek or Greeks? They are to be grateful to the Turks for their fetters, and to the Franks for their broken promises and their lying counsels. They are to be grateful to the artist who engraves their ruins, and to the antiquary who carries them away; to the traveller whose janissary flogs them,

> and to the scribbler whose journal abuses them! This is the amount of their obligations to foreigners.

His view of what the Greeks might hope for was limited:

> The Greeks will never be independent; they will never be sovereigns as heretofore, and God forbid they ever should! But they may be subjects without being slaves. Our colonies are not independent but they are free and industrious, and such may Greece be hereafter.

Byron got back to England in July 1811 with much poetry on paper and more in his head. With the publication of the first two cantos of *Childe Harold* he became an instant literary success, and there was much verse to follow that was inspired by his two years in Ottoman Greece. Perhaps the most famous lines he ever wrote are those which are found in the third canto of *Don Juan* beginning 'The Isles of Greece, the Isles of Greece' and developing into a superb lament for the Greek nation:

> The mountains look on Marathon
> And Marathon looks on the sea;
> And musing there an hour alone,
> I dreamed that Greece might still be free.

The enormous success of *Childe Harold* in particular had an effect that was more than purely literary. As Byron makes plain in the note that I quoted earlier, the Greeks up to that time had generally got a bad press from such visitors as there were, whereas he now opened the eyes of Europe to the existence of a brave Christian people, whose reasonable desires for freedom deserved support.

As well as a literary lion, Byron was also an instant social success. Leslie Stephens, in the *Dictionary of National Biography*, says that 'Byron became the idol of the sentimental part of society. Friends and lovers of notoriety gathered round this fascinating rebel.' Lord Macaulay goes further:

> Among that large class of young persons whose reading is almost entirely confined to works of imagination, the popularity of Lord Byron was unbounded. They bought pictures of him; they treasured up the smallest relics of him; they learned his poems by heart, and did their best to write like him, and to look like him. Many of them practised at the glass in the hope of catching the curl of the upper lip and the scowl of the brow which appeared in some of his portraits. The number of hopeful undergraduates and medical students who became things of dark imaginings, on whom the freshness of the heart ceased to fall like dew, whose passions had consumed themselves to dust, and to whom the relief of tears was denied, passes all calculation. This was not the worst. There were created in the minds of many of these enthusiasts a pernicious and abused association between intellectual power and moral depravity. From the poetry of Lord Byron they drew a system of ethics, compounded of misanthropy and voluptuousness, a system in which the two great commandments were, to hate your neighbour, and to love your neighbour's wife.

It was all too good, if that is the word, to last. Byron made an unsuccessful marriage, and in the murky circumstances of his separation from his wife, popular sympathy was with Lady Byron. There were ugly rumours of an incestuous affair with his half-sister. It seems extraordinary now, but public hostility got to the point that Byron was advised not to go to the theatre or to the House of Lords for fear of insults or even violence. And so, in disgust and in disgrace, he left England again in April 1816, and never came back.

Five years later he was living in Italy, pursuing a complicated liaison with an Italian Countess and dabbling in the affairs of Italian revolutionaries. When the Greek War of Independence broke out in 1821 the Greekness, if there is such a word, was the key to the European reaction. Had it been the Bulgarians or Romanians who were trying to shake off the rule of Turkey, no one except possibly the Russians would have lifted a finger to help them. On any rational view, the Greeks were rebelling against their legitimate government. Hobhouse himself had written that

> It cannot, perhaps be justly determined that the Ottoman empire in the Levant is now to be called a Usurpation, and that the Greeks, when in revolt, are therefore to be regarded, not as rebels, but as patriots fighting for the recovery of their birthright. If the Grand Signor cannot establish a claim to the throne of Constantinople, I know not of any sovereign in Europe whose title will bear an examination.

But the classical education of the ruling classes of Europe swept all that aside, and while the British government remained wary, the wave of sympathy and support for the supposed descendants of Pericles and Leonidas swept through England. A Greek Committee was formed in London, with Hobhouse in the thick of it. In due course two loans, one with a nominal value of £800,000 and one of £2 million, enormous sums for those days, were raised upon no security except the word of a revolutionary government constantly torn by internal quarrels.

Byron offered himself to the Committee to represent and advise them from Greece itself. Who better? The storm of unpopularity had largely blown itself out, and he was an international celebrity. He spoke Italian fluently, and Greek well. Few men were more knowledgeable about the state of the country than he, and although he hesitated at first, he was not only available but keen, for now his chance had come to show himself something more than a poet. W. Alison Phillips says:

> Even before he publicly announced his intention of joining the Greek cause he had exercised an immense influence in arousing the Philhellenic enthusiasm of Europe; and now that the genius whose fame extended throughout the length and breadth of Christendom proclaimed that he was prepared to devote health and fortune and, if need be, life itself to his ideal of a free Hellas, the eyes of the civilised world were directed with a new interest on the affairs of Greece.

So in the autumn of 1823, he arrived in Greece bringing with him the expectation of large sums from the Greek loan, with a good deal of his own money and a willingness to spend much more. Three weeks before his death he wrote to his banker Douglas Kinnaird: 'The Greek Cause up to the present writing hath cost me of my own monies about 30,000 Spanish dollars *advanced*, without counting my own contingent expenses of every kind.' Thirty thousand Spanish dollars was equivalent to £6,000, say £350,000 at today's rates. Not surprisingly, throughout his time in Greece, Byron was bombarded with demands for money from all sides, the klephtic chiefs being particularly anxious to get their hands on as much as possible.

That word 'klephtic' requires some explanation. When it came to the fighting on land in the War of Independence, most of it was done by bandits. These are more respectfully called klephts, and they deserve some special description not just on their own account but also because, as you go around, you see pictures of them in their white skirts and embroidered waistcoats, and statues of them in heroic poses in town squares. W. Alison Phillips writes:

> To be a klepht was, in the popular view, a glory rather than a disgrace; and for whole decades before the War of Independence the klephts were, in the eyes of their countrymen, the defenders of faith and fatherland against the Turk; though, to tell the truth, they plundered Christian and Mussulman with a commendable impartiality. Owning 'no pasha save the naked sword, no vizier save the gun', they looked down upon the Ottomans, and their 'slaves' with equal contempt. A thousand tales were current of their reckless courage, their cruelty, or their generosity; their deeds of valour against the Turk were sung in countless ballads, and the names of their celebrated leaders repeated from mouth to mouth in awe-struck tones. One thing alone they feared: To fall alive into the hands of the Turks; and their accustomed toast was '*to Kalon Moleevi*' – the welcome bullet which should save them from this fate.
>
> The klephts of the Pindus had a priest attached to the band, whose cell was a huge hollow oak. When they made a captive they would lead him up to the tree, and the chief would say: 'Speak, holy oak, which our fathers reverenced, what should we do with our prisoner?'
>
> 'Is he a Christian?' asked the tree, 'or an unbelieving heathen?' 'Thou knowest, sacred tree, that he is a Christian!' 'Then let our brother go on his way rejoicing, after receiving the kiss of fraternal peace, and dedicating his purse for the relief of the needs of his poor brethren!' If the prisoner was a Mussulman the answer would simply be 'Hang the infidel on my holy boughs and confiscate all he has for the use of the true church and her faithful children.'

It was from men like these that the land forces of the revolution were frequently drawn. Two of the first leaders in the field were Petro Mavromichaelis, generally known as Petrobey, at the head of a gang of war-like robbers from the Mani; and Kolokotrones, a klepht who had served in a Greek regiment in the English service in the Ionian Islands, and who had his head on the 5,000-drachma bank note until he was shouldered aside by the euro. The command of the Greek forces in Attica was later given to Karaskakis, who had been bred a robber in the mountains of Epirus. It was lucky for Greece that such men existed, but they waged war with a mixture of ferocity and greed, remaining robbers to the end. According to one historian, they 'were almost all infamous for the sordid perversity of their dispositions'. Not surprisingly, when Lord Byron arrived he found them difficult men to deal with, but it was acknowledged that centuries of foreign oppression combined with domestic lawlessness could not be expected to have raised the general moral tone, nor was it ever denied that the klephts were often brave in the extreme and scored some great military successes.

To say that Byron found the Greeks in disarray would be a massive understatement. He wrote to his sister that they had

> found leisure to quarrel among themselves, and it is not a very easy part to play to avoid appearing partial to one or other of their factions. You can have no idea what an intriguing cunning unquiet generation they are.

To his Italian mistress Madame Guiccioli he wrote: 'Of the Greeks I can't say much good hitherto, and I do not like to speak ill of them, though they do of one another; but I must attend to the Greek cause both from honour and inclination.'

Many of the philhellenes who arrived in the midst of all this went home in disgust, and very many had better not have come at all. Military men were touchy, quarrelsome and given to duelling, and were, says Thomas Moore, 'from their fantastic notions of rank and etiquette far more troublesome than useful'. They also had a different conception of warfare from the Greek chieftains. Their idea, based upon good order and military discipline, was to advance steadily and to stand firm under attack. The Greek idea was to move forward if winning and run away if losing. The great Kolokotrones, he of the 5,000-drachma note, was aware of this difficulty: 'If Wellington had given me an army of 40,000 I could have governed it, but if 500 Greeks had been given to him to lead, he could not have governed them for an hour.' Byron was to find the truth of this later, when he proposed to lead an attack on Lepanto (now Naupactus) at the head of a brigade of his favourite Suliotes. They declined to follow him on the grounds that Suliotes 'did not like the service against stone walls'.

In spite of doubts and difficulties, Byron never wavered. In January of 1824 he arrived in Mesolongi after a crossing from Zante made dangerous by a gale and a close encounter with the Turkish fleet. Mesolongi was the centre of the Greek war effort in western Greece, and when he arrived, says Moore:

> The whole population of the place crowded to the shore to welcome him: the ships anchored off the fortress fired a salute as he passed; and all the troops and dignitaries of the place, civil and military, met him on his landing, and accompanied him, amidst the mingled din of shouts, wild music and discharges of artillery, to the house that had been prepared for him. 'I cannot easily describe,' says Count Gamba [the brother of Byron's Italian mistress], 'the emotions which such a scene excited. I could scarcely refrain from tears.

Byron came prepared to give his life for Greece. Count Gamba also wrote that 'to an honourable death, in some such achievement as that of storming Lepanto, he looked forward as the most signal and lasting service that a name like his – echoed as it would be, among the watch-words of Liberty from age to age – could bequeath to her cause.' *Dis aliter visum* – the gods decided otherwise. Mesolongi was a dreadfully marshy and unhealthy place, and his friends had pleaded with him not to go there. 'If we are not taken off with the sword we are likely to march off with an ague in this mud basket,' wrote Byron to Charles Hancock on 5 February. 'The dykes of Holland, when broken down, are the Deserts of Arabia for dryness, in comparison.' Thomas Moore reports that ten days later Byron had a convulsive fit – 'his teeth were closed, his speech and senses gone and he was in strong convulsions.' Byron wrote to his sister that the attack 'had a strong appearance of *epilepsy* – why – I know not, for it is late in life – its first appearance at 36.' The day after this attack says Moore, he

> complained much of a sensation of weight in his head. The doctors therefore thought it right to apply leeches to his temples; but found it difficult, on their removal, to stop the blood, which continued to flow so copiously, that from exhaustion he fainted.

Colonel Stanhope, who was an eyewitness to the scene, adds:

> when, faint with over-bleeding, he was lying on his sickbed, with his whole nervous system completely shaken, mutinous Suliotes, covered with dirt and splendid attires, broke into his apartment, brandishing their costly arms and loudly

> demanding their wild rights. Lord Byron, electrified by this unexpected act, seemed to recover from his sickness; and the more the Suliotes raged the more his calm courage triumphed.

'A more undaunted man in the hour of peril never breathed' says Count Gamba.
Both aspects of this episode were typical of the remaining days of his life. Moore says:

> From the period of his attack he more than once complained of vertigos which made him feel, he said, as if intoxicated. He was also frequently affected with shiverings and tremors. At the same time, the demands on his exertions, personal and pecuniary, poured in from all sides. He was met in the details of his duty, by every possible variety of obstruction and distraction that rapacity, turbulence and treachery could throw in his way. Such vexations, too, as would have been trying to the most robust health here fell upon a frame already marked out for death.

Perhaps the most remarkable thing of all was the steadiness with which this sometimes volatile and often dilatory man refused to be discouraged. 'The very firmness', says Moore, 'with which a position so lone and disheartening was sustained serves to increase our sympathy, till we almost forget admiration in pity, and half regret that he should have been great at such a cost.'

He was finally struck down with a 'marsh fever', which I take to mean malaria. On 14 April his doctors again proposed to bleed him, but at first he refused: 'Do with me whatever else you like, but bleed me you shall not,' he said. Finally they wore him down, 'and he cast the fiercest glance of vexation and throwing out his arm, said, in the angriest tone "there – you are, I see, a damned set of butchers, take away as much blood as you like, but have done with it!"' They bled him twice according to Moore – five times according to his valet Fletcher. They blistered his legs, they gave him two doses of 'antispasmodic potion'; he fell into a coma on 18 April 1824, and 24 hours later he was dead. Fletcher, his valet, and Tita, his Italian gondolier, had nursed him continuously.

The Greeks regarded this as the greatest calamity, but Byron's was by no means a wasted death. The difficulties he faced in trying to unite the squabbling factions were probably insuperable, and for the role of military commander he really had no qualifications beyond courage. On his deathbed he said of Greece 'I have given her my time, my means, my health – and now I give her my life – what could I do more?' His death was the best service that he could render, for in sacrificing his life he increased beyond measure the public sympathy and support for the cause that he had taken up.

Mesolongi instantly became famous throughout the world as the place where Byron died, but a year later it achieved a glorious reputation in its own right. The town had been briefly besieged and successfully defended against the Turks in 1822/23 but in 1825 Sultan Mahmoud determined that there should be no second failure. He dispatched Reshid Pasha from Ioannina with 20,000 troops and the warning that if he failed to take Mesolongi, his head would be forfeit.

Partly owing to Byron's efforts, the defences were in good order. There was a garrison of 4,000 men, but there was also a civilian population of 12,000 who were a serious drain on food supplies. On 7 May 1825 the siege began; the town was shelled and largely reduced to ruins; the defenders heroically repelled all attacks; a Hydriot fleet twice got through with fresh supplies, and finally chased away the Turkish fleet; vigorous sorties were made by the garrison, followed by crowds of people with spades and pickaxes to demolish the Ottoman earthworks. By November death and desertion had reduced Reshid's forces to 3,000, and he was pinned down with Mesolongi in front and armed Greeks in the mountains behind. A Turkish fleet arrived in the nick of time to save him from starvation.

Finally, on the Sultan's orders, the Egyptian Ibrahim Pasha came with reinforcements fresh from victory in the Peloponnese, and, says W. Alison Phillips,

> the mere presence of the Egyptian was a wound to Reshid's pride, and Ibrahim rubbed salt into the sore. 'What!' he cried when he saw Mesolongi, 'were you kept out eight months by this fence? Why, I took Navarino in eight *days*!'

He shelled the town for three days and on 28 February 1826 he launched his Egyptians to the attack.

> Three times the Arab guard gained a footing on the wall; three times they recoiled before the furious onslaught of the Greeks; and at midday the attempt was relinquished. Ibrahim was beside himself with rage. Reshid, not altogether displeased, asked him what he *now* thought of the 'fence!'

However, the Turks had got command of the sea and settled to the business of starving the garrison out. Ibrahim offered honourable terms of surrender, which were rejected: 'What the future had in store for them or their foes, they answered, God only knew; but of terms they would have none, and were determined to live, or die, free!'

Mesolongi was now doomed. W. Alison Phillips writes:

> The town was reduced to the most miserable plight. The starved inhabitants wandered amid the ruins of their homes, looking more like ghosts than living men. For days they had been reduced to subsisting upon the most loathsome food; now even rats and mice were luxuries no longer obtainable. The sick and wounded, for whose care it was impossible to make provision, lay in neglect and filth, rotting in a living death. The brave defenders of the shattered walls, weakened by hunger, could scarcely any longer bear the weight of their arms. Yet no voice was raised in favour of surrender.

Notaris Botzares, the Greek commander, resolved on a dash for freedom. He divided the Mesolongiots into two bands, one to attack the camp of Reshid, and the other, with the women and children, to try to cut its way through the Egyptians. The attempt was made on the night of 22 April 1826. As soon as they advanced they were mown down by a murderous fire from the Turkish trenches, for the plan had been betrayed by a Bulgarian deserter. Some managed to fight on, and of all the defenders some 1,300, including a few women and children, eventually reached safety. Many though, in panic, rushed back into the town with the Turks at their heels.

Mesolongi then was given over to sack and slaughter, but not without further deeds of heroism. A lame man sat waiting in the powder magazine with a lighted match, and when the Turks arrived, he blew them and himself to smithereens. The same feat was repeated in the cartridge factory by Christos Capsalis, who sat surrounded by those too old or ill to take part in the sortie. W. Alison Phillips continues:

> Truly, had Byron lived to see this night, he would have admitted, in spite of all his disillusion and disappointment, that at last 'Grecian mothers had given birth to men.'

> The effect of the news was profound. Mesolongi, the scene of Byron's romantic activity, appealed in itself to the imagination of a world which had not yet shaken off the spell of the poet's genius; the defence and fall of Mesolongi then gave an immense impetus to the wave of Philhellenic feeling which was already sweeping all before it throughout Europe. The crimes, the follies, the selfishness of the Greeks were forgotten. The empty coffers of the Greek government continued to be replenished with European gold, and the Greek armies reinforced by European volunteers, till Reshid Pasha could exclaim, with bitterness and with truth, 'We are no longer fighting the Greeks, but all Europe!'

If now you would like to imagine yourself (or if you would rather, imagine me) in Mesolongi, a pilgrim to this place of pilgrimage to which few pilgrims come (at least they don't in May), with a head full of all the moving and stirring matter of which this appendix is comprised – then the place to start is what they call the Old Town Hall. This is a fine neo-classical building housing a superb museum and art gallery. It is very largely given over to Byron and to the siege. There is a copy of the Athens oil painting of Byron's arrival at Mesolongi, to be welcomed by Prince Mavrocordatos, by the Bishop and a man I take to be Notaris Botzares the commander, amidst a crowd of cheering irregular soldiers and wondering women. There is a whole room of Byron prints and pictures of Byronic matters, such as the strange helmets which he brought with him to Greece; there are books, plates, busts, even three Byronic clocks with Byron on top of them.

Then there are great paintings of the siege – one called *The Exodus*, depicting the attempted breakout; one of the Bishop giving Holy Communion to the soldiers beforehand; one of Capsalis about to blow up the cartridge factory. There is a copy of a painting by Delacroix, *Freedom*

Rising from the Ruins of Mesolongi, and another called *The Assault of Ibrahim* in which Ibrahim is depicted on a prancing horse with the powder magazine exploding in the background. Also there are paintings of many Greek heroes, splendidly arrayed in their white kilts and embroidered jackets, their belts bristling with daggers and pistols. And then again, to my great delight, there is a portrait of Frank Abney Hastings, he whose bust I had come across at Etoliko.

After you have drunk in the contents of this superb collection, the next step is to go in search of Byron's house, and here there is a mystery. In trying to unravel it I had a demonstration of something I had been told by a distinguished writer of guidebooks, now dead. 'It's perfectly easy,' he said. 'You just get together a number of books already written about the place, make an amalgam of them, sprinkle it with a few reminiscences from whenever you went there yourself, and the job is done.' It is also said that a famous television personality, whose name I suppress in fear of the libel laws, composed a glowing description of a bridge which had fallen down ten years before he had supposedly walked across it. All of which explains why, if a piece of nonsense creeps into one guidebook, it is likely to be perpetuated by all subsequent guidebooks by other authors.

The mystery of Byron's house and its solution are as follows:

It is agreed that Byron's house no longer exists, but that there is a memorial garden to mark the spot. The Rough Guide, in its annoyingly condescending description of Mesolongi, copies the Blue Guide and says that to find it you go to the *end* of Trikoupis Street and turn left into Levidou Street. No you don't, you only go partway down

Trikoupis Street (the significance of this will become clear) but you do find the garden in Levidou. Both guides say that the house was destroyed in the Second World War. Rubbish!

a) My Baedeker of 1894 says: 'The house in which he lived stands no longer.'

b) The local guidebook (in Greek) says the house was destroyed when Capsalis blew up the cartridge factory in 1826.

c) Simplest of all, if you go there and use your eyes, you find a pillar on which the inscription plainly says that it was erected in 1924, exactly 100 years after the poet's death, upon the site of the house where Byron stayed.

If the house wasn't there in 1894 or 1924, I think we can say with confidence that the Second World War had nothing to do with its disappearance.

So far so good, but now comes a further complication. I have a postcard on which is reproduced a painting in the Benaki Museum at Athens, on the back of which is written 'Lord Byron's House at Mesolongi. Engraving after the painting by W. Purser, 1834.' The problems are:

a) This house as shown in the picture is on the shore of the lagoon, whereas the memorial garden is well inland.

b) If this picture was painted in 1834, how can it depict the house that was destroyed in 1826?

It took me a long time to unravel this conundrum, but I will tell you briefly that W. Purser was in Greece and Italy between 1817 and 1820, and therefore must have worked up the 1834 picture from a sketch that he had made earlier. The fact that he happened to have a sketch of the house where Byron subsequently stayed was just a bit of good luck for him. He showed the house as being beside the lagoon because, at the time he made the sketch, it was;

the memorial garden is no longer beside the lagoon because there has been a lot of land reclamation since then. Whenever the first Blue Guide was written, or whenever that book was written which the first Blue Guide copied, no doubt Trikoupis Street ended near the garden, since when the shore has been pushed back and Trikoupis Street made longer without anyone noticing, except me.

So you may, with perfect confidence, take your stand in the memorial garden in the certain knowledge that here stood the house where the unruly Suliotes burst into the dying poet's bedroom, and from which he tried to reconcile the squabbling factions, and to fend off unreasonable demands for money. A large outer room was given over to his personal bodyguard of 50 Suliotes, and here Count Gamba says he used to walk a great deal, particularly in wet weather, accompanied by his favourite dog Lion. You may, if you wish, pace the paving stones where the house once was, and imagine to yourself the Suliotes, Byron and the dog.

Finally you should make your way to the magnificent Garden of the Heroes. This is lovely in its own right – a cool and spacious garden, planted with mature trees and interspersed with statues and monuments. These are all dedicated to heroes of the War of Independence and in particular to heroes of the great siege. To most of us, most of the names will be unknown, but never mind, the inscriptions (translated for you in the guidebook) speak for themselves:

Skarlatos Spyros: He fell on the islet of Vasiladi on February 25th, 1826.
A. Kolias: He was killed at the 'Terrible' bastion on September 10th, 1825.

Tusias Zervas: A Commander from Souli. He fell in the Exodus (1826).

And so they go on. There are memorials to the foreign philhellenes, to Italians, to Poles, to Frenchmen, to Swedes, to Germans, to Americans, to the Swiss John-Jacob Mayer and to Gustav-Adolf Sess from Finland. There is a general tomb with the bones of many of those killed at the siege, and looking toward this, in pride of place and raised above the rest, stands Lord Byron.

The Blue Guide and the Rough Guide will tell you that the base of this fine imposing statue contains his heart, and I rather wish it was so, but it is not. Byron was buried at Hucknall Torkard in Nottinghamshire, having been refused burial in Westminster Abbey. Had anyone taken so drastic a step as removing his heart and placing it elsewhere, it would be known and mentioned by several authorities, who are, on this point, silent. There is, perhaps, some part of him in Mesolongi. Moore says that the citizens had wanted him to be buried there 'And it was thought it advisable so far to accede to their desires as to leave them, for interment, one of the vessels in which his remains, after embalmment, were enclosed.' According to the local guidebook of the Garden of the Heroes, the vessel that they were given contained his lungs, and this was duly enclosed within the base of the statue. Possibly so. The vessel was first deposited in the church of St Spiridon, and how or whether it survived the siege is not known. Still, the town to its eternal credit has given him glorious recognition.

Here he wrote a poem headed 'On This Day I Complete My Thirty-Sixth Year' and dated 'Missolonghi, January 22nd, 1824'. The first four verses have references to a Greek boy called Lukas Chalandritsanos; the rest of it is plain enough.

'Tis time this heart should be unmoved,
Since other it hath ceased to move:
Yet though I cannot be beloved,
Still let me love!

My days are in the yellow leaf;
The flowers and fruits of love are gone;
The worm – the canker, and the grief
Are mine alone!

The fire that on my bosom preys
Is lone as some Volcanic Isle;
No torch is kindled at its blaze
A funeral pile!

The hope, the fear, the jealous care,
The exalted portion of the pain
And power of Love I cannot share,
But wear the chain.

But 'tis not *thus* – and 'tis not *here*
Such thoughts should shake my Soul, nor *now*
Where glory decks the hero's bier
Or binds his brow.

The Sword, the Banner, and the Field,
Glory and Greece around us see!
The Spartan borne upon his shield
Was not more free!

Awake (not Greece – she *is* awake!)
Awake, my Spirit! think through *whom*
Thy life-blood tracks its parent lake
And then strike home!

Tread those reviving passions down
Unworthy Manhood – unto thee
Indifferent should the smile or frown
Of Beauty be.

If thou regret'st thy Youth, *why live?*
The land of honourable Death
Is here – up to the field, and give
Away thy Breath.

Seek out – less often sought than found –
A Soldier's Grave, for thee the best;
Then look around, and choose thy Ground,
And take thy Rest!

Reading this poem aloud in the Garden of the Heroes made a fitting conclusion to my BBC programme and makes therefore, I trust, a fitting conclusion to this appendix.

Select Bibliography

Of the writing of many books about Byron there is no end, and there is a huge literature about nineteenth-century Greece. I have drawn on a small miscellaneous collection of my own, assembled in a fairly haphazard way over the years.

Baedeker, Karl *Greece – Handbook for Travellers*, 2nd edn (Dulau and Co, 1894)

Bowen, George Ferguson *Glimpses of Eastern Life and Manners: Mount Athos, Thessaly and Epirus – A Diary of a Journey* (Rivington, 1852)

Brassey, Annie *Sunshine and Storm in the East* (Longmans, Green and Co., 1880)

The British Museum *Elgin and Phigaleian Marbles* (M. A. Nattali, 1846)

Byron, Lord *The Works of Lord Byron*, vol. IX (London, Knight and Lacey, 1824)

The Works of the Right Honourable Lord Byron, vols. X and XI (John and Henry L. Hunt, 1824)

Don Juan, vols. I and II (Printed for the Booksellers, 1826)

The Works of Lord Byron in Six Volumes (John Murray, 1827)

The Letters of Lord Byron, ed. R. G. Howarth (J. M. Dent and Sons Ltd, 1948)

Byron's Letters and Journals Volume I 'In My Hot Youth', 1798–1810, ed. Leslie A. Marchand (Harvard University Press, 1973)

Lord Byron: Selected Letters and Jounals, ed. Leslie A. Marchand (John Murray, 1982)

Davenport, R. A. *The Life of Ali Pasha of Tepeline* (Thomas Tegg and Son, 1837)

Disraeli, Benjamin *Home Letters*, 2nd edn (John Murray, 1885)

Ellingham, Mark (ed.) *The Rough Guide to Greece*, 2nd edn (Routledge & Kegan Paul, 1984)
Hobhouse, John Cam *A Journey through Albania* (M. Carey and Son, 1817; Arno Press and the New York Times, 1971)
Jervis, Henry Jervis-White *The History of the Island of Corfu* (Colburn and Co., 1852; Argonaut Inc., 1970)
Kinglake, A. W. *Eothen*, 2nd edn (John Oliver, 1845)
Kolokotrones, Theodore *The Old Man of the Morea*, tr. Elizabeth M. Edmonds (Unwin, 1892; Hellenic College Press)
Lear, Edward *Journals of a Landscape Painter in Albania and Illyria* (Richard Bentley, 1851)
Edward Lear in Corsica: The Journal of a Landscape Painter (Robert John Bush, 1870; William Kimber, 1966)
Edward Lear: The Corfu Years – A Chronicle Presented through his Letters and Journals, ed. Philip Sherrard (Denise Harvey & Company, 1988)
Leigh Fermor, Patrick *Mani* (John Murray, 1958)
Mahaffy, J. P. *Rambles and Studies in Greece*, 4th edn revised and enlarged (Macmillan and Co., 1892)
Marchand, Leslie A. *Byron: A Biography* (Alfred A. Knopf, 1957)
Moore, Thomas *Letters and Journals of Lord Byron with Notices of his Life* (Baudry's European Library, 1833)
Parry, Maj. Gambier *Sketches of a Yachting Cruise* (W. H. Allen & Co., 1889)
Phillips, W. Alison *The War of Greek Independence* (Smith, Elder & Co., 1897)
Rossiter, Stuart (ed.) *The Blue Guide: Greece*, 2nd edn (Ernest Benn Ltd, 1973)
Thackeray, W. M. *Notes of a Journey from Cornhill to Grand Cairo*, 3rd edn (Smith, Elder & Co., 1865)
Trelawny, E. J. *Recollections of the Last Days of Shelley and Byron* (Edward Moscon, 1858)

Trypanis, C. A. (ed.) *The Penguin Book of Greek Verse* (Penguin, 1984)

Wheeler, W. *Letters of Private William Wheeler 1809–1828*, ed. Sir B. Liddell-Hart (Michael Joseph, 1951)

Williams, H. W. *Travels in Italy, Greece and the Ionian Islands* (Archibald, Constable and Co., and Hurst, Robinson, and Co, 1820)

Wordsworth, Christopher *Greece – Pictorial, Descriptive and Historical*, new edn (John Murray, 1882)

The Hotel on the Roof of the World

Five Years in Tibet

Alec Le Sueur

ISBN : 1 84024 199 3
£7.99 Paperback
129 x 198 mm, 352 pages

Few foreigners have been lucky enough to set foot on Tibetan soil – Alec Le Sueur spent five extraordinary years there, working for an international hotel chain. Against the breathtaking beauty of the Himalayas he unfolds a highly amusing and politically enlightening account of his experiences.

Fly infestations at state banquets, hopeful mountaineers, unexpected deliveries of live snakes, a predominance of yaks and everything yak-related, the unbelievable Miss Tibet competition, insurmountable communication problems and a dead guest are just some of the entertainments to be found at the 'Fawlty Towers' of Lhasa.

Daily challenges are increased by the fragile political situation. Le Sueur, the only foreigner since the days of Heinrich Harrer to spend so long in Tibet, examines its intriguing cultural background, thus providing a fascinating insight into a country that is virtually impenetrable to today's traveller.

Short Walks in Shangri-La

Peter Francis Browne

ISBN : 1 84024 194 2
£7.99 Paperback
129 x 198 mm, 320 pages

Isn't an earthly paradise what everyone's dreams are made of? Should such a utopia exist, surely it would be amongst the mountains of the Himalayas, the writer James Hilton reasoned, and in 1933 he wrote about such a place, the hidden valley of his novel, Lost Horizon. He called it Shangri-La.

Clinging to the vague hope that he'd be able to heave his backpack up the mountains, let alone discover his personal Shangri-La, Peter Francis Browne decides to embark on the madness that is taking a stroll in the Himalayas.

With his friend and guide, Iman, and visiting the places that tourists eschew, Browne discovers both the Nepal that the Nepalese government wants to promote and the Nepal it doesn't. Shangri-La? Not for most of the Nepalese. Isolated from the rest of the world for the past fifty years, a series of corrupt governments sees a country imposed upon, impoverished and corrupted. However, still finding its joys in its people, the stoic walker learns a lot about Nepal and a little more about himself.

At once a personal tale of friendships, an amusing lesson in taking a long, hard look at oneself, and a passionate tale of a paradise lost, A Short Walk in Shangri-La is a rich and very readable brew from a well-loved author.

www.summersdale.com